KeepersDolly[
Favorite 19th Century *Des*

GW01418771

By Eve Coleman

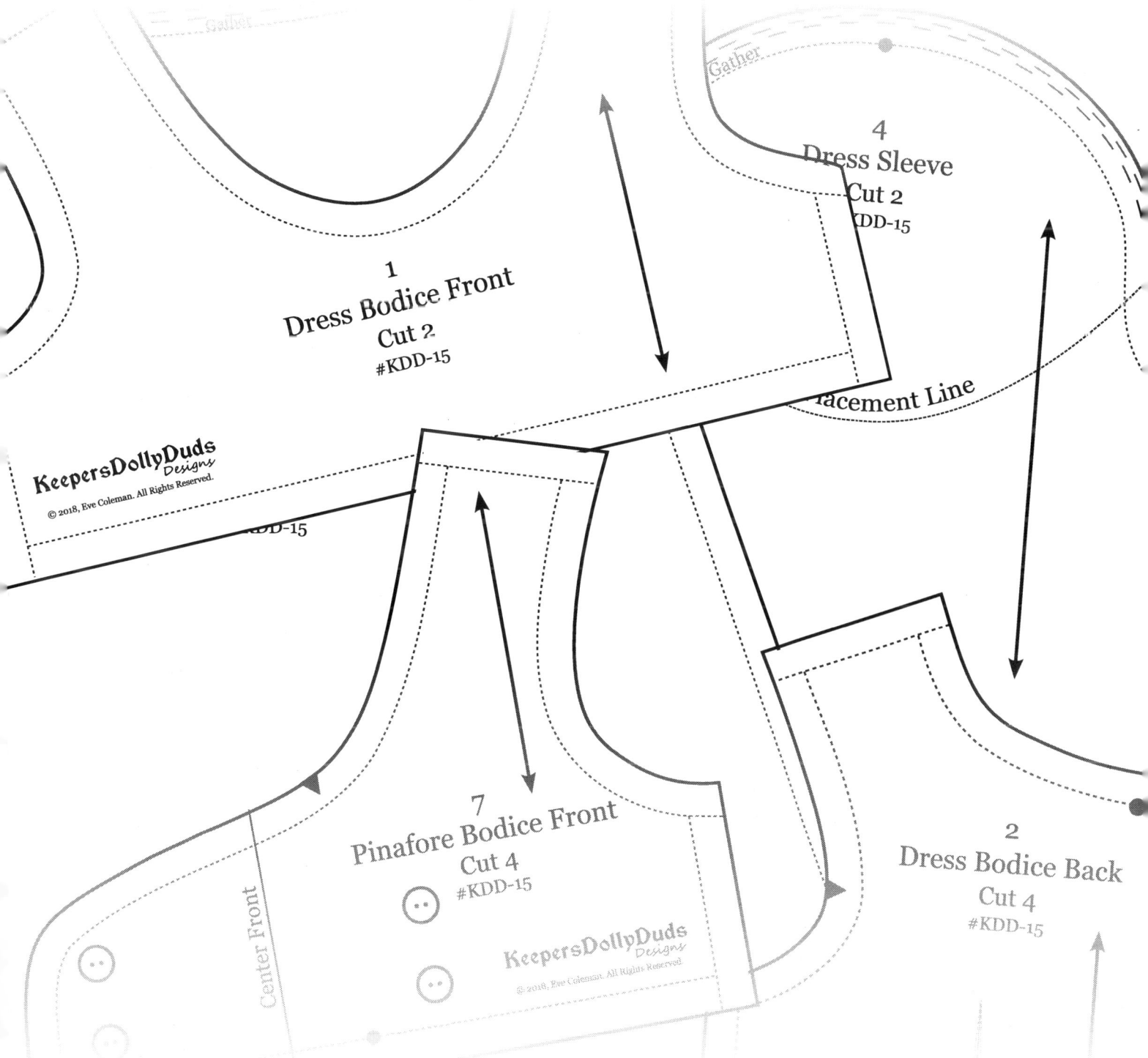

Gather

Gather

4
Dress Sleeve
Cut 2
KDD-15

1
Dress Bodice Front
Cut 2
#KDD-15

lacement Line

KeepersDollyDuds
Designs
© 2018, Eve Coleman. All Rights Reserved.

DD-15

7
Pinafore Bodice Front
Cut 4
#KDD-15

Center Front

KeepersDollyDuds
Designs
© 2018, Eve Coleman. All Rights Reserved.

2
Dress Bodice Back
Cut 4
#KDD-15

Published By Thimbles and Acorns Esko, Minnesota
Making History Memorable

KeepersDollyDuds Designs

...real clothes for real dolls

www.thimblesandacorns.com
www.pixiefaire.com

Thimbles and Acorns Publishing
www.thimblesandacorns.com
email: sharifuller@thimblesandacorns.com

ISBN-13: 978-093226621 (Black and White Interior)
ISBN-13: 978-1094786513 (Full Color Interior)

Pattern photography by Eve Coleman. Images copyright 2012.

Special Thanks to Project Consultants
Linda Blaker, VintiqueDesigns
Karen Dosier, Threads of Troy
Heidi Mittiga, Flossie Potter Patterns

Table of Contents

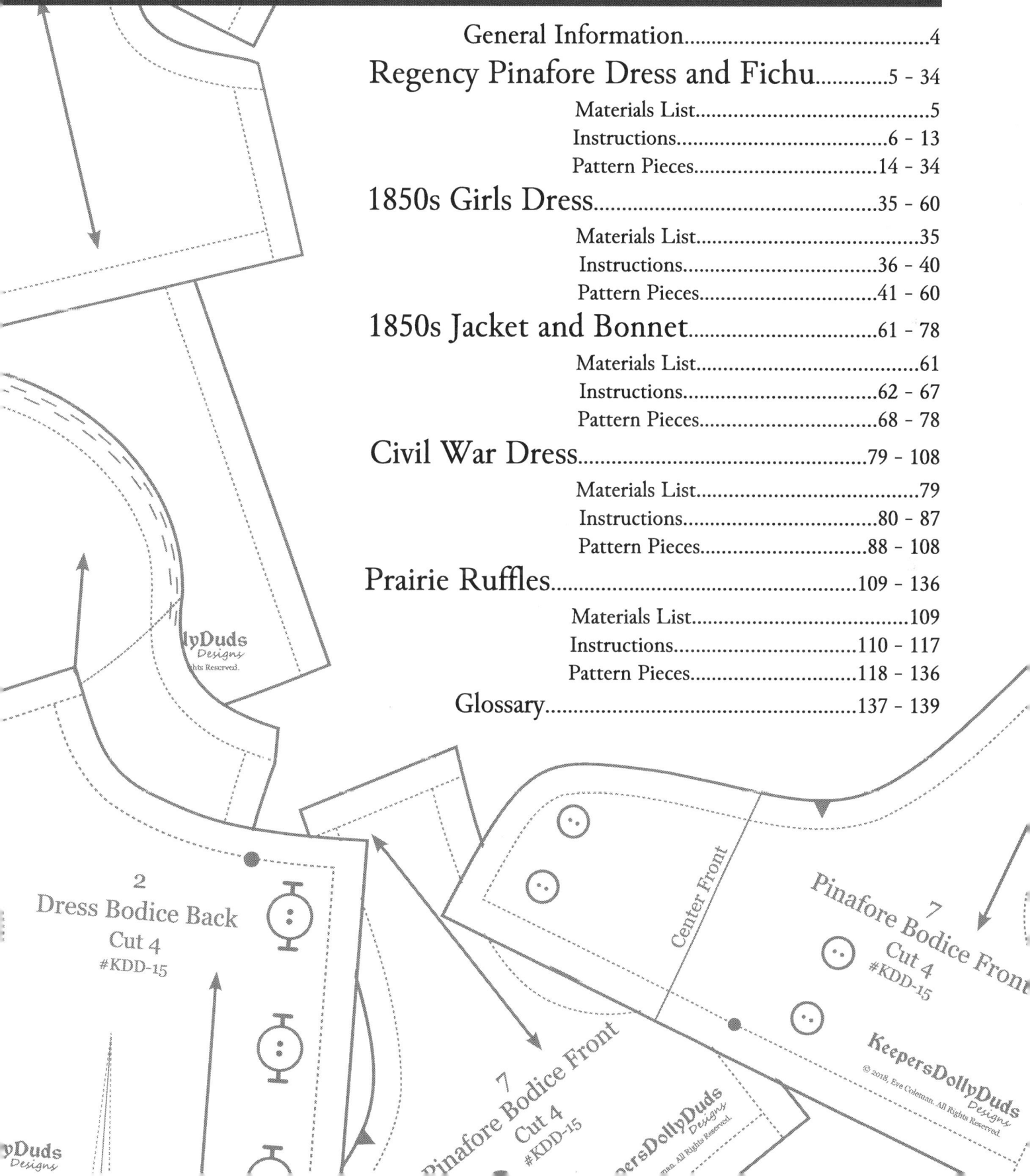

2
Dress Bodice Back
Cut 4
#KDD-15

Center Front

7
Pinafore Bodice Front
Cut 4
#KDD-15

7
Pinafore Bodice Front
Cut 4
#KDD-15

KeepersDollyDuds
Designs
© 2018, Eve Coleman. All Rights Reserved

General Information

General Sewing Instructions

- Read through the instructions before beginning.
- Pre-wash washable fabrics to help reduce shrinkage.
- Before sewing, transfer all pattern markings to the fabric where indicated on the pattern pieces.
- All seams are 1/4-inch (6mm) unless otherwise indicated.
- In the illustrations, the right side of the fabric is colored or shaded and the wrong side of the fabric is left white.

Pattern Information

This pattern is designed to fit 18-inch dolls such as American Girl®; however, it is suitable to use with other dolls with similar body shapes. Small variations in size can usually be accommodated with minor modifications such as adjusting the closure placements or hemlines.

Body measurements for soft bodied dolls often vary.	18-inch (46 cm) American Girl® Harmony Club® Maplelea®, and Other Similarly Sized Dolls
Bust	11" (28 cm)
Waist	11" (28 cm)
Hip	12.25" (31 cm)
Back-neck to Waist	4" (10 cm)
Shoulder to Wrist	5.5" (14 cm)
Arm	4" (10 cm)
Wrist	3.5" (9 cm)
Widest Hand	4.5" (11.5 cm)
Shoulder to Floor	13.5" (34.25 cm)
Neck	6" (15.25 cm)
Inseam	7" (17.75 cm)
Waist to Floor	10" (25.5 cm)
Head	12.25" (31 cm)

Sewing Skill Level

Skill levels vary with each project and are indicated with the title.

● **Beginner**
basic skills such as straight stitching, some hand sewing, and applying snaps

●● **Confident Beginner**
gathering, hook & loop tape

●●● **Intermediate**
fold over elastic, stretch lace, bias tape, pleats, darts, zippers, and pockets

●●●● **Experienced**
beading, buttonholes, and welt pockets

●●●●● **Advanced**
couture techniques, French seams

Dres

ance

Regency Pinafore Dress and Fichu

Materials List

● ● ●

#KDD-15

Suggested Fabrics: *Dress and Pinafore* in lightweight fabric such as cotton, cotton blends, linen, or silk. Not suitable for knits. *Fichu* in semi-sheer cotton batiste, cotton voile, silk voile, dotted Swiss, or handkerchief linen. Not suitable for knits

Fabric Yardage:
Dress ~ 1/3 yard (0.3 m) 45-inch wide fabric
Dress Sleeves and Ruffle ~ 1/2 yard (0.5 m) 45-inch wide fabric
Pinafore ~ 1/2 yard (0.5 m) 45-inch wide fabric
Fichu ~ 1/4 yard (0.25 m) 45-inch wide fabric

Notions:

__Thread
Dress
__2/3 yard (0.6 m) 1/2-inch (12 mm) wide lace
__Three small snaps OR 3-inches of
    1/2-inch (12 mm) wide hook and loop tape
    OR three 3/8-inch (9 mm) buttons
Pinafore
__ 2/3 yard (0.6 m) 1/2-inch (12 mm) wide lace
__four 1/4-inch (6 mm) decorative buttons
__four small snaps

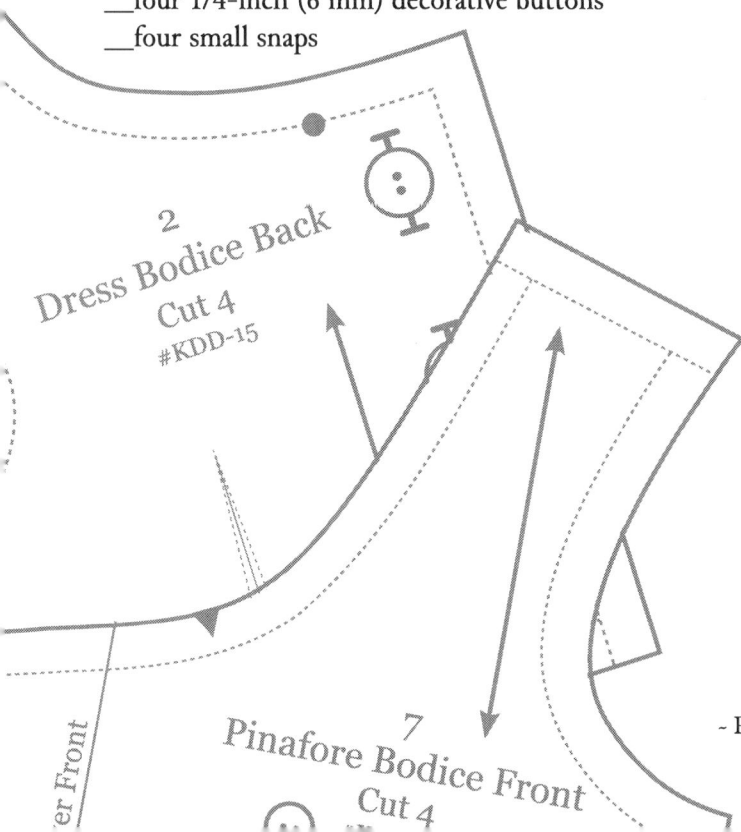

2
Dress Bodice Back
Cut 4
#KDD-15

7
Pinafore Bodice Front
Cut 4

er Front

Gather

4
Regency Dress Sleeve
Cut 2
#KDD-15

Regency Dress Bodice

Step 1: Sew darts where indicated on the pattern on the bodice back. Press toward center back. Finish the shoulder seam allowances if desired.

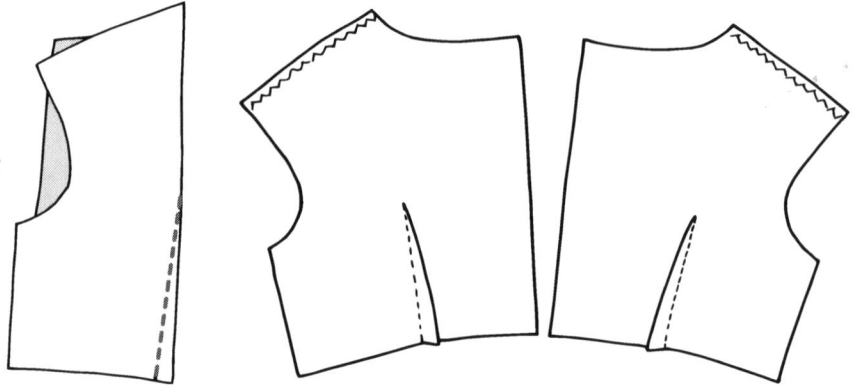

Step 2: Pin the bodice front to the bodice back pieces right sides together along the shoulders. Stitch. Press the seam allowances open. Repeat for the bodice lining pieces.

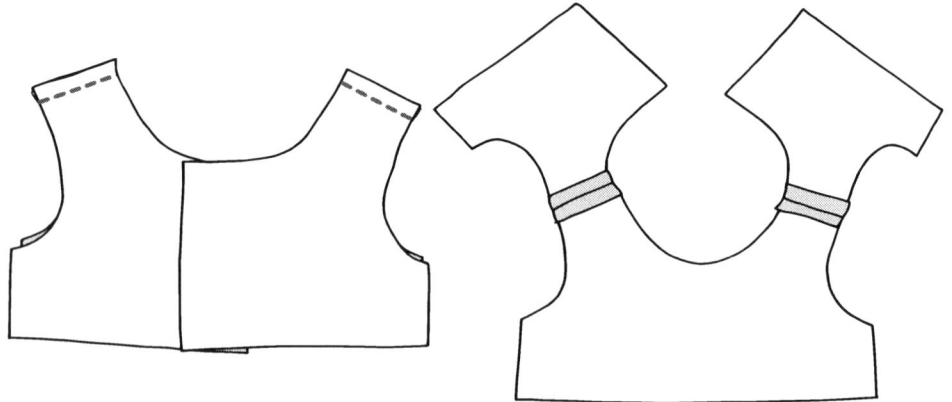

Step 3: Fold the neck ruffle in half along the fold line, right side out. Press. Sew two rows of gathering stitches along the raw edge.

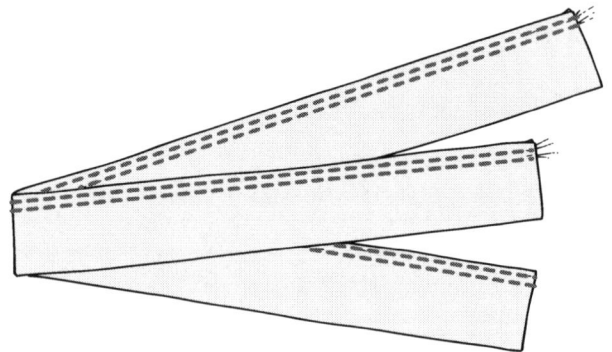

Step 4: Pin the neck ruffle to the bodice between the dots on the back neckline. Draw up the gathering stitches to fit, arranging the fullness evenly around the neckline. Turn the ends of the ruffle inside the seam allowance. Baste to secure.

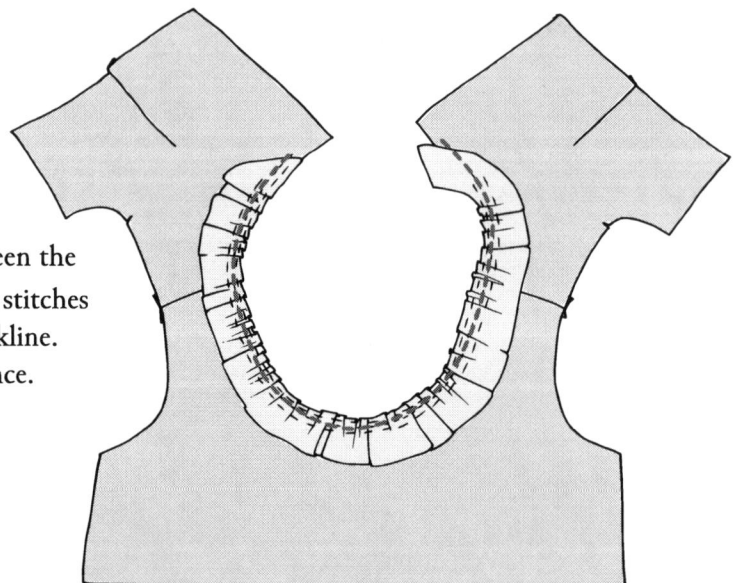

Regency Dress Sleeves

Step 5: Mark the placement lines for the sleeve trim on the right side of each sleeve. Attach trim along the marked lines.

Step 6: With the right sides together, pin the top edge of the lace to the bottom edge of each sleeve. Stitch. Finish the seam allowances, if desired. Press the seam allowance toward the sleeve. Topstitch along the bottom edge of the sleeves to secure the seam allowance. Sew two rows of gathering stitches along the top of each sleeve where indicated on the pattern.

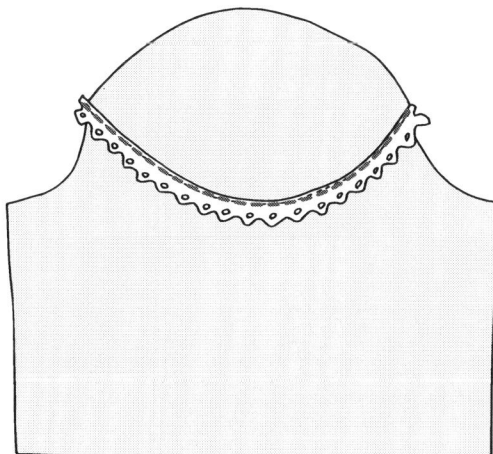

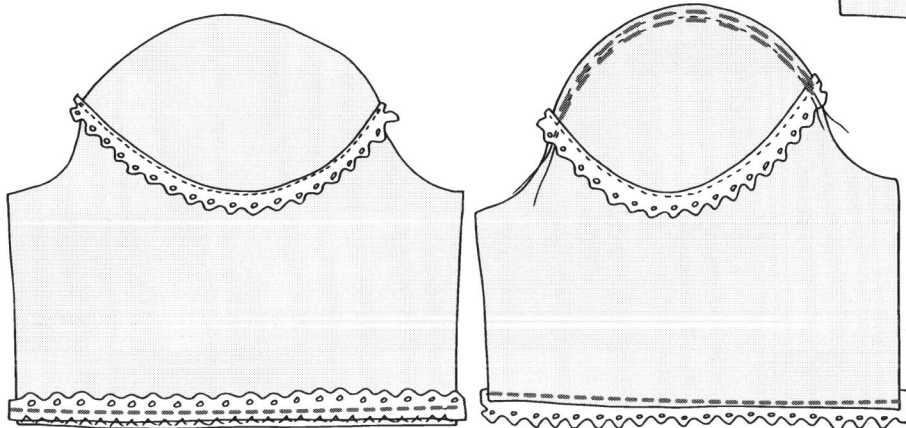

Step 7: With the right sides together, pin the sleeves to the armscyes of the dress bodice, matching the notches. Draw up the gathering stitches to fit, arranging the fullness evenly. Stitch. Clip the curves and finish the seam allowances, if desired. Press the seam allowances toward the bodice. Finish the side seam allowances, if desired.

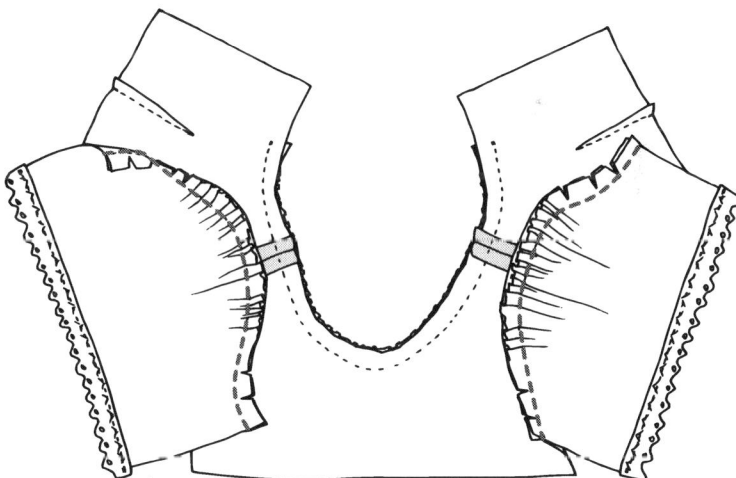

Step 8: Pin the side seam allowances right sides together, matching the seamlines of the armscyes and the bottom edges of the sleeves and bodice. Stitch. Press the seam allowances open.

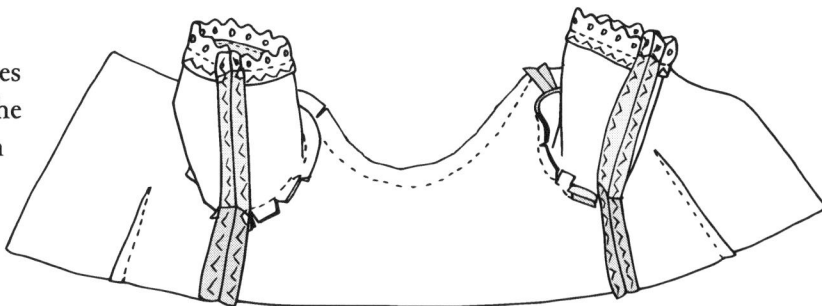

Regency Bodice Lining

Step 9: Stay-stitch along the armscyes of the bodice lining. Clip the curves and press the seam allowances toward the bodice along the stay-stitching.

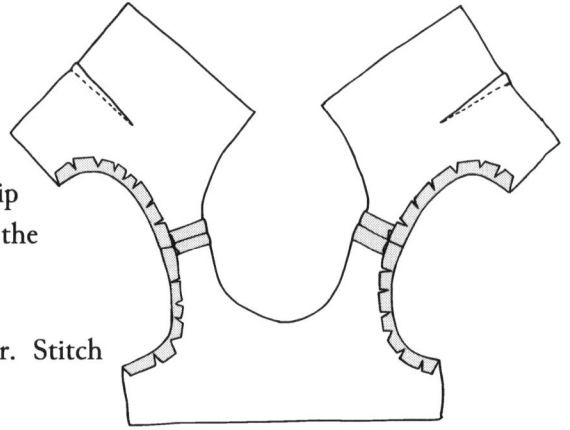

Step 10: Pin the sides of the bodice lining right sides together. Stitch and press the seam allowances open.

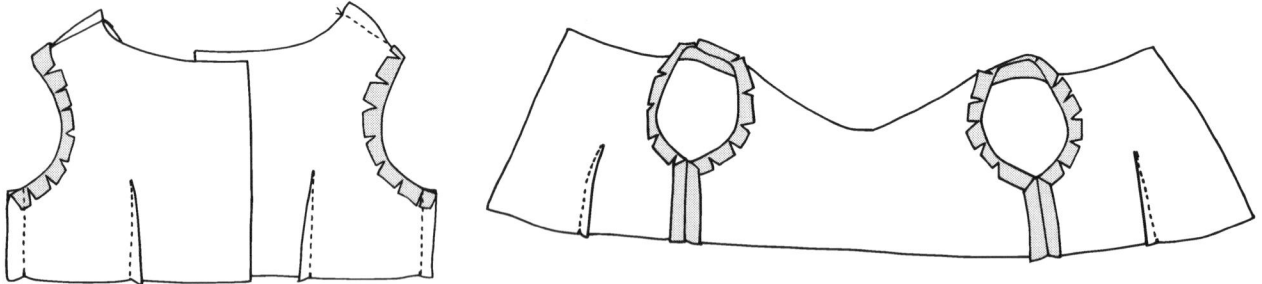

Step 11: With the right sides together, pin the bodice lining to the bodice along the back edges and neckline. Pull the sleeves of the bodice through the armscyes of the lining to help the bodice lay flat. Stitch. Clip the corners and curves. Turn the bodice right side out, squaring the corners with a blunt needle. Press, following the seamlines.

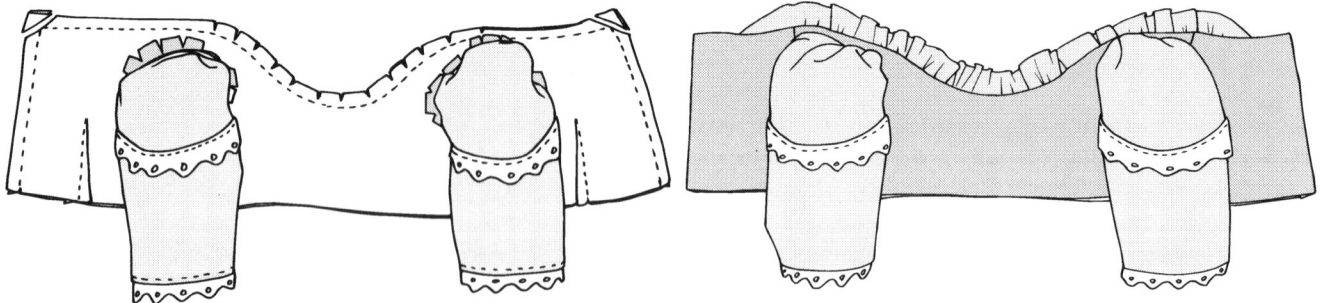

Regency Dress Skirting

Step 12: Finish the back and side seam allowances of the dress front and back skirting. Pin the skirting front and backs right sides together, matching the notches. Stitch. Press the seam allowances open.

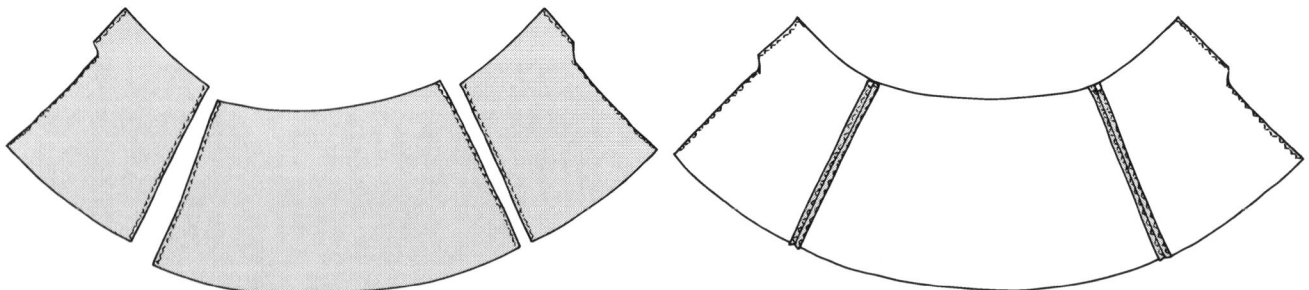

Step 13: Turn the sides of the skirt plackets under 1/4-inch (6 mm). Press. Topstitch 1/8-inch (3 mm) from the folded edge to secure. Sew two rows of gathering stitches along the top edge of the skirting where indicated on the pattern. Turn the plackets under 3/4-inch (9 mm), the fold line should line up with the back seam line. Pin to secure.

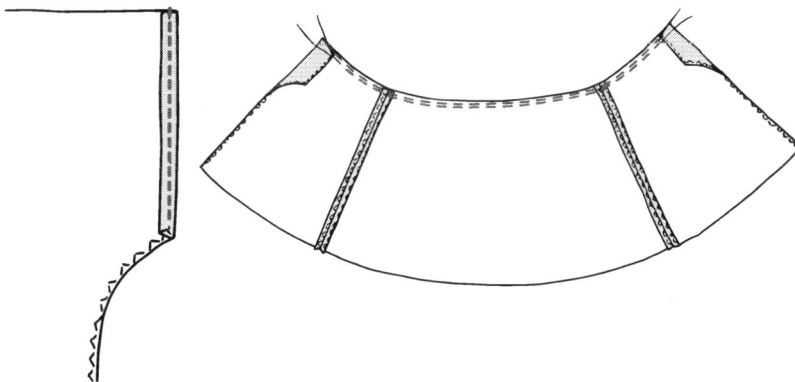

Step 14: With the right sides together, pin the dress skirting to the dress bodice between the back edges of the bodice, matching the center front notches. Do not pin the skirting to the lining. Draw up the gathering stitches and arrange the fullness evenly along the bodice. Stitch, being careful not to catch the lining in the seam. Press the seam allowance toward the bodice, being careful not to crush the gathers.

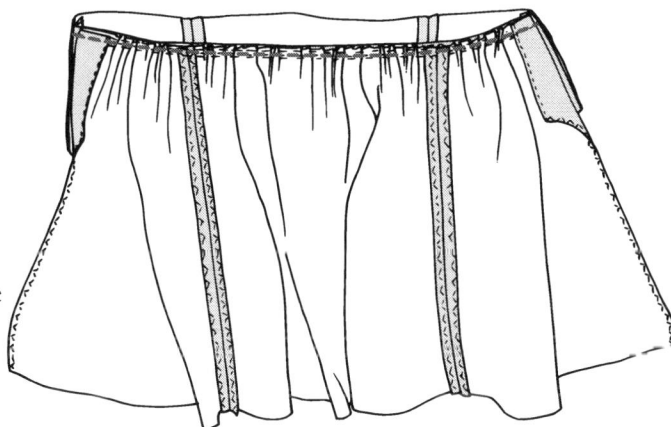

Step 15: Turn the bottom edge of the bodice lining under and pin along the waistline seam. Hand stitch to secure. Turn the seam allowances of each bodice lining armscye under and pin along the seam lines of the bodice armscyes. Hand stitch to secure. Pin the back edges of the skirting right sides together. Stitch from the dot to the bottom edge. Press the seam allowance open.

Finishing the Dress

Step 16: Finish the bottom edge of the skirting. Turn under a 3/8-inch (9 mm) hem. Press and pin in place. Hand or machine stitch to secure. If preferred, finish the bottom edge of the skirt with a double-fold hem.

Step 17: Make buttonholes on the proper left side of the bodice and attach buttons on the proper right where indicated on the pattern. Snaps or hook and loop tape can be used as closures if prefered.

Regency Pinafore

Step 18: Sew darts on the pinafore back where indicated on the pattern. Press the darts toward the center back. Repeat for the pinafore back lining, only press the darts in the opposite direction to reduce bulk. Omit darts for thicker-bodied dolls.

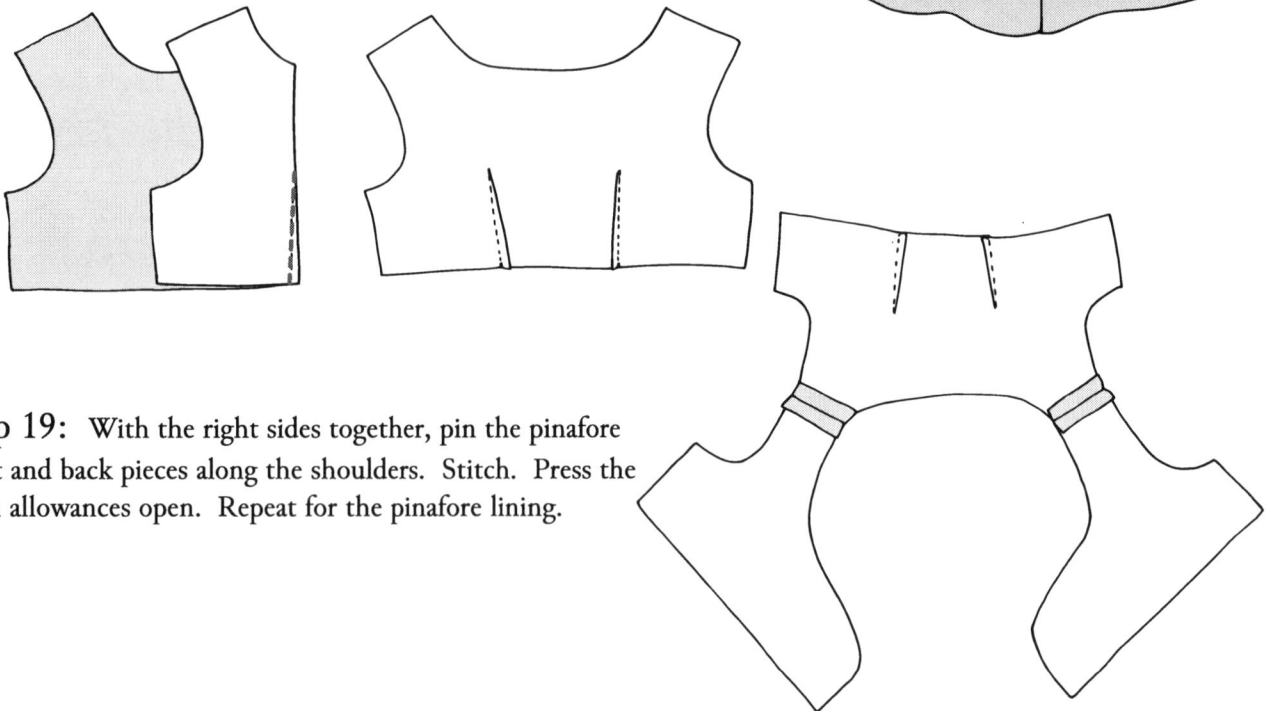

Step 19: With the right sides together, pin the pinafore front and back pieces along the shoulders. Stitch. Press the seam allowances open. Repeat for the pinafore lining.

Step 20: With the decorative edge facing the bodice, pin lace to the neckline of the pinafore bodice. Pin the bodice lining over the bodice along the neckline and armscyes, right sides together. Stitch the neckline and armscyes. Clip the curves and trim the seam allowances to 1/8-inch (3 mm). Turn right side out by pulling the bodice fronts through the shoulders. Press, following the seam lines.

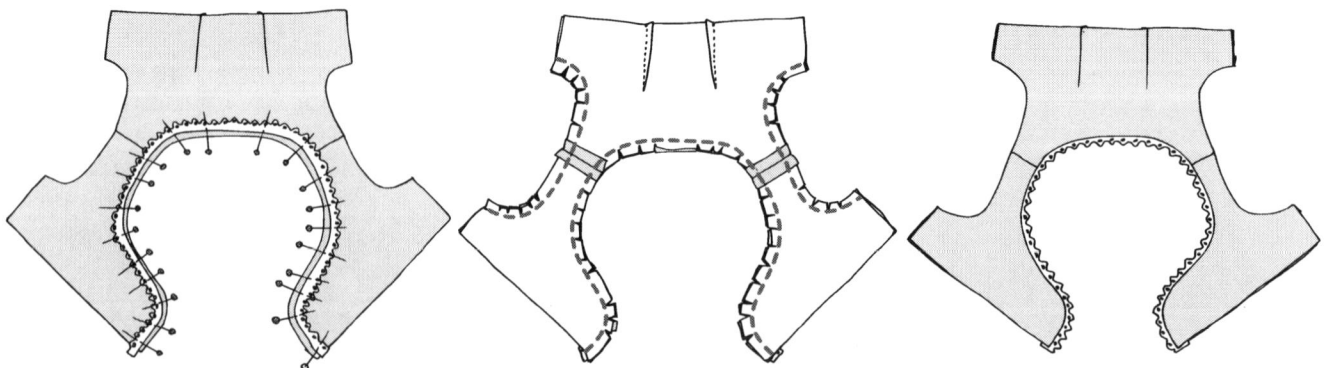

Step 21: With the right sides together, sew the side seams of each bodice and bodice lining together as one seam. Press the seam allowances open. Turn right side out and press.

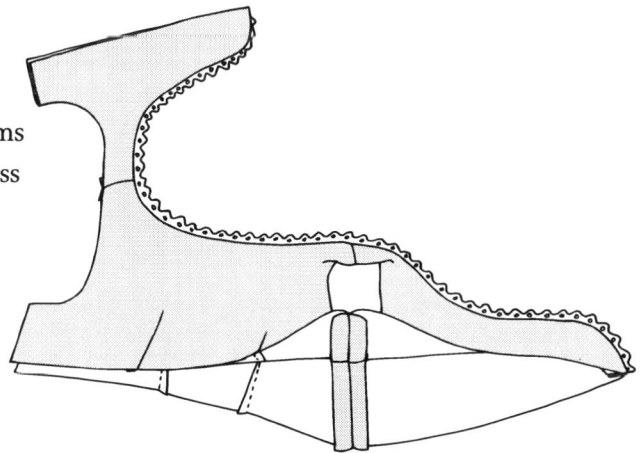

Pinafore Skirting

Step 22: Finish the back and side seam allowances of the pinafore front and back skirting. Pin the pinafore skirt back and fronts right sides together, matching the notches. Stitch. Press the seam allowances open.

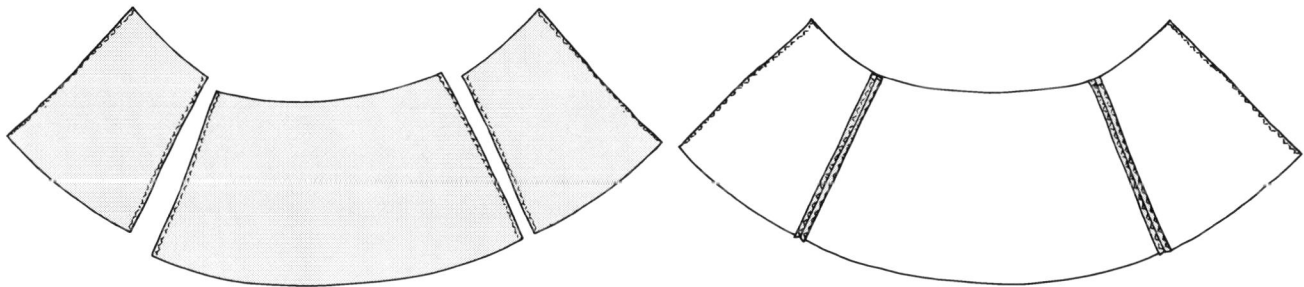

Step 23: With the right sides together, turn each back facing under at the bottom edge along the fold line. Pin in place. Stitch across the facing 1/2-inch (12 mm) from the bottom edge. Finish the bottom edge of the skirting. Turn the facing right side out, squaring the corners with a blunt needle. Press a 1/2- inch (12 mm) hem under along the bottom edge of the skirting and pin in place. Stitch the hem by machine or by hand.

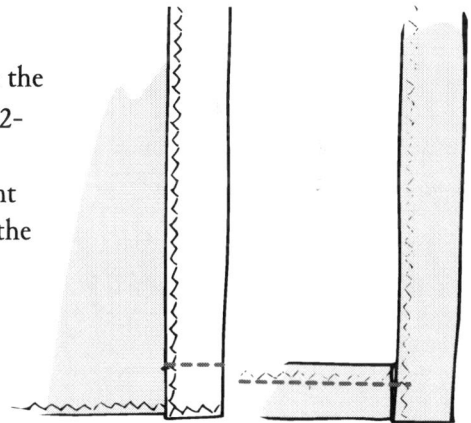

Step 24: Sew two rows of gathering stitches along the top edge of the skirting where indicated on the pattern.

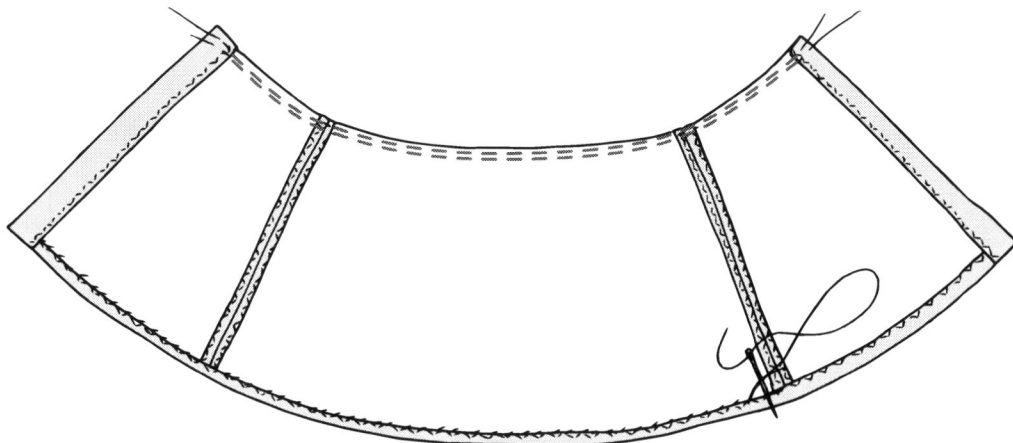

Step 25: With the right sides together, pin the pinafore skirting to the pinafore bodice between the front dots and matching the center back notches. Draw up the gathering stitches and arrange the gathers evenly along the bodice. Stitch, being careful not to catch the bodice lining in the seam. Press the seam allowance toward the bodice, being careful not to crush the gathers.

Step 26: Turn the bodice wrong side out along the front flaps. With the wrong sides together, pin the bodice lining to the bodice along the bottom edge of each front flap just past the front edges of the skirting. Stitch. Clip the corners and turn right side out, squaring the corners with a blunt needle. Press, following the seam lines. Turn the bottom edge of the lining under along the seam allowance and pin along the waistline seam. Hand stitch to secure.

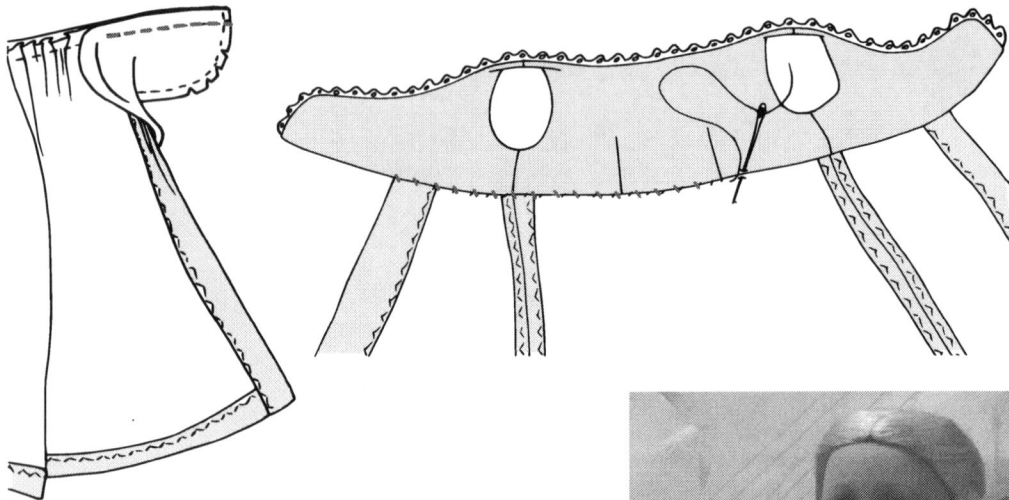

Finishing the Pinafore

Step 27: Attach decorative buttons where indicated on the pattern on the proper right flap. Attach snaps between the flaps directly under the buttons.

Fichu

Step 28: Pin the fichu pieces right sides together. Stitch, leaving the space between the dots on the inside curve open. Clip the corners and curves. Trim the seam allowance to 1/8-inch (3 mm).

Step 29: Turn the fichu right side out, squaring the corners and rounding the curves with a blunt needle. Press following the seam lines. Turn the seam allowances of the opening inside and whipstitch it closed.

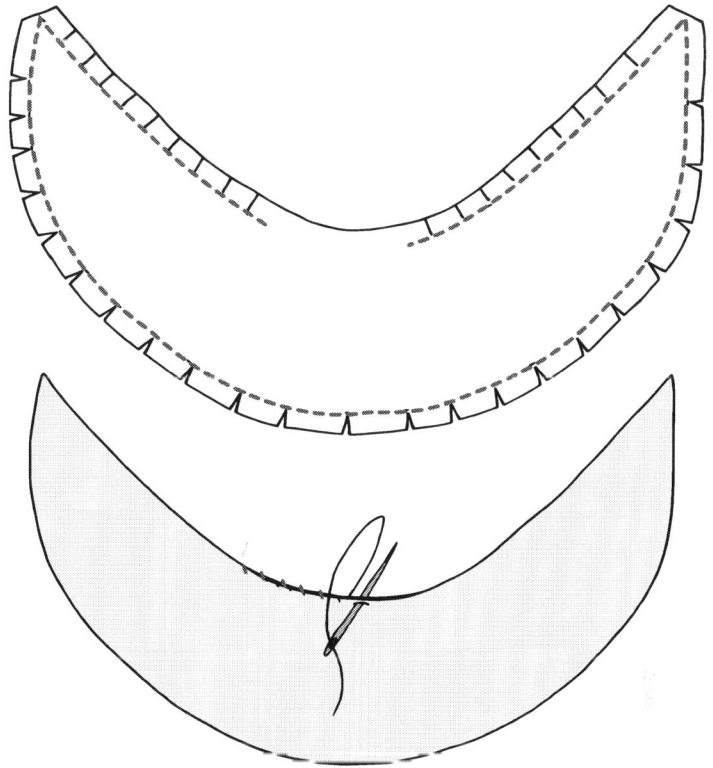

Pattern Pieces

Cutting Layout for 45-inch (1.14 m) wide Fabric
11 Pieces

1 ~ Regency Dress Bodice Front
2 ~ Regency Dress Bodice Back
3 ~ Regency Neck Ruffle
4 ~ Regency Dress Sleeve
5 ~ Regency Dress Front Skirting
6 ~ Regency Dress Back Skirting
7 ~ Regency Pinafore Bodice Front
8 ~ Regency Pinafore Bodice Back
9 ~ Regency Pinafore Front Skirting
10 ~ Regency Pinafore Back Skirting
11 ~ Regency Fichu

Regency Dress
Use pieces: 1, 2, 5, and 6

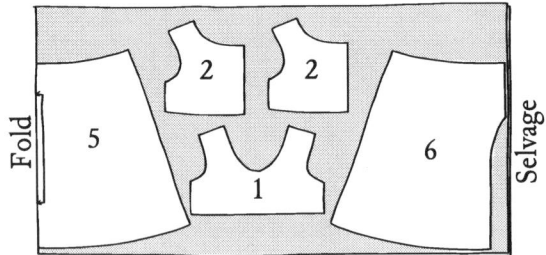

Regency Fichu
Use piece: 11

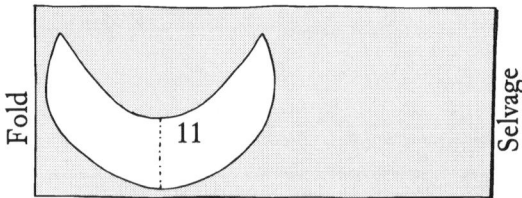

Regency Dress Contrast
Use pieces: 3 and 4

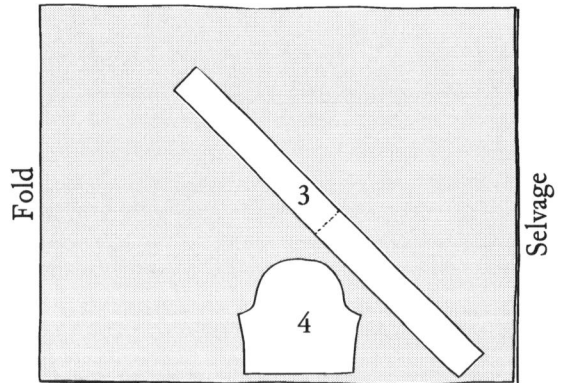

Regency Pinafore
Use pieces: 7, 8, 9, and 10

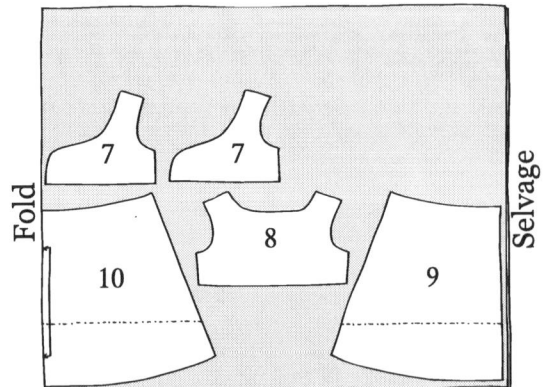

Regency Dress and Pinafore

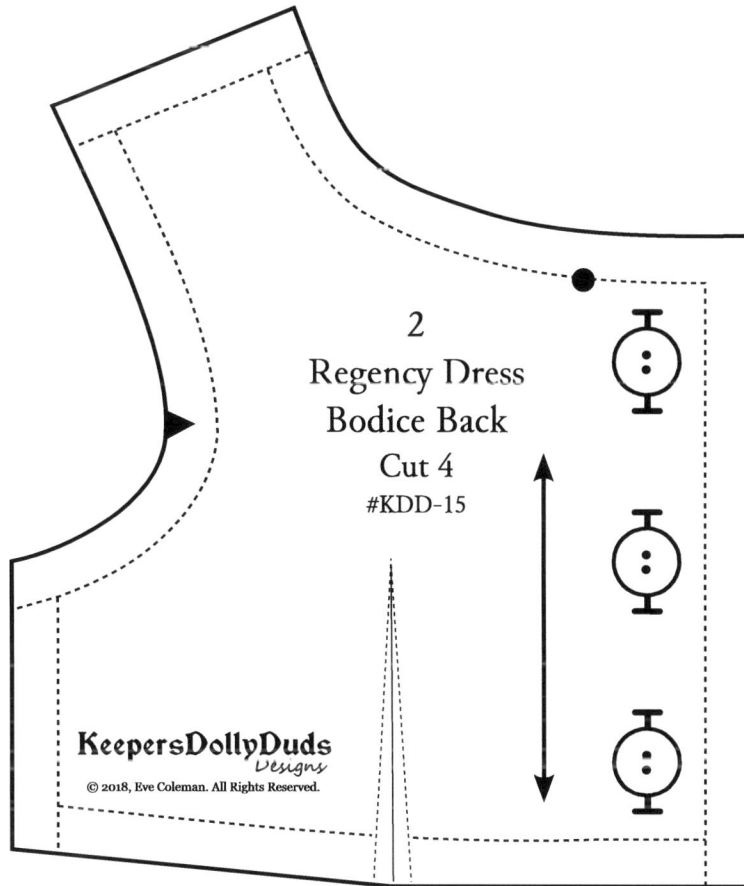

2
Regency Dress
Bodice Back
Cut 4
#KDD-15

KeepersDollyDuds
Designs
© 2018, Eve Coleman. All Rights Reserved.

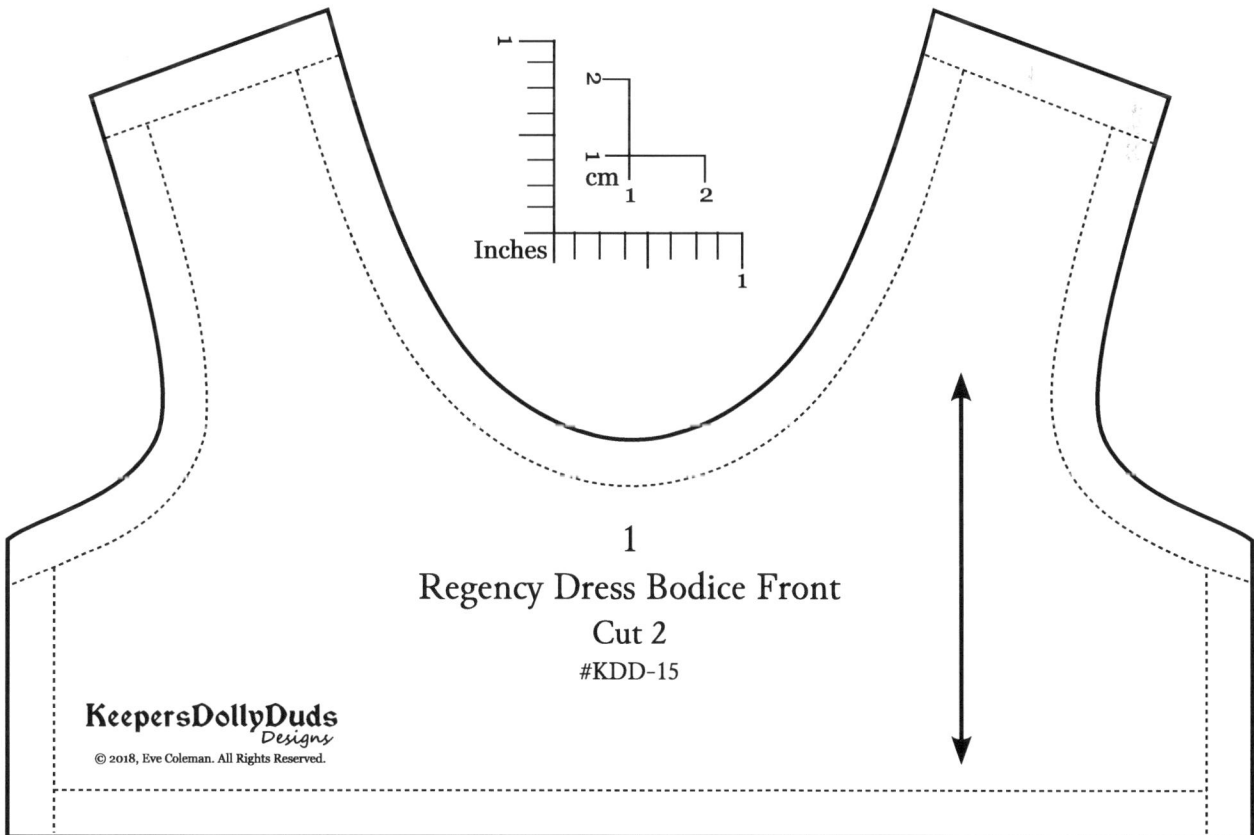

1
cm
Inches

1
Regency Dress Bodice Front
Cut 2
#KDD-15

KeepersDollyDuds
Designs
© 2018, Eve Coleman. All Rights Reserved.

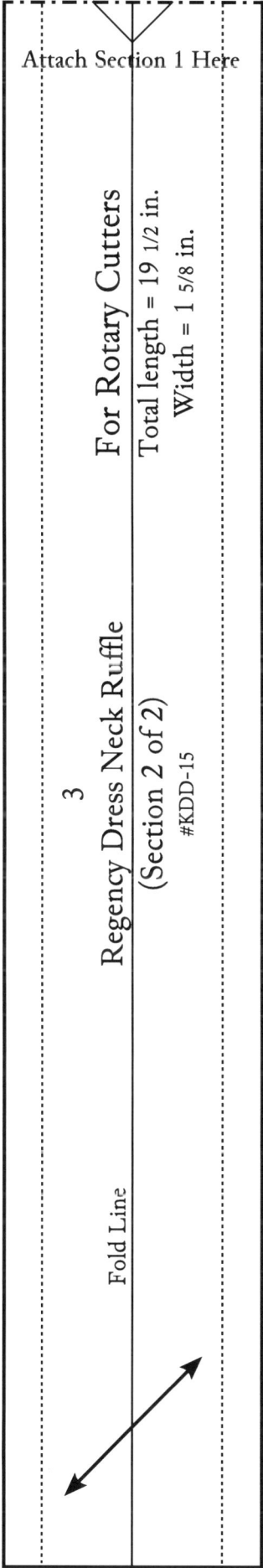

Attach Section 1 Here

For Rotary Cutters

Total length = 19 1/2 in.
Width = 1 5/8 in.

3

Regency Dress Neck Ruffle

(Section 2 of 2)

#KDD-15

Fold Line

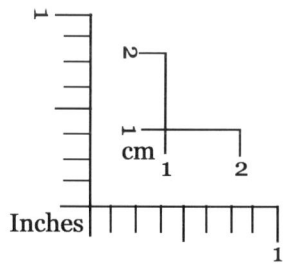

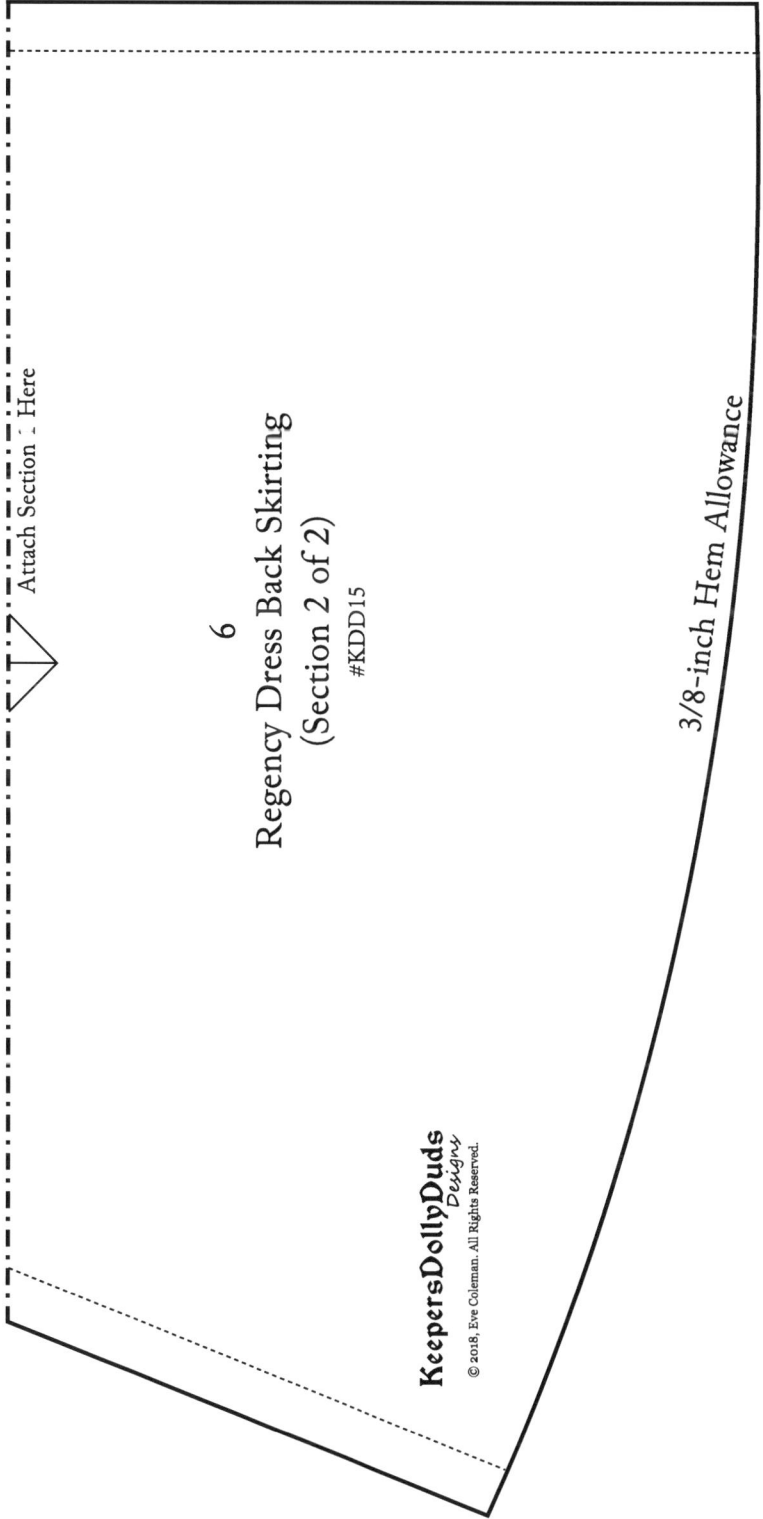

Inches

Attach Section 2 Here

6

Regency Dress Back Skirting

(Section 2 of 2)

#KDD15

3/8-inch Hem Allowance

Lace Placement Line

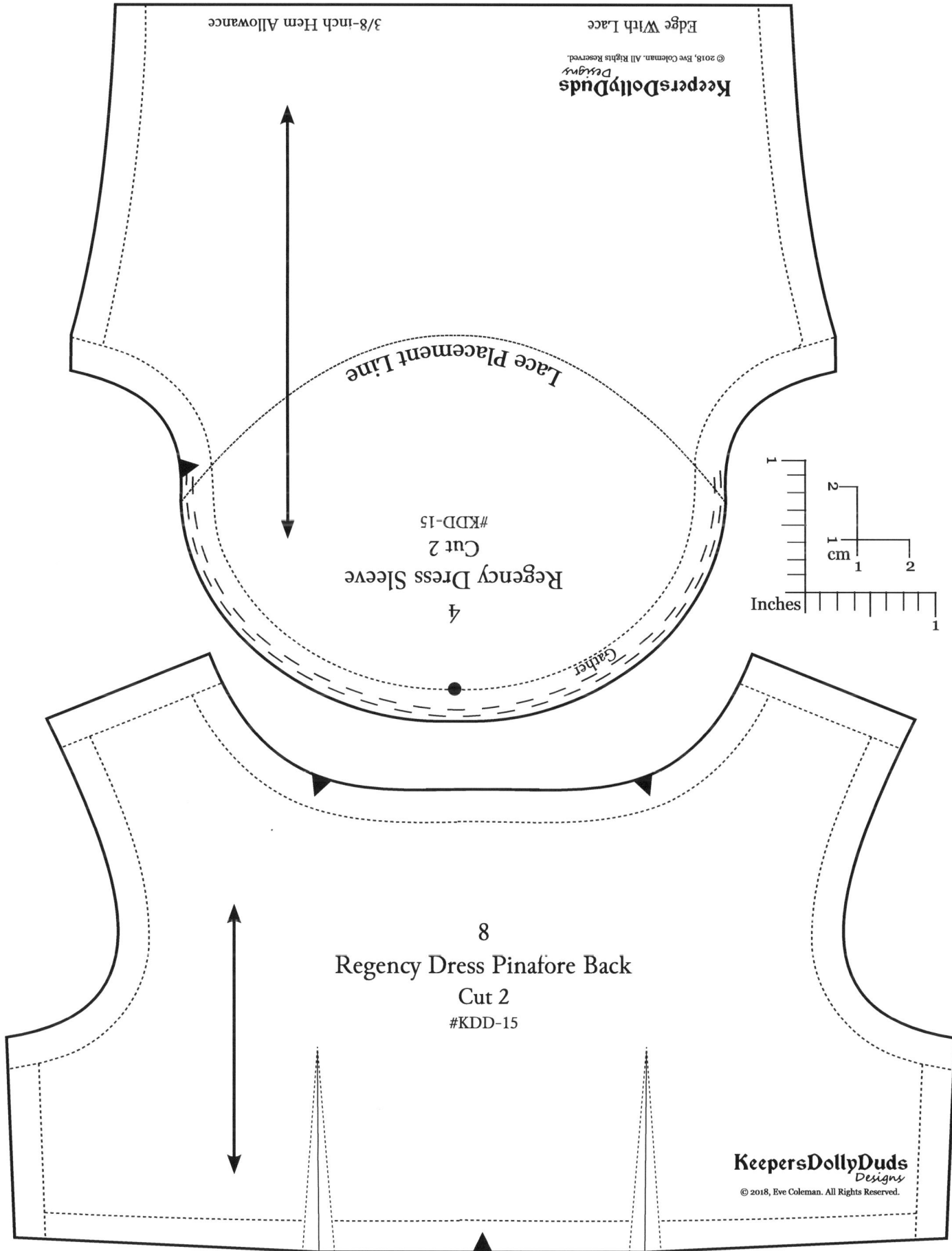

4
Regency Dress Sleeve
Cut 2
#KDD-15

Gather

1

2

1
cm   1   2

Inches
1

8
Regency Dress Pinafore Back
Cut 2
#KDD-15

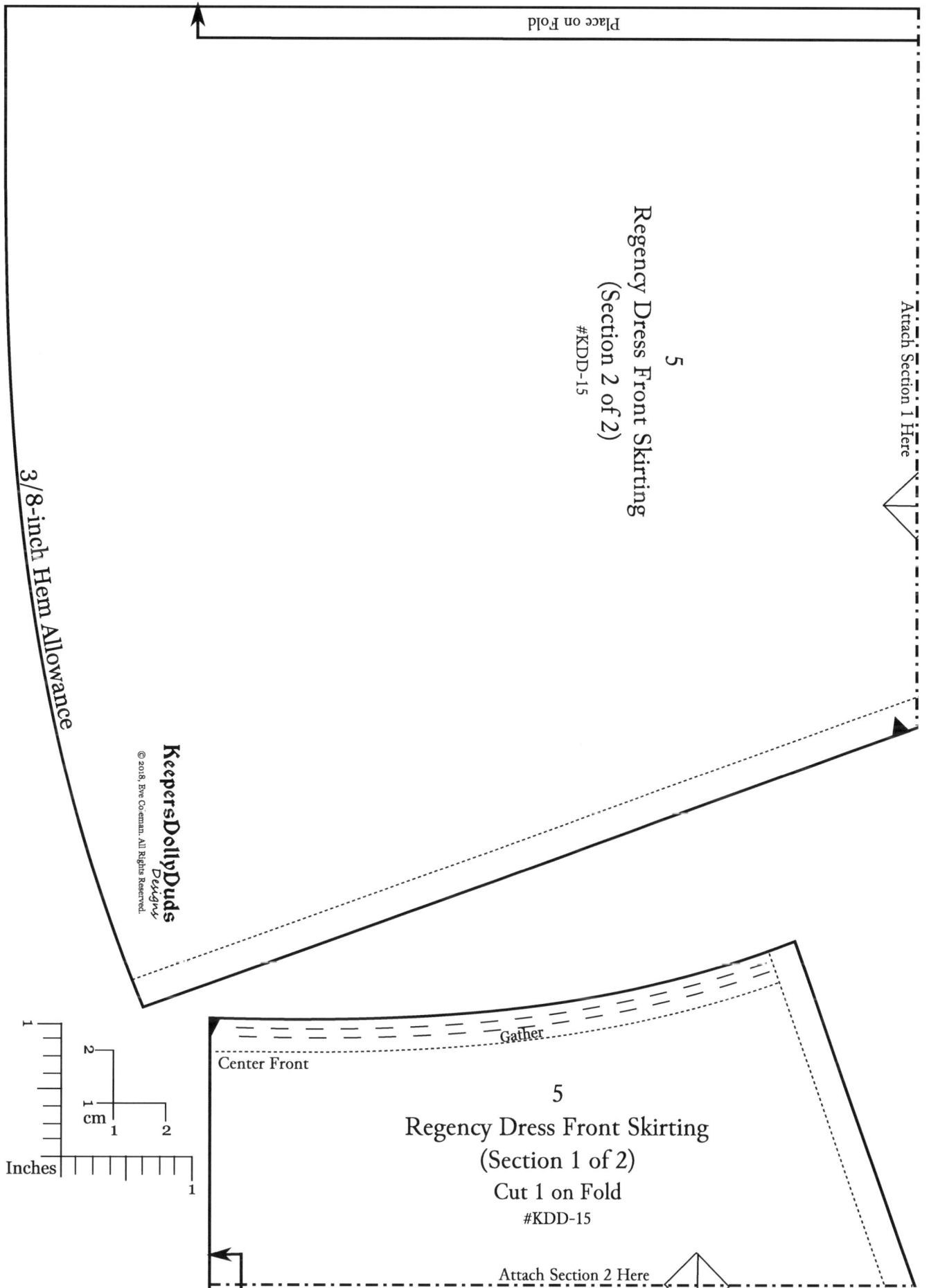

Attach Section 1 Here

5

Regency Dress Front Skirting

(Section 2 of 2)

#KDD-15

3/8-inch Hem Allowance

KeepersDollyDuds
Designs
© 2018, Eve Coleman. All Rights Reserved.

Center Front

Gather

5

Regency Dress Front Skirting

(Section 1 of 2)

Cut 1 on Fold

#KDD-15

Attach Section 2 Here

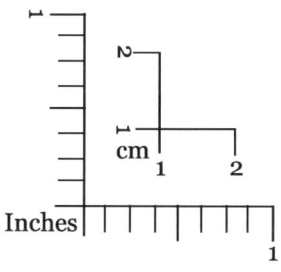

1
2
cm   1   2
1
Inches
1

Inches

cm

2

1

1

2

Fold Line

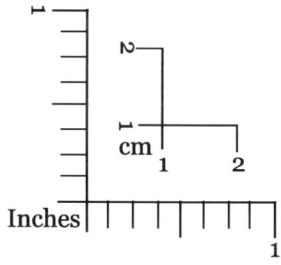

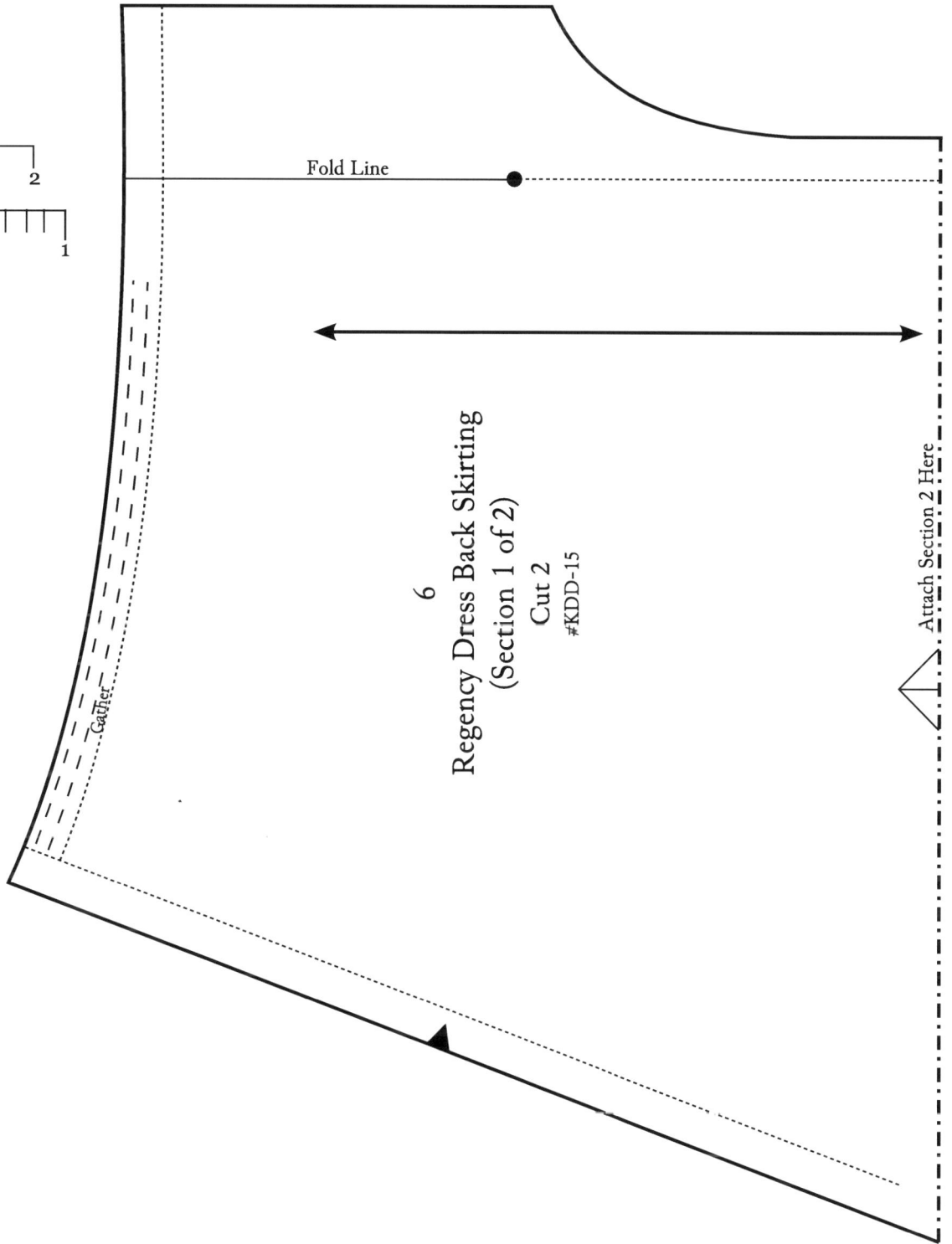

6
Regency Dress Back Skirting
(Section 1 of 2)
Cut 2
#KDD-15

Gather

Attach Section 2 Here

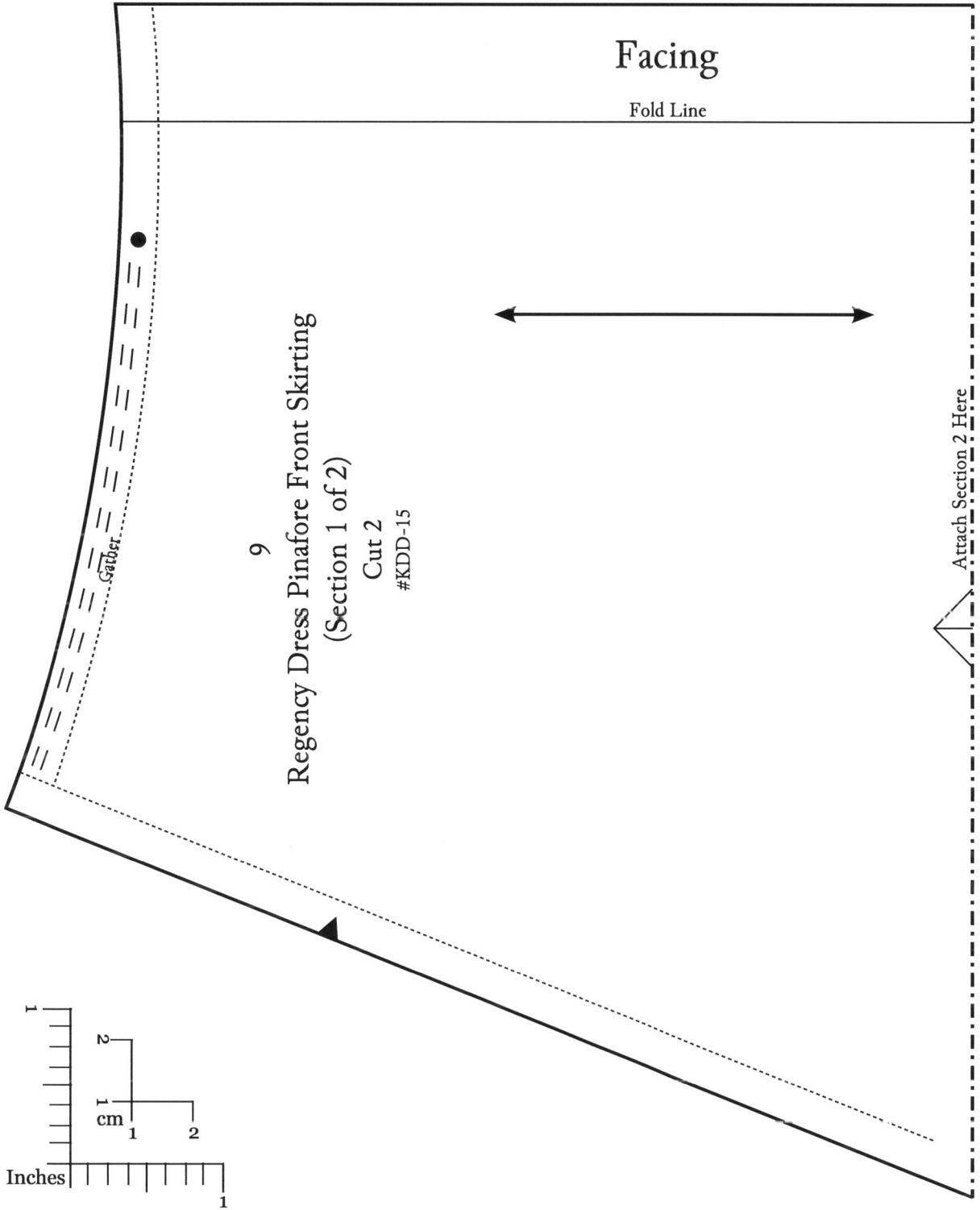

Facing

Fold Line

Gather

9
Regency Dress Pinafore Front Skirting
(Section 1 of 2)
Cut 2
#KDD-15

Attach Section 2 Here

1

2

1
cm   1   2

Inches

1

Inches

cm

10

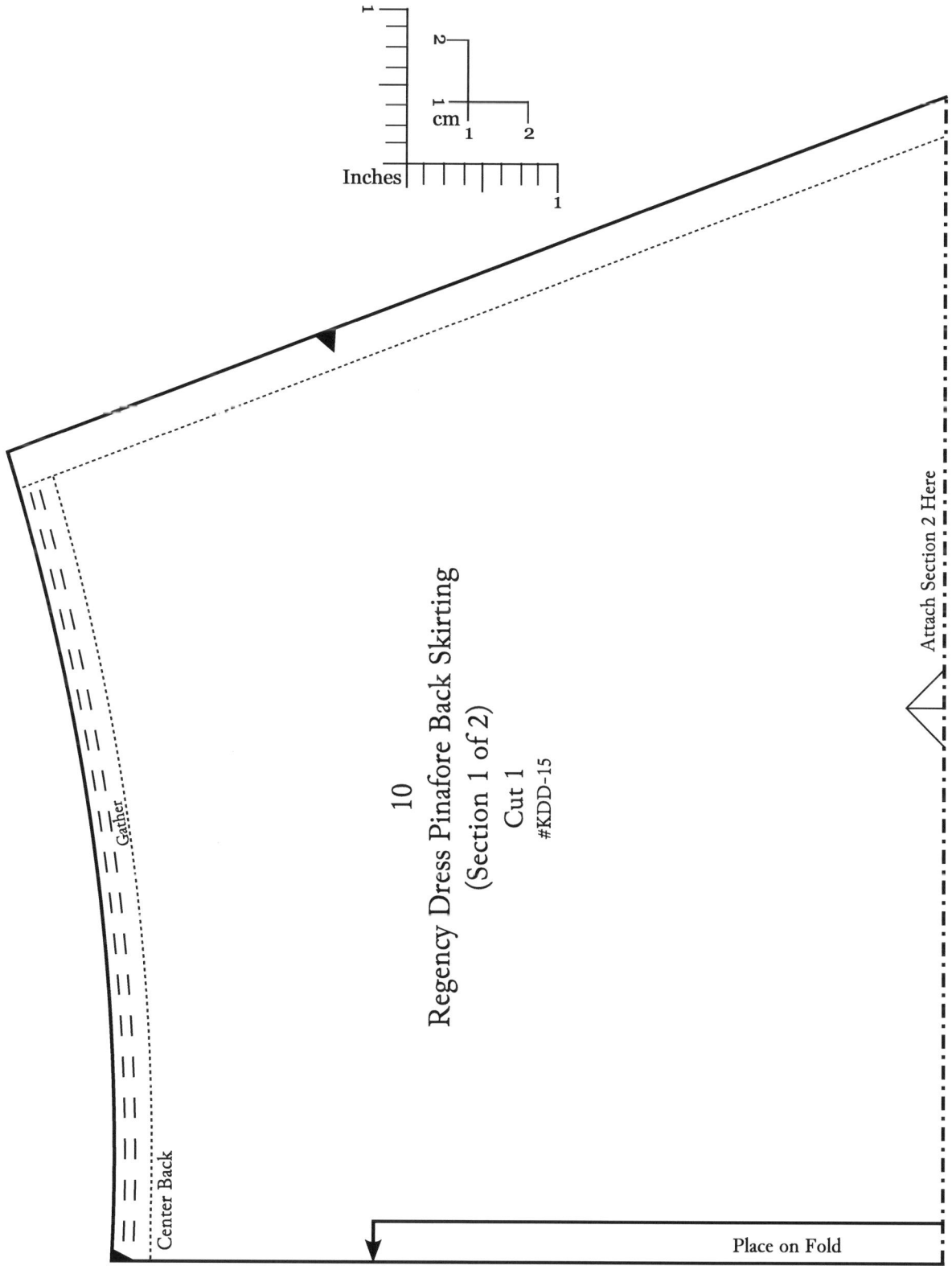

Regency Dress Pinafore Back Skirting
(Section 1 of 2)

Cut 1

#KDD-15

Gather

Center Back

Attach Section 2 Here

Place on Fold

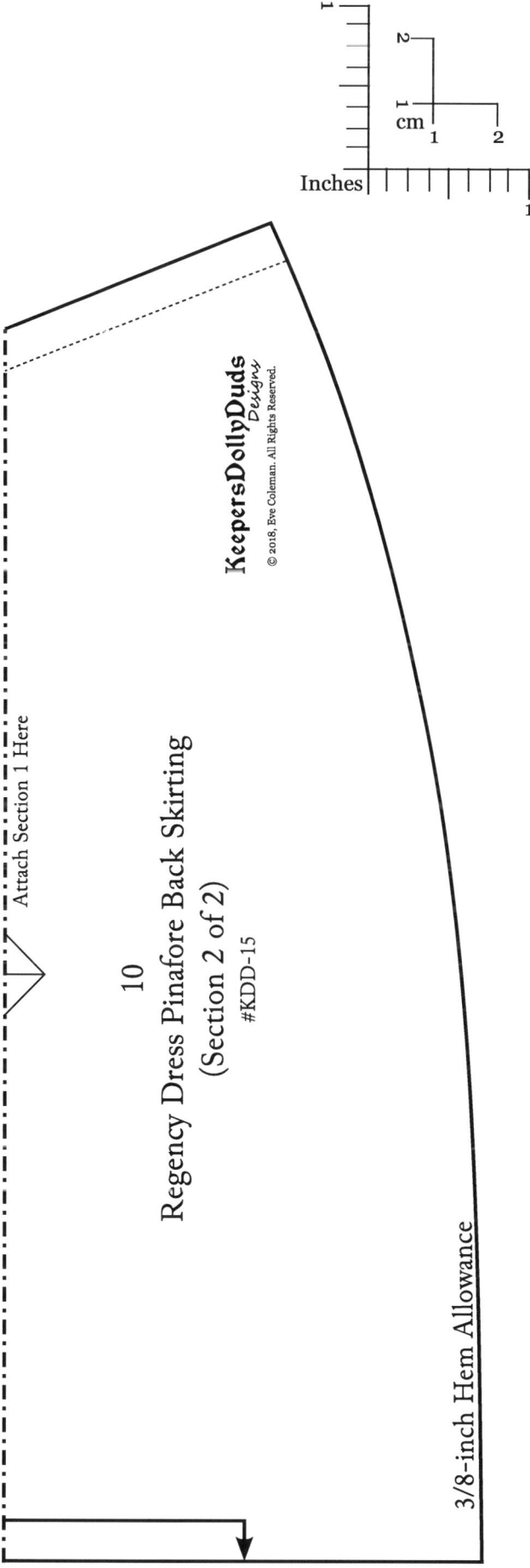

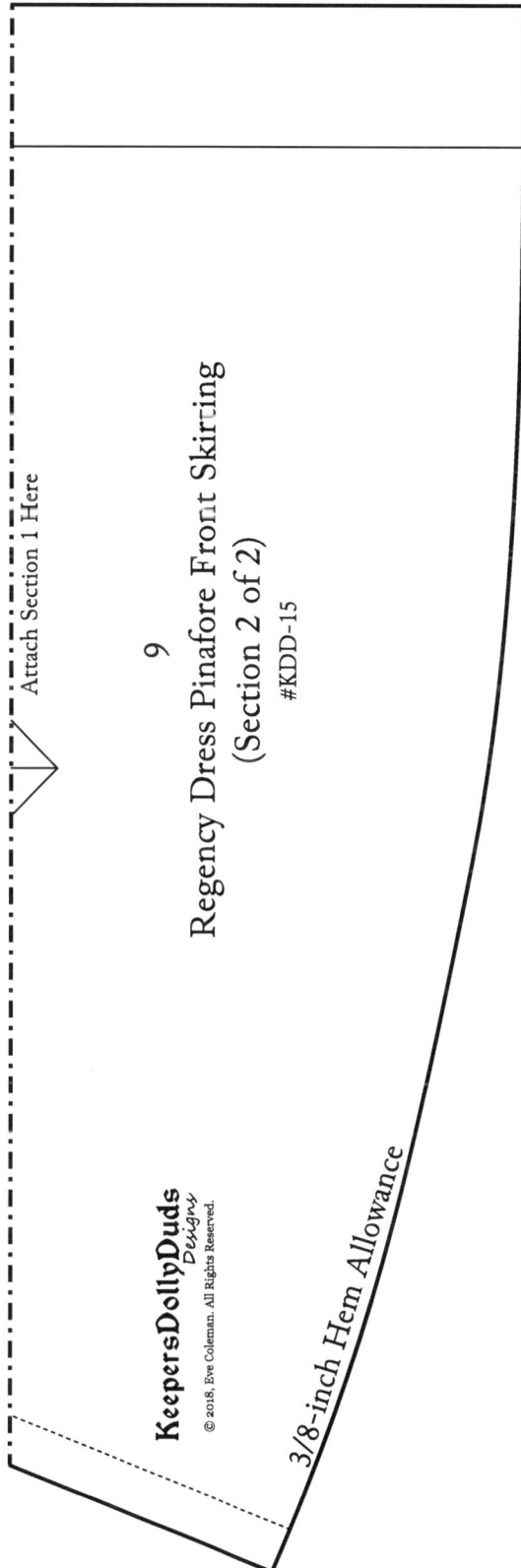

1
2
1
cm 1 2
Inches 1

Attach Section 1 Here

KeepersDollyDuds
Designs
© 2018, Eve Coleman. All Rights Reserved.

10
Regency Dress Pinafore Back Skirting
(Section 2 of 2)
#KDD-15

3/8-inch Hem Allowance

Attach Section 1 Here

9
Regency Dress Pinafore Front Skirting
(Section 2 of 2)
#KDD-15

KeepersDollyDuds
Designs
© 2018, Eve Coleman. All Rights Reserved.

3/8-inch Hem Allowance

Inches

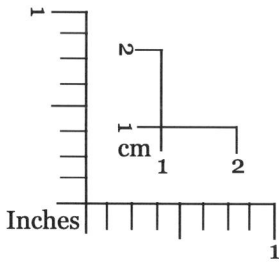

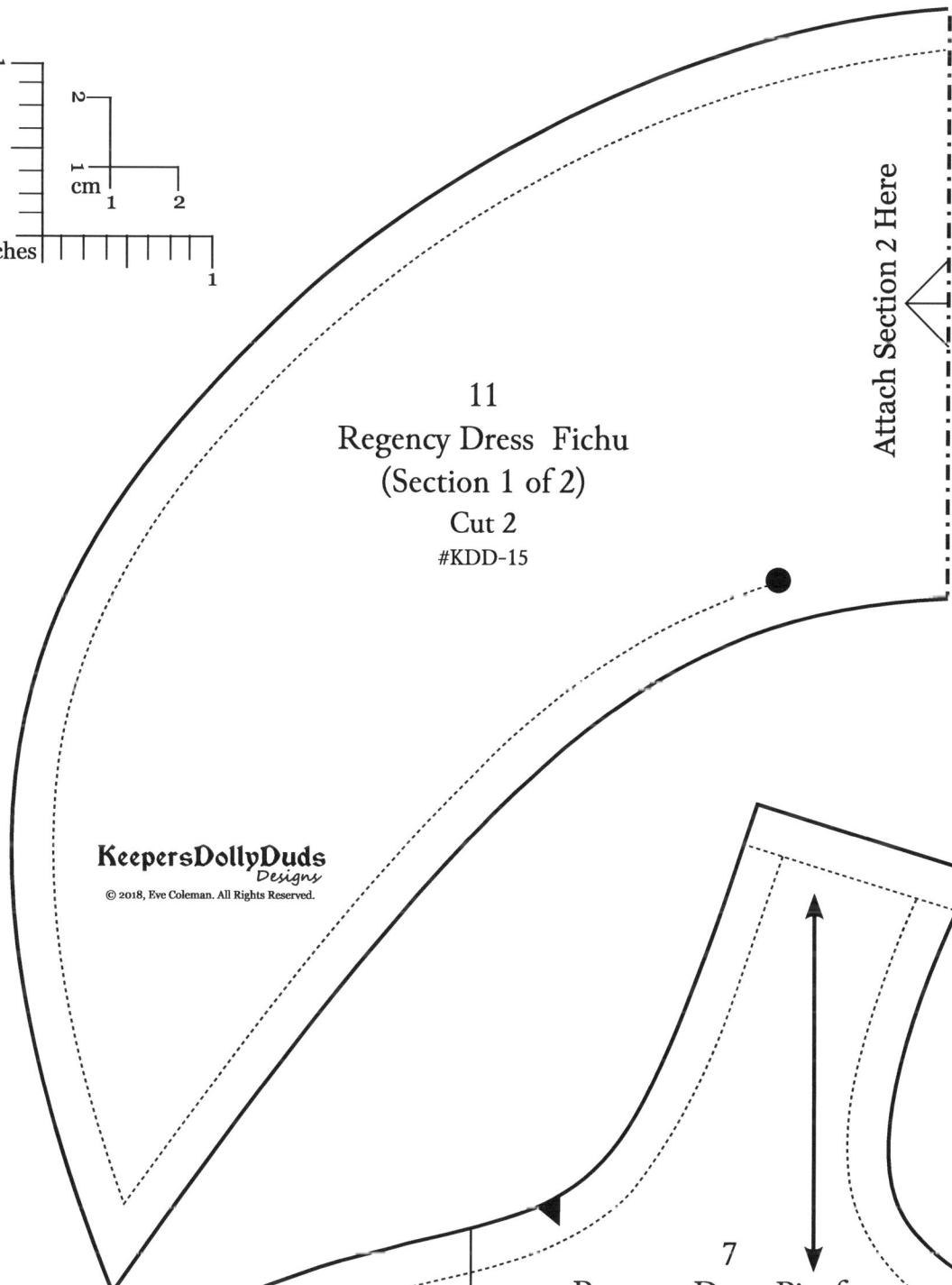

11
Regency Dress Fichu
(Section 1 of 2)
Cut 2
#KDD-15

Attach Section 2 Here

KeepersDollyDuds
Designs
© 2018, Eve Coleman. All Rights Reserved.

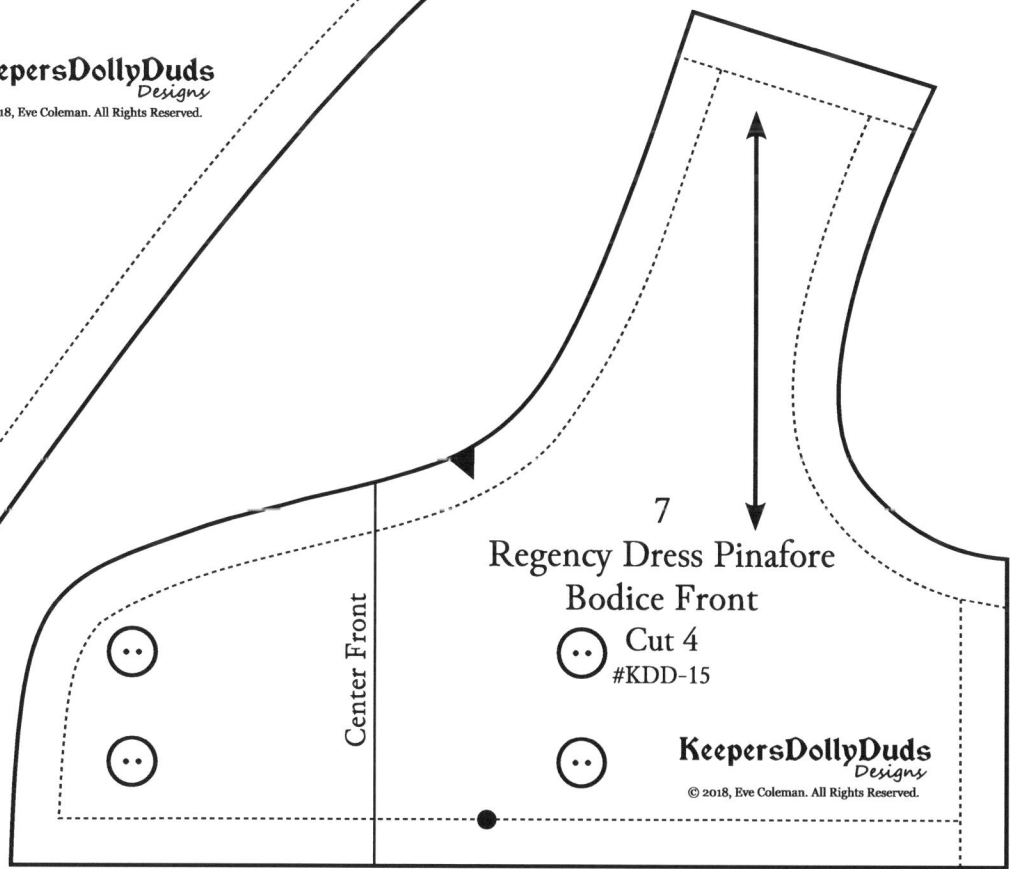

7
Regency Dress Pinafore
Bodice Front
Cut 4
#KDD-15

Center Front

KeepersDollyDuds
Designs
© 2018, Eve Coleman. All Rights Reserved.

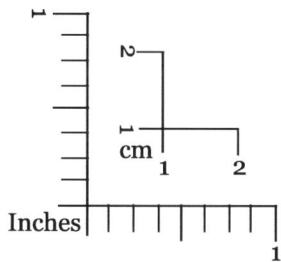

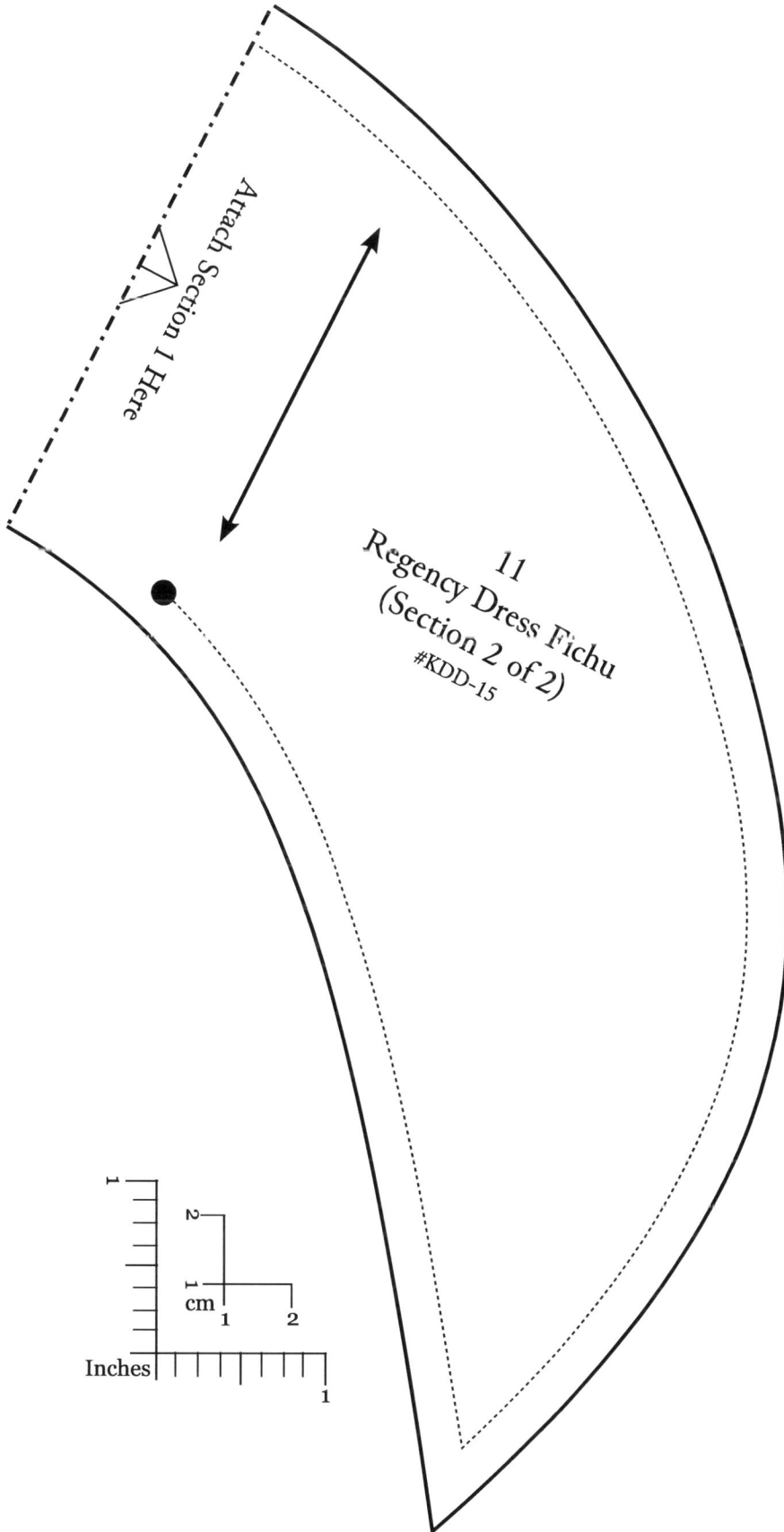

Attach Section 1 Here

11
Regency Dress Fichu
(Section 2 of 2)
#KDD-15

1

2
1
cm   1   2
Inches   1

Fold Line

3
Regency Dress Neck Ruffle
(Section 1 of 2)
Cut 1
#KDD-15

Attach Section 2 Here

1850s Girls Dress

Materials List

#KDD-01

Suggested Fabrics: *Dress* in lightweight fabric such as cotton, linen, or silk. Not suitable for knits.

Fabric Yardage:

Dress ~ 2/3 yard (0.6 m) 45-inch wide fabric

Notions:

__Thread

View A and View B Dress

__3 yards 1/2-inch (12 mm) wide lace or trim

__10-inch square of lightweight fusible
    interfacing

__Small ribbon bow

__ Three small snaps OR 3-inches of
    1/2-inch (12 mm) wide hook and loop tape
    OR three 3/8-inch (9 mm) buttons

View B Dress

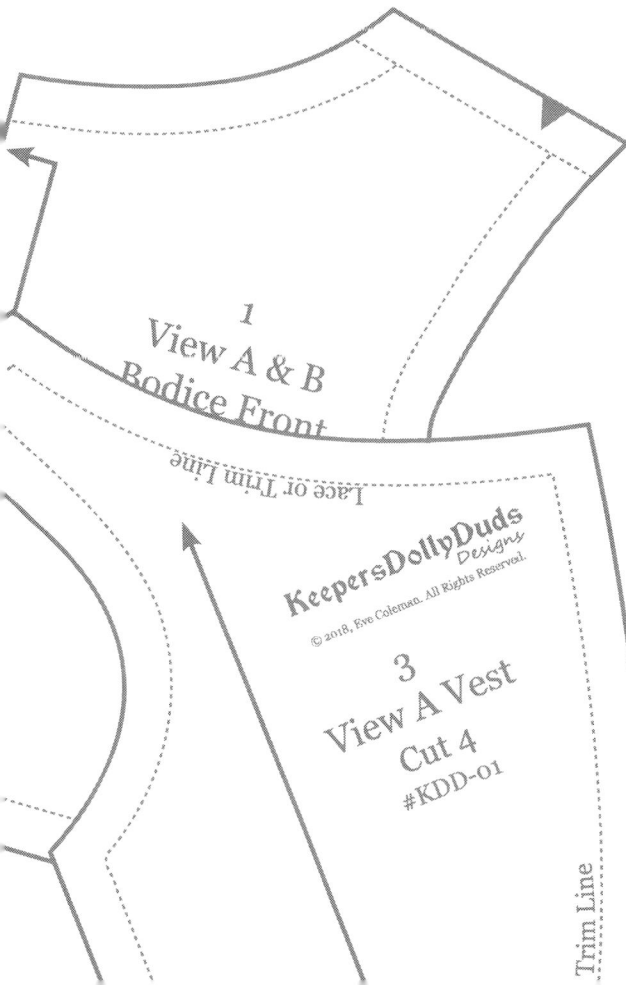

1
View A & B
Bodice Front

Lace or Trim Line

KeepersDollyDuds
Designs
© 2018, Eve Coleman. All Rights Reserved.

3
View A Vest
Cut 4
#KDD-01

Trim Line

Gather

Lace Trim for Sleeves and Skirt

Step 1: *For View A*, use under-sleeve only. *For View B*, use both the under-sleeve and over-sleeve. Sew the top edge of the lace along the lower edges of the sleeve pieces being used. Turn and press. Topstitch close to the edge.

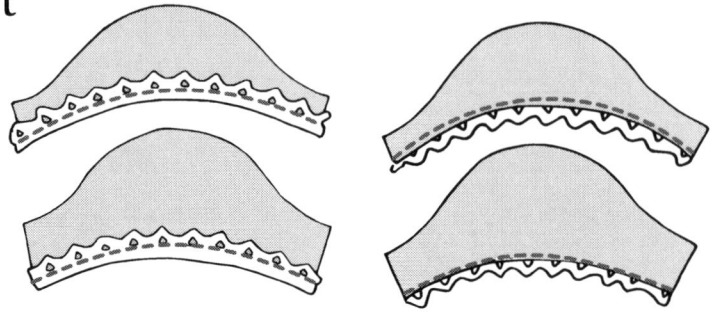

Step 2: *For View B*, lay an over-sleeve on top of each corresponding under-sleeve right side up. For both views, stitch two rows of gathering stitches on the top edge of each sleeve where indicated on the pattern.

Step 3: Clip the inside corners of the scallops on the overskirt where indicated. Sew lace along the edge, easing the lace around the curves and opening the inside corners so the skirt can follow the edge of the lace. Finish the edge if desired. Clip the lace at the inside corners up to the seam so that it will lay flat. Turn, press, and topstitch the hem close to the folded edge.

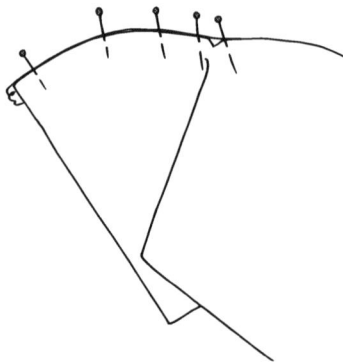

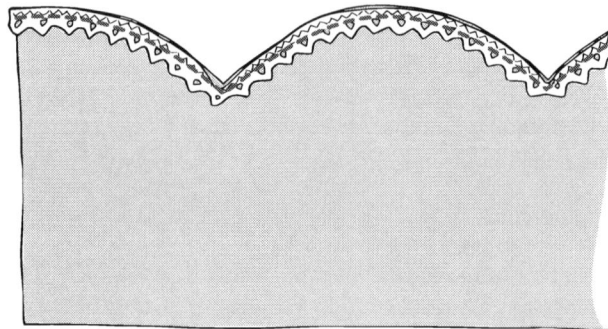

Step 4: View B, skip to Step 5

For View A, Pin or baste lace to the right side of the vest pieces where indicated on the pattern. Clip the lace at the corners of the vest to make the turns. With the right sides together, pin a vest lining piece over each of the vest pieces along the edges with the lace. Clip the corners and curves. Turn right side out, squaring the corners with a blunt needle. Press and topstitch along the edge of the vest.

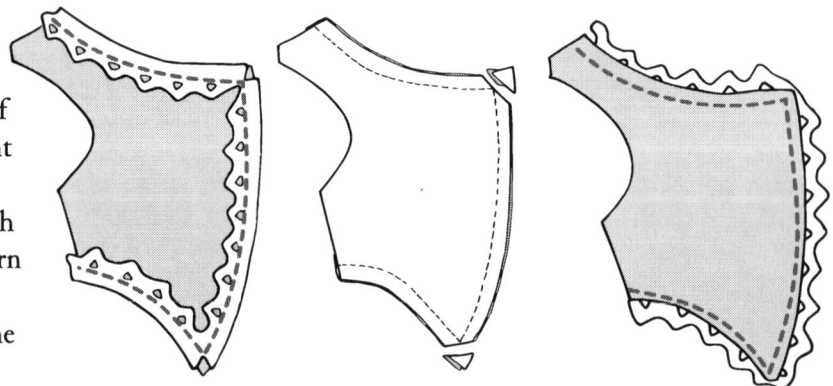

Step 5: *For View B,* with right sides together, attach lace to the side edges of both bodice overlays. Turn the lace along the seam line and press flat.

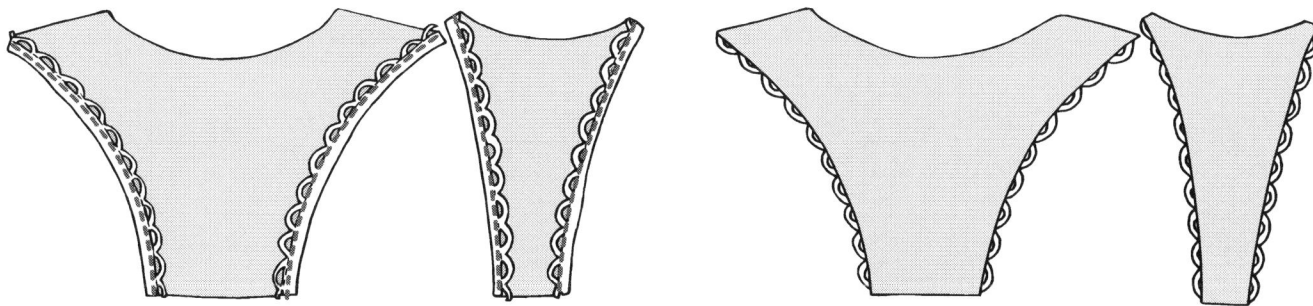

Bodice

Step 6: *For View B,* skip to Step 7. *For View A,* pin the vest pieces to t[...] bodice front. Continue on to Step 8.

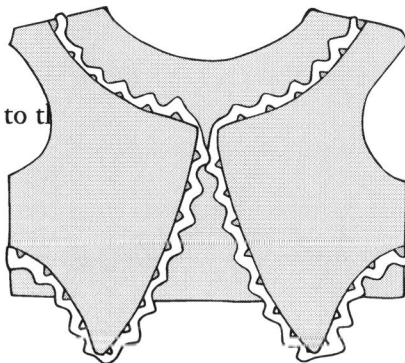

Step 7: *For View A,* skip to Step 8. For View B, Pin the bodice overlays to [...] the bodice front. Stitch in place, closely following the side edges.

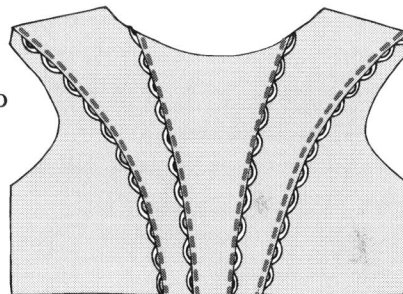

Step 8: Sew the darts on the bodice back. Press them toward the back opening.

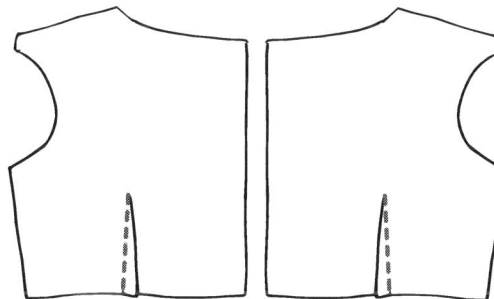

Step 9: Sew the bodice back pieces to the bodice front at the shoulders. Finish the seam allowances and press them toward the back.

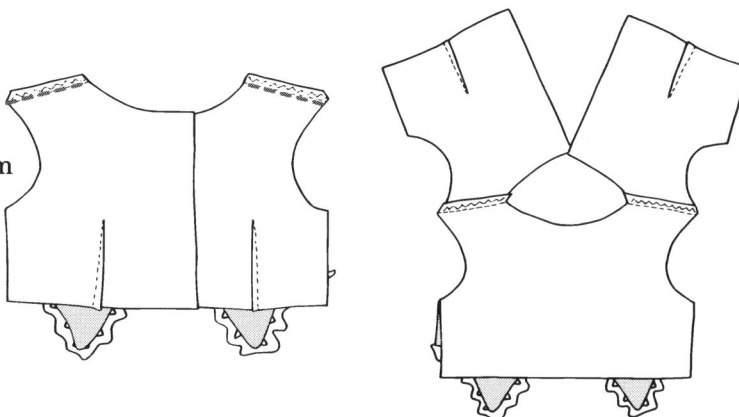

Step 10: Apply interfacing to facings following the manufacturers instructions. Finish the shoulder seam allowances on the facing pieces if desired. Sew the facing pieces together at the shoulders. Press the seams open. Finish the outside edge if desired.

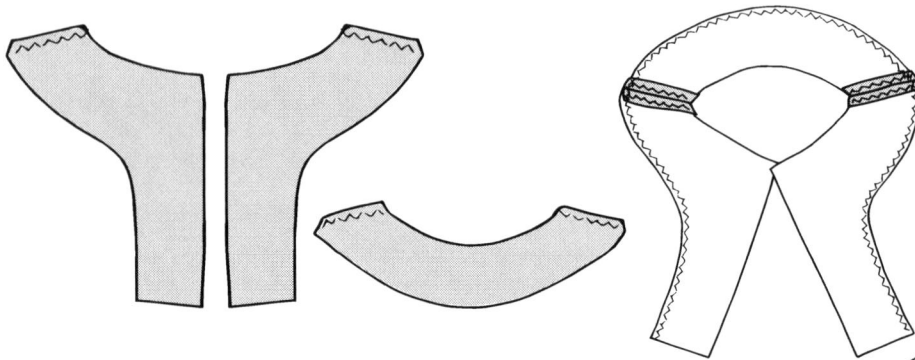

Step 11: Pin the facing to bodice, matching the shoulder seams. Stitch in place. Clip corners and curves. Turn right side, squaring the corners with a blunt needle. Press, following the seamline. Understitch the neckline.

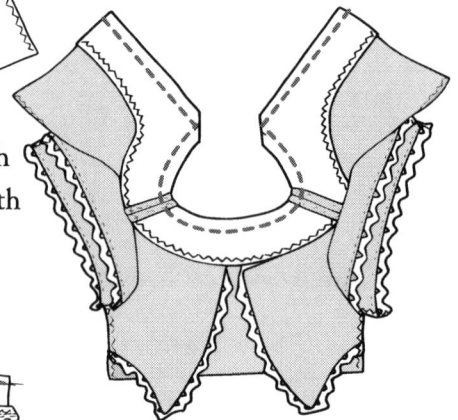

Step 12: With the right sides together, pin each sleeve into an armscye, drawing the gathering stitches to ease the fit. Stitch. Clip the curves and finish the seam allowances if desired. Finish the side seam allowances if desired.

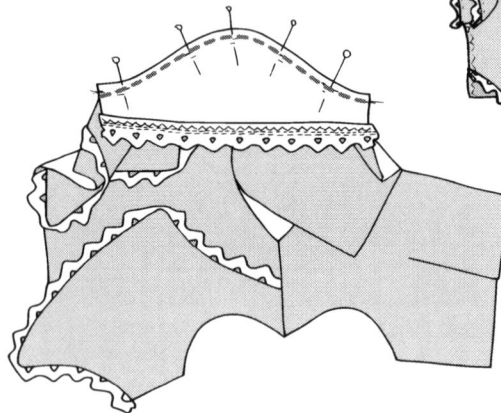

Step 13: Fold the ties along the fold line right sides together. Using a 1/8- inch (3 mm) seam allowance, stitch where indicated on the pattern. Clip the corners and turn right side out, squaring the corners with a blunt needle. Press along the seamline.

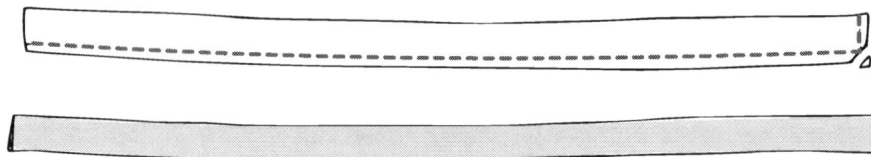

Step 14: With the seam side facing down, pin the open end of a tie to each side of the bodice front where indicated on the pattern. Finish the side seam allowances of the bodice front and back.

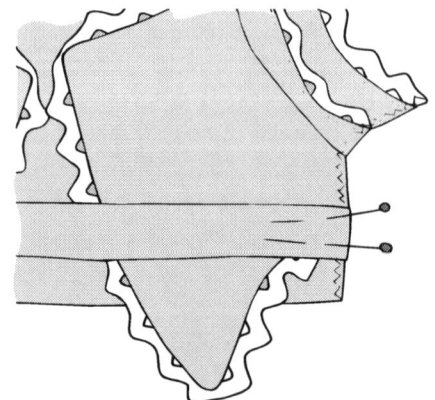

Step 15: Sew the side seams of the sleeves and bodice right sides together, taking care to line up the bottom edges of the sleeves and bodice and the seam allowances on the armscyes. Press the seam allowances open.

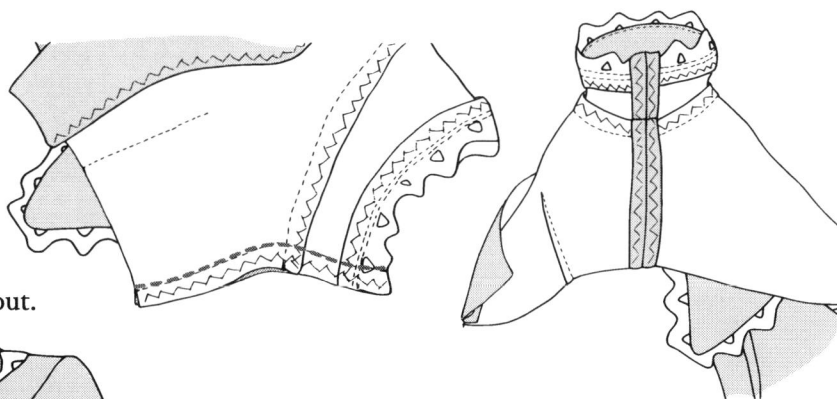

Step 16: Turn the bodice right side out.

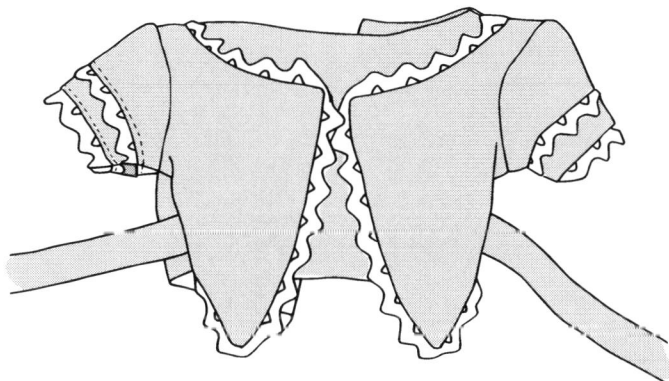

Step 17: With the right sides facing up, lay the overskirt on top of the underskirt. Pin in place and sew two rows of gathering stitches along the top edge to secure. Finish the back edges if desired.

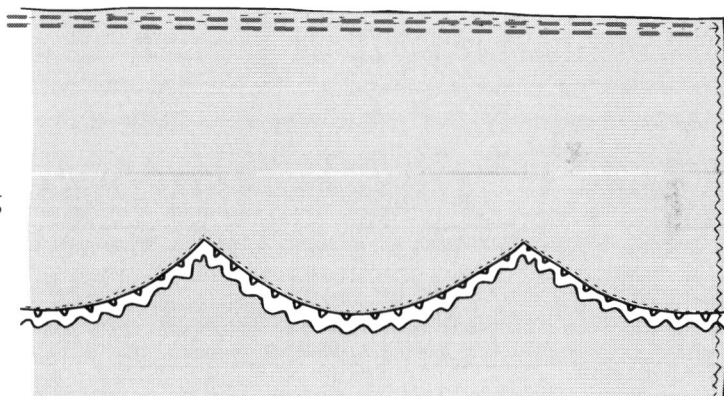

Step 18: Pin the back edges of the skirting right sides together. Stitch with a 1/2 inch (12 mm) seam allowance from the dot to the hem. Press the seam allowances open along the seam and fold lines.

Step 19: With the right sides together, pin the skirting to the bodice. Wrap the back facings around the back edge of the skirting and pin to the wrong side at the top edge. Draw up the gathering stitches to fit along the bodice, arranging the fullness evenly. Stitch, being careful not to catch the View A vest in the seamline. Finish the seam allowance if desired. Turn the bodice back facings right side out. Press the seam allowance up toward the bodice, being careful not to crush the gathers.

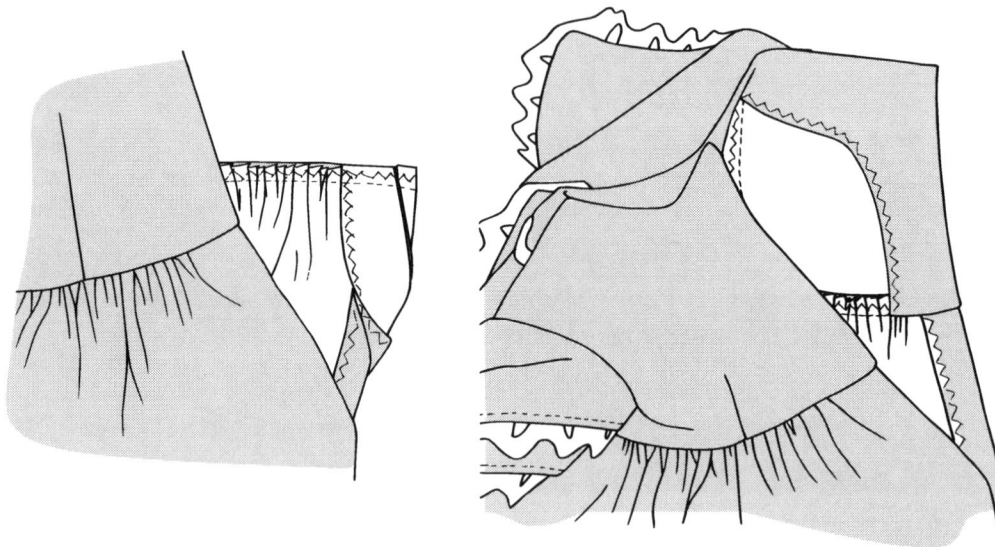

Step 20: *For View A,* tack the vest to the bodice front at the upper corners.

Step 21: Make buttonholes on the proper left bodice back and attach buttons on the proper right bodice back where indicated on the pattern. Snaps or hook and loop tape can be used if preferred.

Step 22: Finish the lower edge of the underskirt with a narrow hem .

Step 23: For both views, attach a small bow at the center front.

View B

Pattern Pieces

Cutting Layout for 45-inch (1.14 m) wide Fabric
12 Pieces

1 ~ 1850s View A & B Bodice Front
2 ~ 1850s View A & B Bodice Back
3 ~ 1850s View A Vest
4 ~ 1850s View A & B Front Facing
5 ~ 1850s View A & B Back Facing
6 ~ 1850s View A & B Undersleeve
7 ~ 1850s View B Oversleeve
8 ~ 1850s View A & B Ties
9 ~ 1850s View A & B Overskirt
10 ~ 1850s View A & B Underskirt
11 ~ 1850s View B Bodice Overlay #1
12 ~ 1850s View B Bodice Overlay #2

View A Dress

View A 1850s Dress Girls Dress
Use pieces: 1, 2, 3, 4, 5, 6, 8, 9, and 10

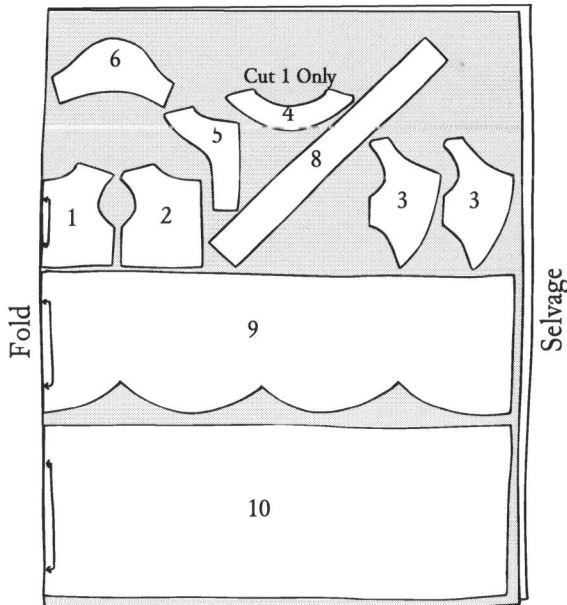

View B 1850s Girls Dress
Use pieces: 1, 2, 4, 5, 6, 7, 8, 9, 10, 11, and 12

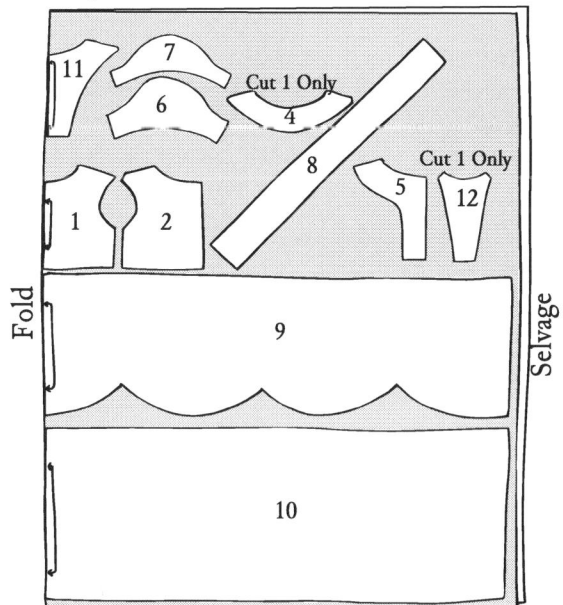

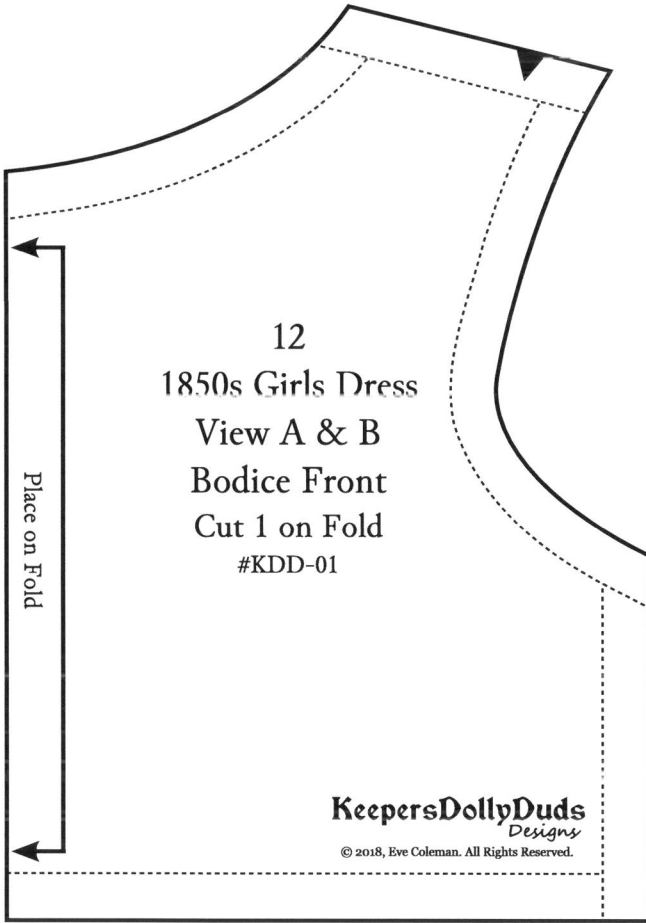

12
1850s Girls Dress
View A & B
Bodice Front
Cut 1 on Fold
#KDD-01

Place on Fold

KeepersDollyDuds
Designs
© 2018, Eve Coleman. All Rights Reserved.

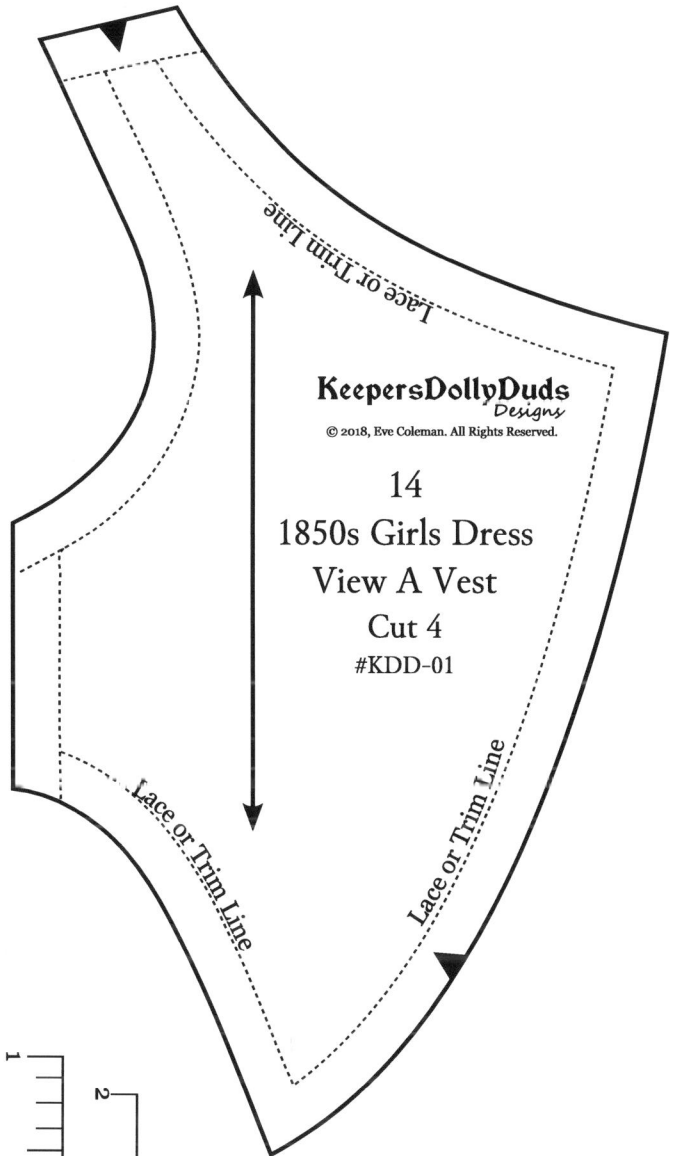

Lace or Trim Line

KeepersDollyDuds
Designs
© 2018, Eve Coleman. All Rights Reserved.

14
1850s Girls Dress
View A Vest
Cut 4
#KDD-01

Lace or Trim Line

Lace or Trim Line

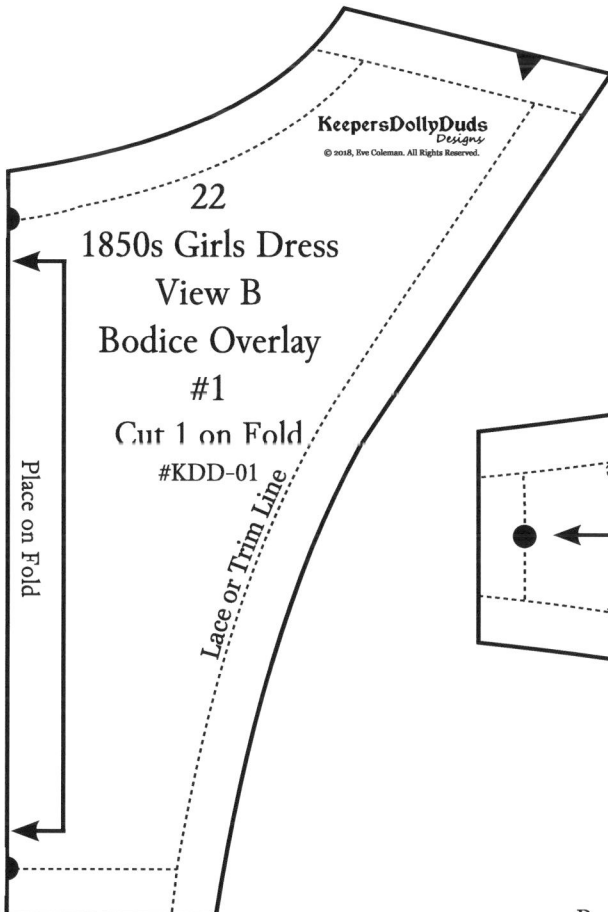

KeepersDollyDuds
Designs
© 2018, Eve Coleman. All Rights Reserved.

22
1850s Girls Dress
View B
Bodice Overlay
#1
Cut 1 on Fold
#KDD-01

Place on Fold

Lace or Trim Line

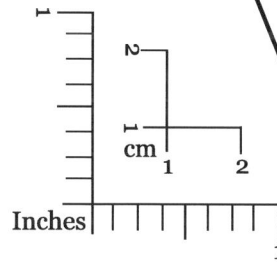

1
2
1
cm 1 2
Inches 1

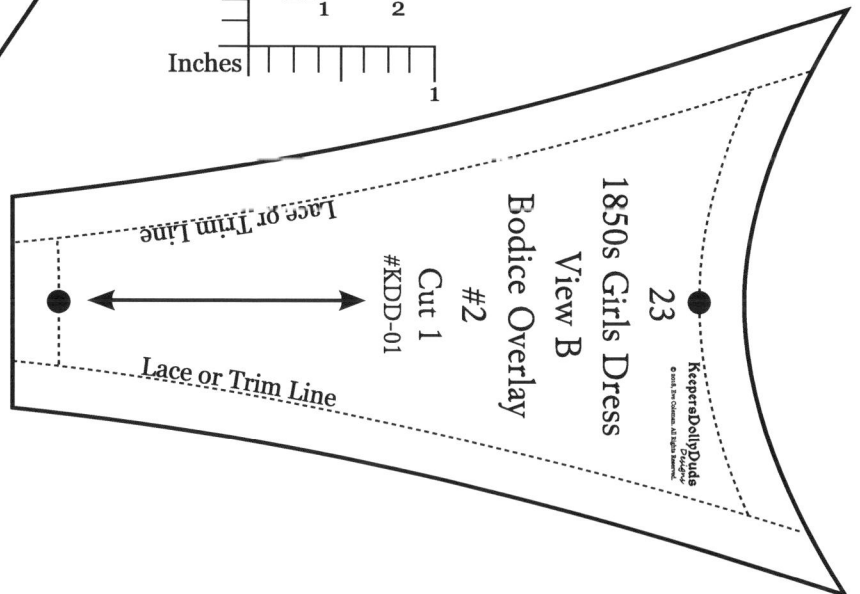

Lace or Trim Line

1850s Girls Dress
View B
Bodice Overlay
#2
Cut 1
#KDD-01

23

KeepersDollyDuds
Designs

Lace or Trim Line

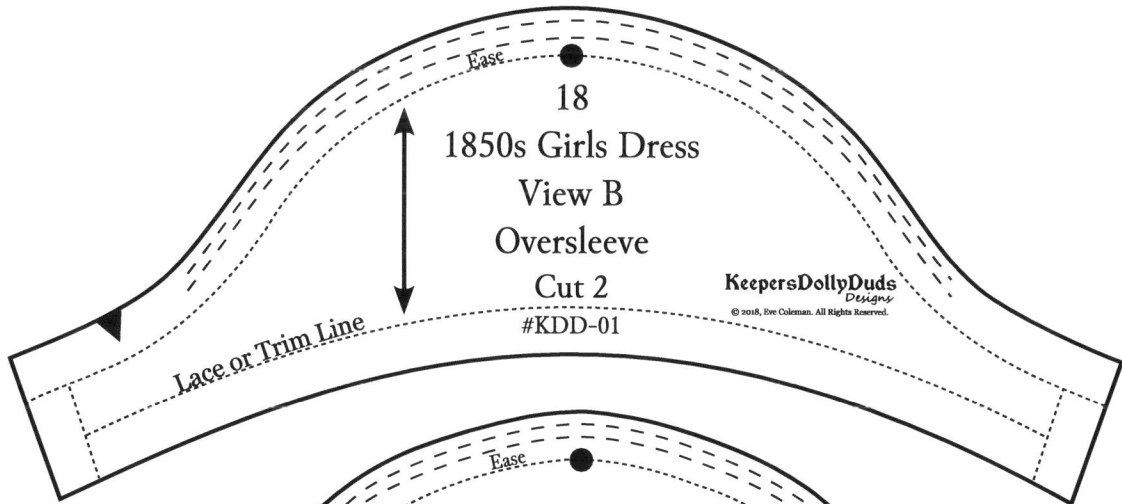

Ease

18
1850s Girls Dress
View B
Oversleeve
Cut 2

KeepersDollyDuds
Designs
© 2018, Eve Coleman. All Rights Reserved.

#KDD-01

Lace or Trim Line

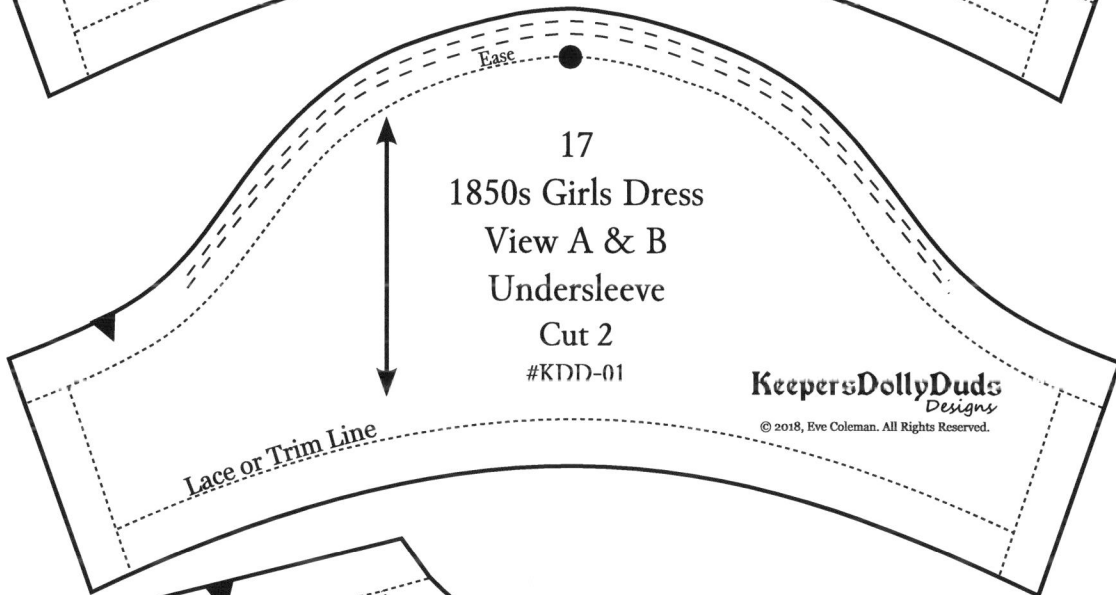

Ease

17
1850s Girls Dress
View A & B
Undersleeve
Cut 2
#KDD-01

KeepersDollyDuds
Designs
© 2018, Eve Coleman. All Rights Reserved.

Lace or Trim Line

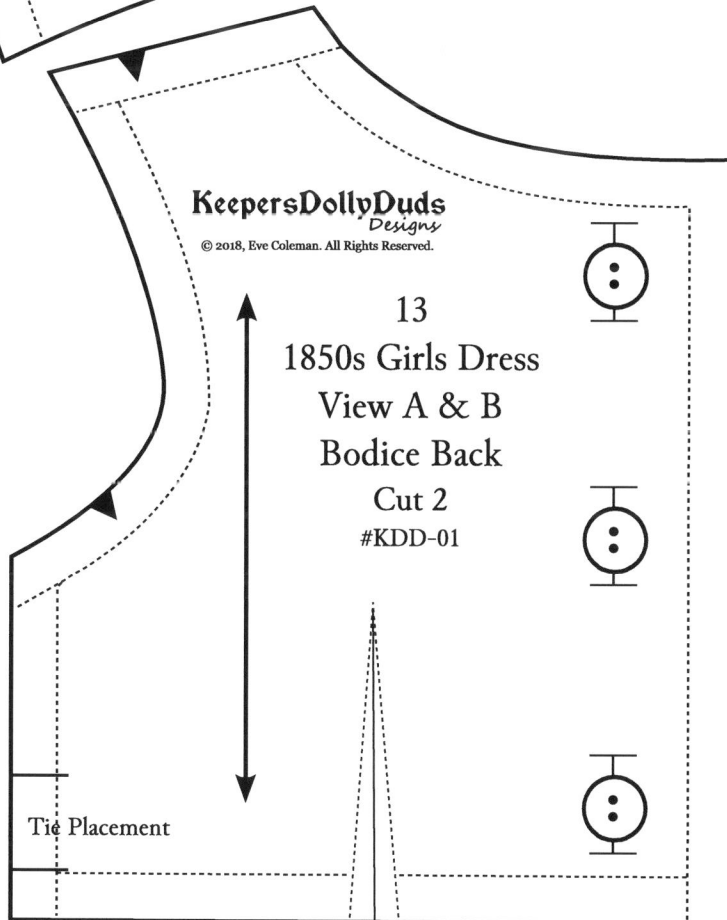

KeepersDollyDuds
Designs
© 2018, Eve Coleman. All Rights Reserved.

13
1850s Girls Dress
View A & B
Bodice Back
Cut 2
#KDD-01

Tie Placement

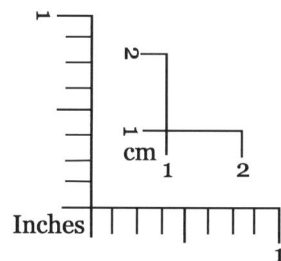

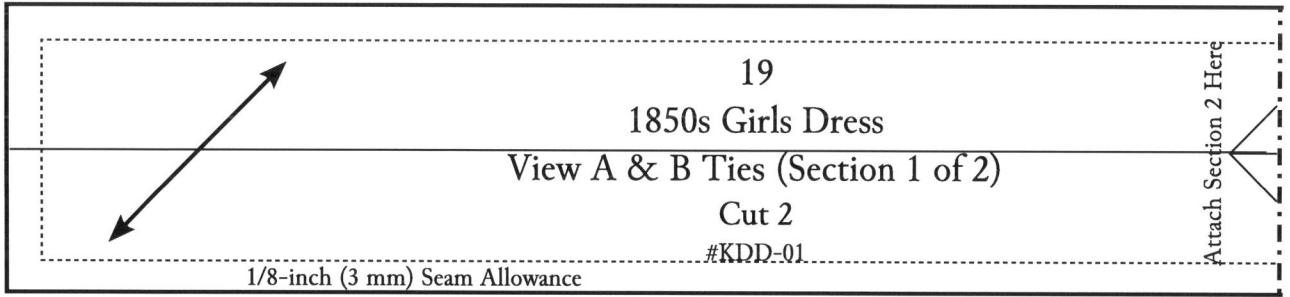

19
1850s Girls Dress
View A & B Ties (Section 1 of 2)
Cut 2
#KDD-01
1/8-inch (3 mm) Seam Allowance

Attach Section 2 Here

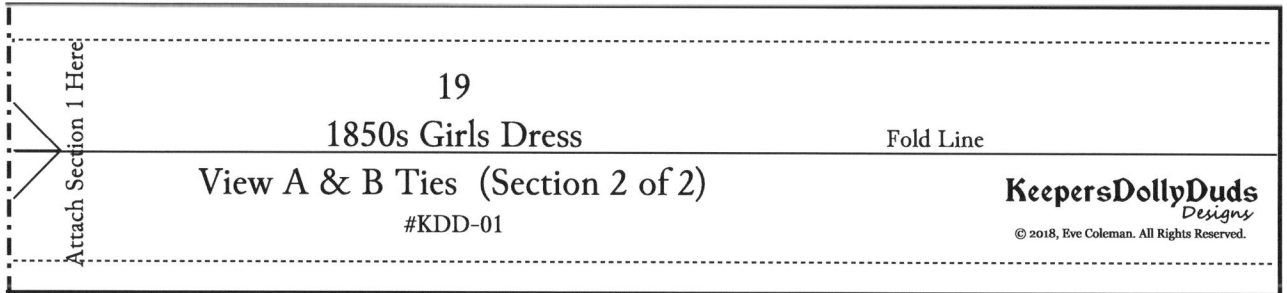

Attach Section 1 Here

19
1850s Girls Dress
View A & B Ties (Section 2 of 2)
#KDD-01

Fold Line

KeepersDollyDuds
Designs
© 2018, Eve Coleman. All Rights Reserved.

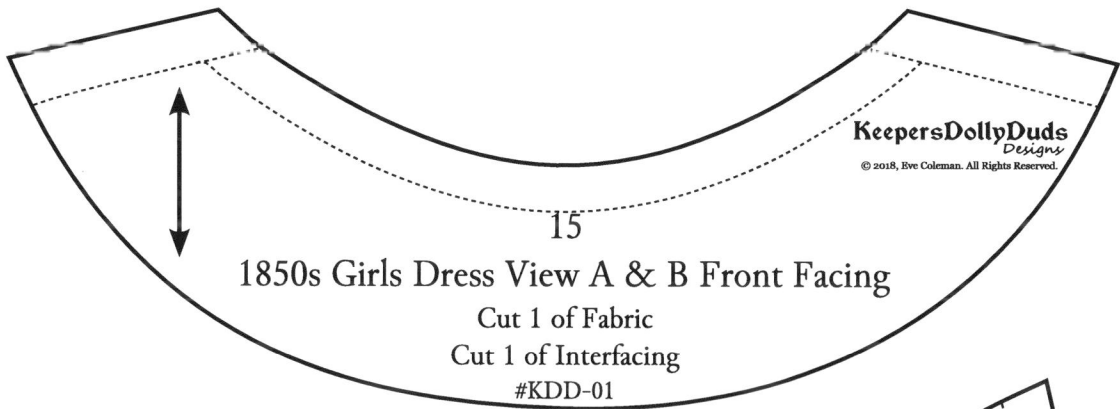

KeepersDollyDuds
Designs
© 2018, Eve Coleman. All Rights Reserved.

15
1850s Girls Dress View A & B Front Facing
Cut 1 of Fabric
Cut 1 of Interfacing
#KDD-01

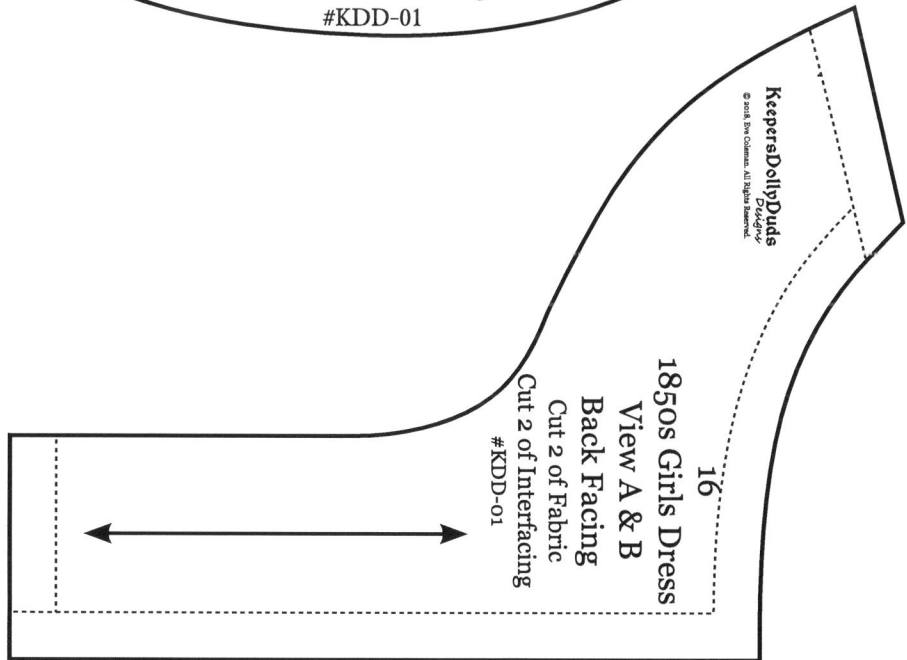

KeepersDollyDuds
Designs
© 2018, Eve Coleman. All Rights Reserved.

16
1850s Girls Dress
View A & B
Back Facing
Cut 2 of Fabric
Cut 2 of Interfacing
#KDD-01

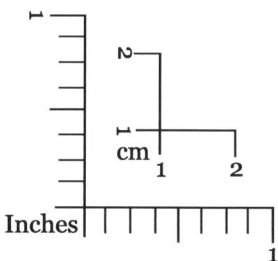

1
2
1
cm   1   2
Inches
1

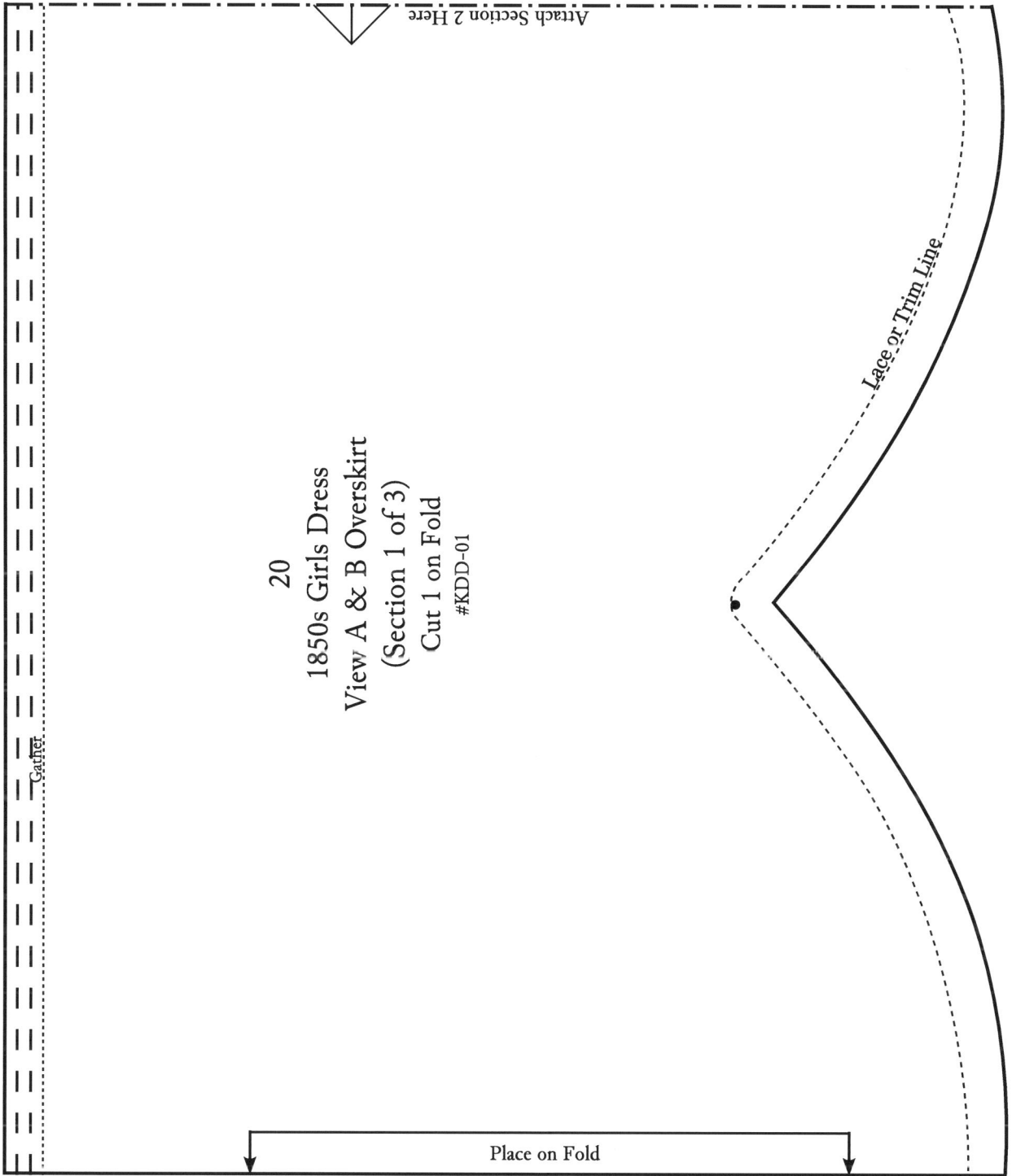

Attach Section 2 Here

Lace or Trim Line

20
1850s Girls Dress
View A & B Overskirt
(Section 1 of 3)
Cut 1 on Fold
#KDD-01

Gather

Place on Fold

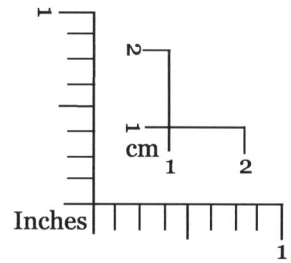

20
1850s Girls Dress
View A & B Overskirt
(Section 2 of 3)
#KDD-01

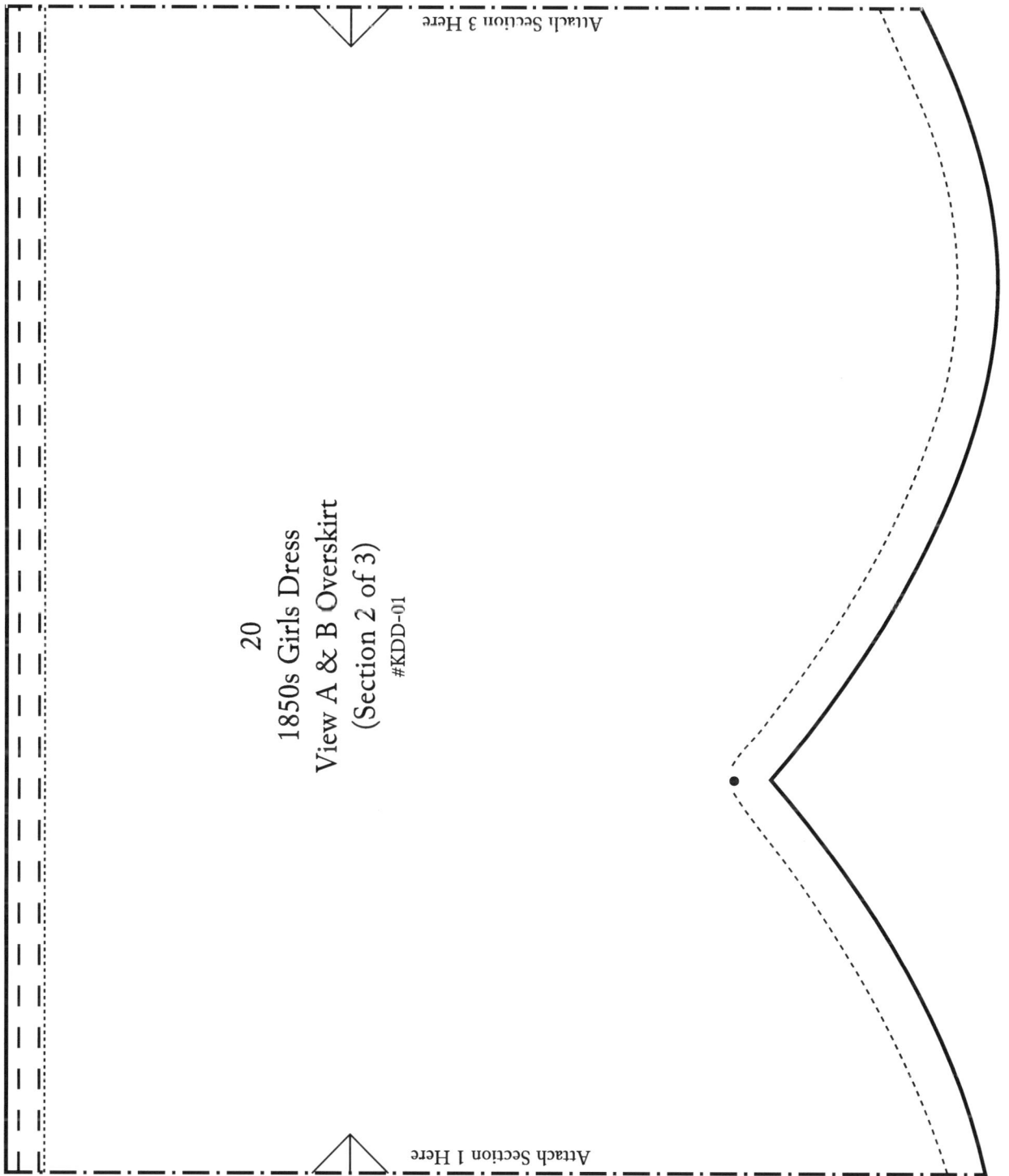

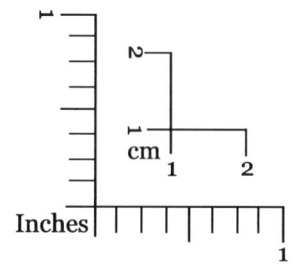

Attach Section 3 Here

Attach Section 1 Here

1

2

1

cm   1   2

Inches   1

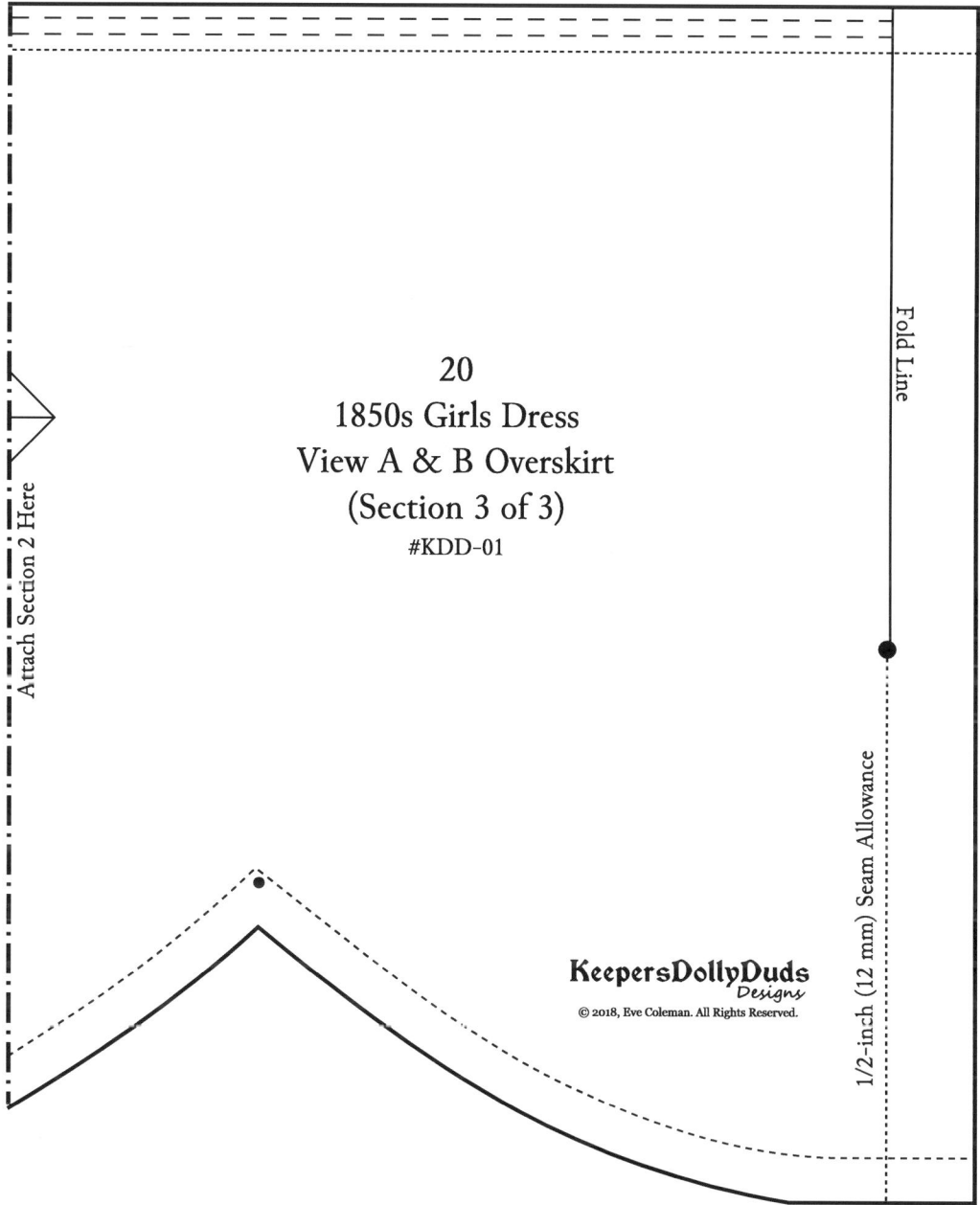

20
1850s Girls Dress
View A & B Overskirt
(Section 3 of 3)
#KDD-01

Attach Section 2 Here

Fold Line

1/2-inch (12 mm) Seam Allowance

KeepersDollyDuds
Designs
© 2018, Eve Coleman. All Rights Reserved.

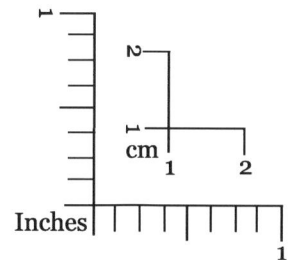

Gather

Place or Fold

Attach Section 2 Here

21
1850s Girls Dress
View A & B Underskirt
(Section 1 of 3)
Cut 1 on Fold
#KDD-01

1/4-inch (6 mm) Narrow Hem Allowed

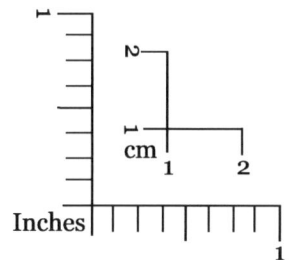

cm

Inches

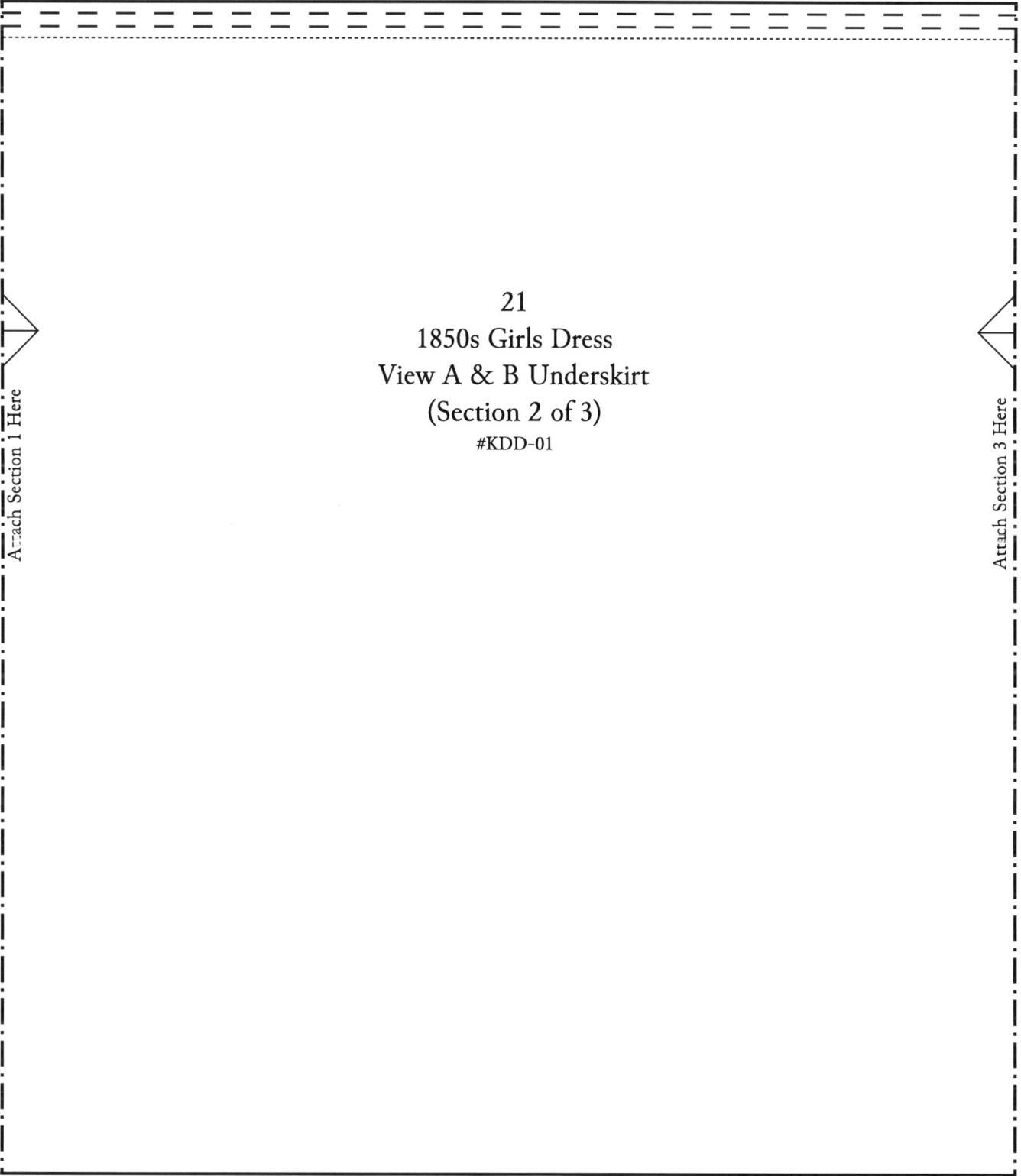

21
1850s Girls Dress
View A & B Underskirt
(Section 2 of 3)
#KDD-01

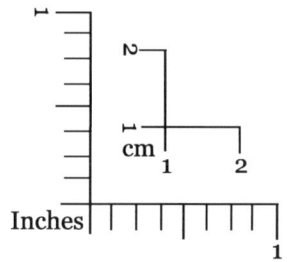

cm

Inches

21
1850s Girls Dress
View A & B Underskirt
(Section 3 of 3)
#KDD-01

Fold Line

1/2 inch (12 mm) Seam Allowance

Attach Section 2 Here

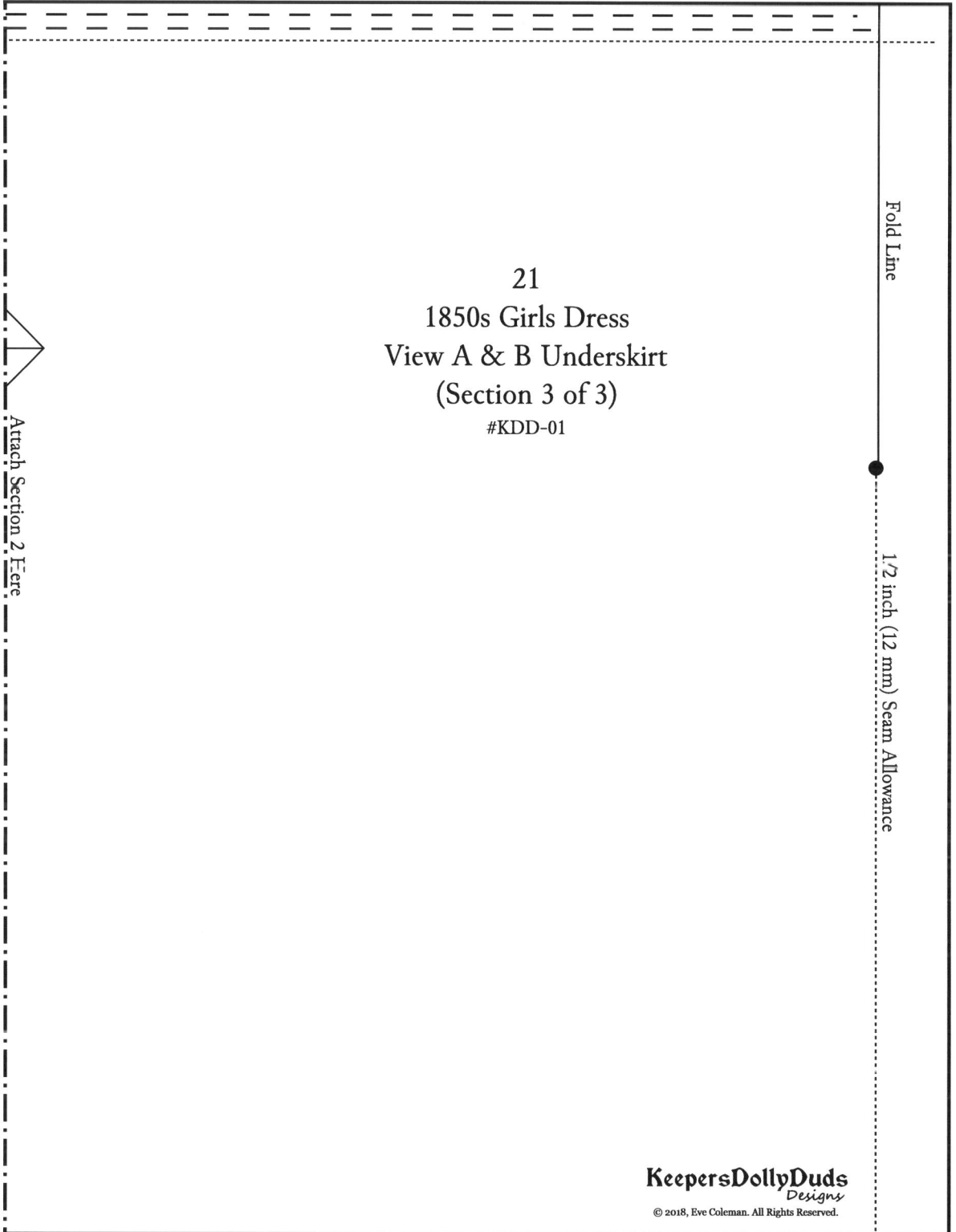

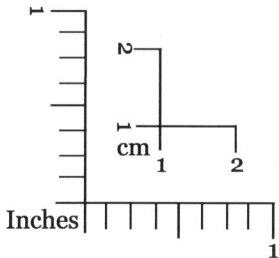

cm
Inches

1850s Girls Jacket and Bonnet

Materials List

⬤⬤⬤

#KDD-02

Suggested Fabrics: *Jacket and Bonnet* in woven fabric such as cotton or cotton blends, wool, velveteen, or twill. Not suitable for knits. *Jacket and Bonnet Lining* in synthetic suit lining, silk, satin, cotton or cotton blends. Not suitable for knits.

Fabric Yardage:

Jacket and Bonnet - 1/2 yard (0.5 m) 45-inch wide fabric
Lining - 1/2 yard (0.5 m) 45-inch wide fabric

Notions:

__Thread
View A Jacket
__Six 3/8-inch (9 mm) buttons
View B Jacket
__Eight 3/8-inch (9 mm) buttons
__Bobby pin for turning fabric tubes
Bonnet
__6-inch by 20-inch piece of woven, lightweight, fusible interfacing
__13-inches 1-inch wide gathered lace
__2/3 yard 1/2-inch wide ribbon

View A Jacket and Bonnet

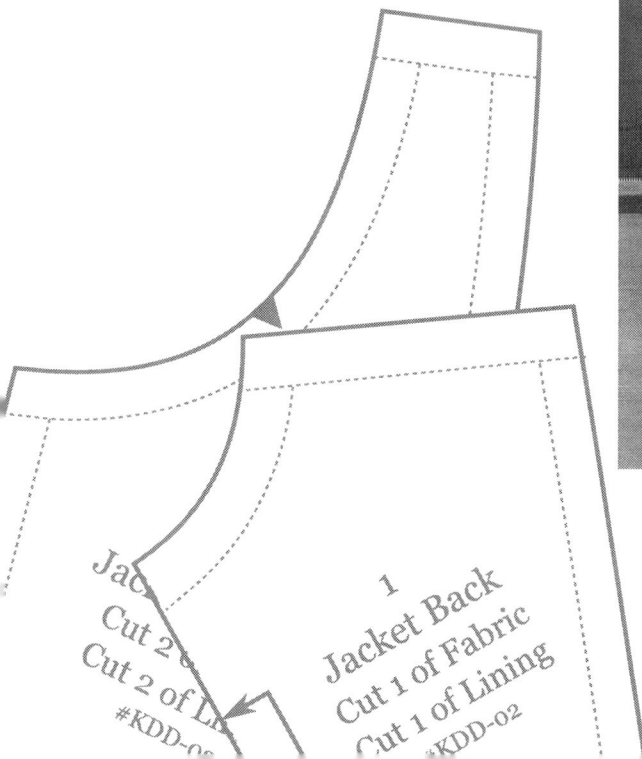

Jacket

Step 1: Stay-stitch the jacket front, jacket side front, jacket back and jacket side back just inside the seam allowances where indicated on the pattern. Clip the curves up to the stitching line.

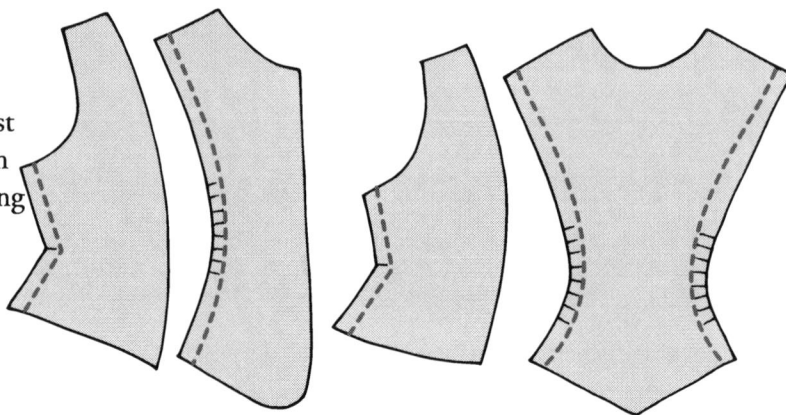

Step 2: Pin jacket back and jacket side back pieces together, matching notches and easing fabric along the curves. Stitch. Press the seam allowances toward the center back and top stitch through all layers 1/8-inch (3 mm) from the seam line.

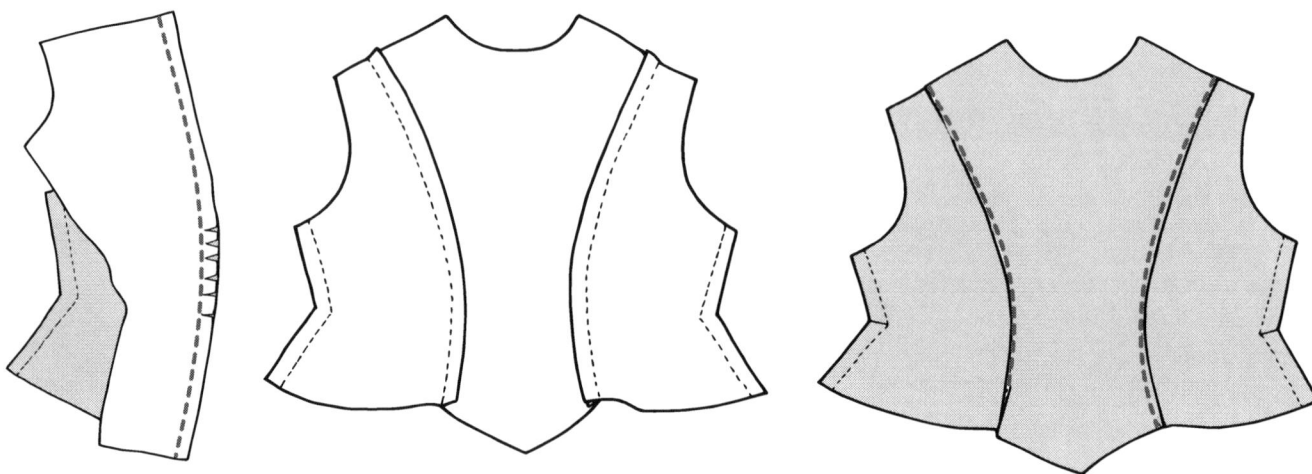

Step 3: Follow the instructions in Step 2 for the jacket front pieces.

Loop Closures ~ View B

For View A, Skip to Step 6

Step 4: To make the button loops, fold the bias trim piece in half right sides together along the fold line. Using a narrow zig-zag stitch, sew a seam 1/4- inch from the folded edge. to turn the tube, snip the folded edge up to the seamline about 1/2-inch from the end. Slip a bobby pin onto the cut end of the tube and slide it into the tube through the slit. Push the bobby pin through the tube. Once you work the end of the tube inside, the rest of the tube should slide through easily.

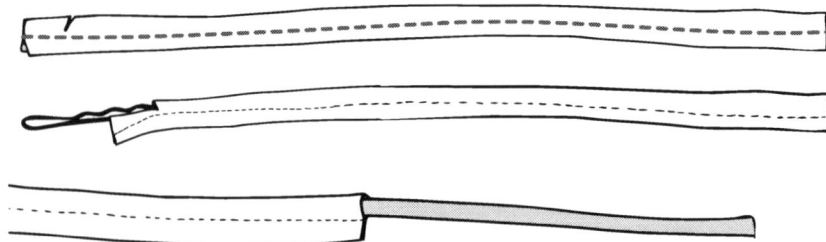

Step 5: Cut eight 1-3/4-inch (4.5 cm) long loop sections from the tube. Fold them in half and pin them to the proper right jacket front where indicated on the pattern. Line up the rounded ends of the loops 3/4-inch (2 cm) from the front edge. Baste to secure.

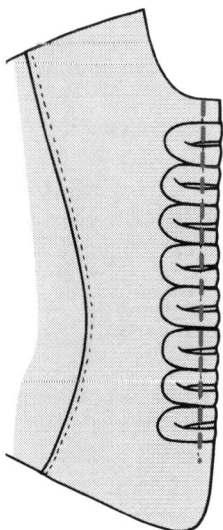

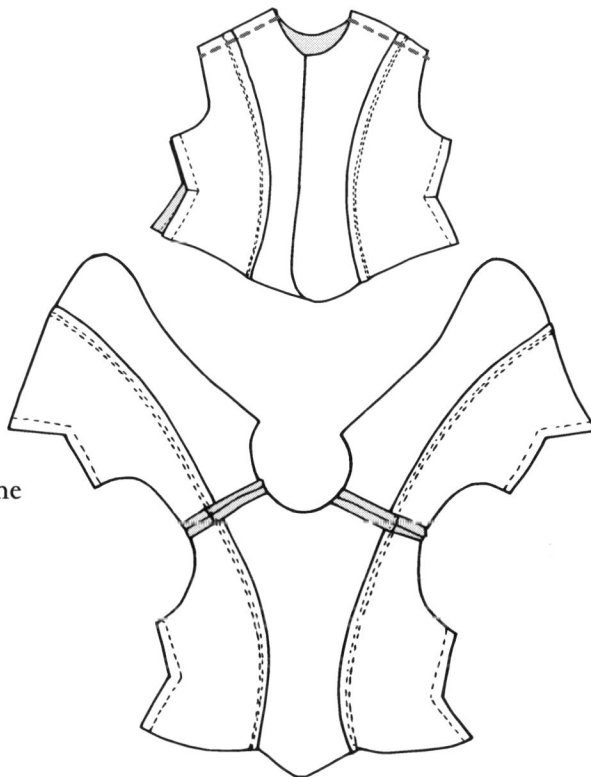

Step 6: With right sides together, pin the jacket front to the jacket back at the shoulder seams. Stitch and press the seam allowances open.

Sleeves

Step 7: Sew two rows of gathering stitches on the sleeves where indicated on the pattern.

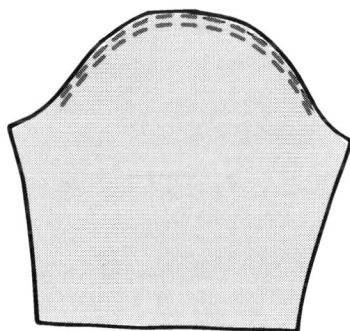

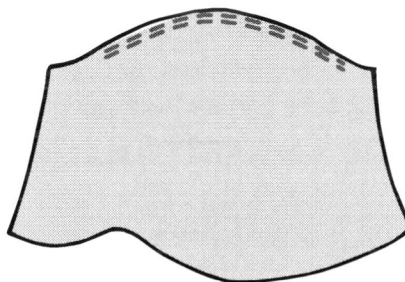

View A Sleeve   View B Sleeve

Step 8: With the right sides together, pin the sleeves to the armscyes matching the notches. Draw up the gathering stitches to ease or gather the tops of the sleeves to fit the armscyes. Arrange the fullness evenly. Stitch. Clip the curves and trim the seam allowances to 1/8-inch (3 mm). Press seam allowances towards the jacket bodice.

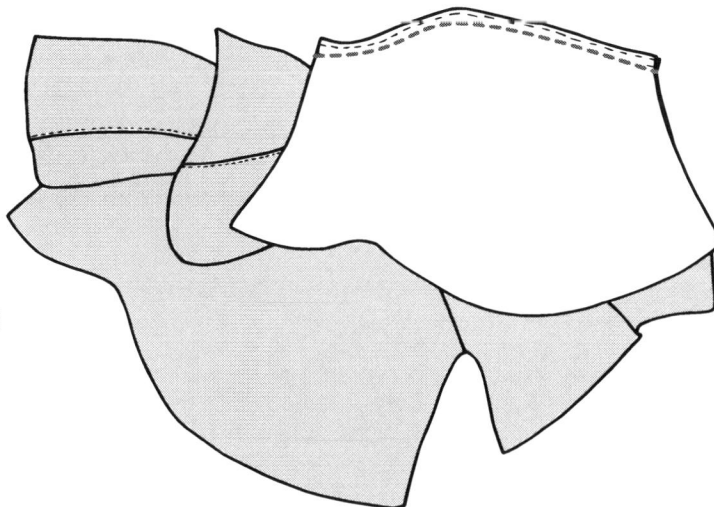

Jacket Lining

Step 9: Repeat Steps 1 through 3 and 6 through 7 for the jacket lining, except press the armscy seam allowances toward the sleeves.

Step 10: Pin the lining to the jacket right sides together, along the bottom edges of the sleeves, the bottom edges of the jacket back, and the bottom, front, and neckline edges of the jacket front. Stitch the pinned edges. Clip the corners and inside curves and notch the outside curves.

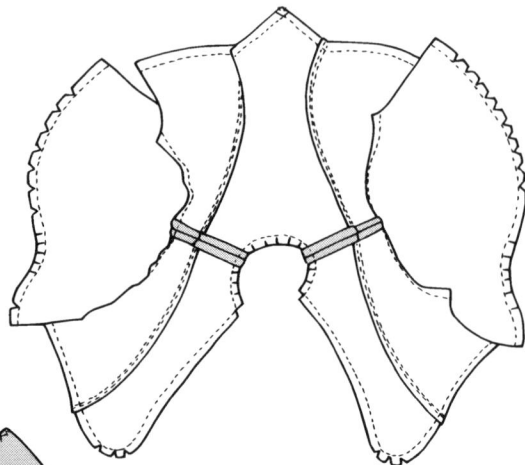

Step 11: Turn the jacket right side out. Press, following the seam lines. Line up the side seam allowances of the jacket and jacket lining finish the seam allowances, if desired.

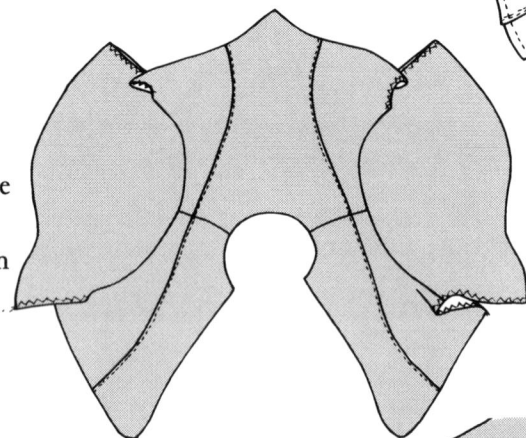

Step 12: Pin the side seam allowances of the jacket and sleeves right sides together, matching the armscyes and hemlines. Stitch. Press the seam allowances open. Tack down the ends of the seam allowances at the hemline and bottom edge of the sleeves. On inside of jacket tack the lining to the jacket at the armscye and shoulders to keep lining from shifting.

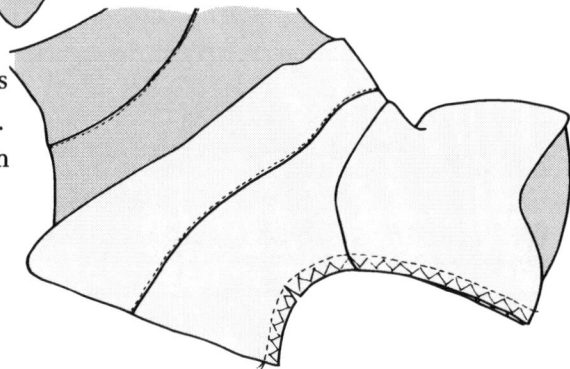

Tab Closures ~ View A

For View B, skip to Step 16

Step 13: With right sides together, pin each tab to a tab lining. Stitch with a 1/8-inch (3 mm) seam allowance, leaving the space between the dots open for turning. Clip the corners.

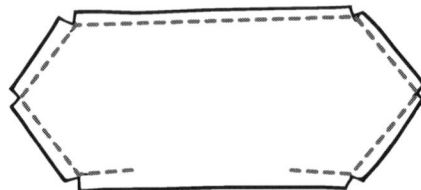

Step 14: Turn each tab right side out, squaring the corners with a blunt needle. Tuck seam allowances of the opening in and press, following the seamlines.

Step 15: Topstitch all the way around the tabs close to the edge being careful to seal the opening.

Note: To help manipulate the small tabs, lay them on a piece of paper while sewing the topstitching and buttonholes. When finished, tear the paper away.

Step 16: Make a 3/8-inch (9 mm) buttonhole on the proper left side of each tab where indicated on the pattern. Position tabs where indicated on the jacket front and attach the tab with buttons on the proper right side. Align the right and left Jacket fronts so they meet in the middle and do not overlap. Attach buttons on the proper left directly underneath the buttonhole on each tab.

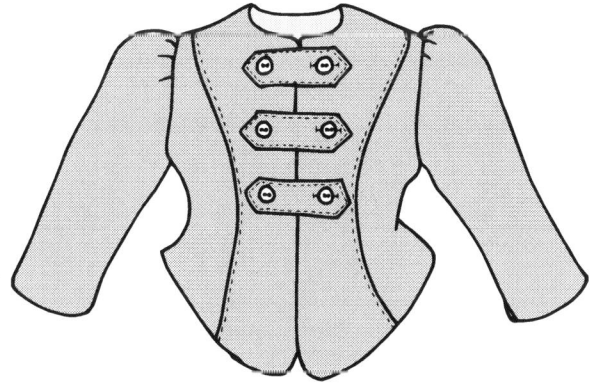

Button Placement ~ View B

Step 17: Align the right and left jacket fronts so they meet in the middle and do not overlap. Attach buttons on the proper left directly underneath each of the button loops.

Bonnet

Step 18: Apply fusible interfacing to wrong sides of bonnet brim and bonnet back following the manufacturers' instructions.

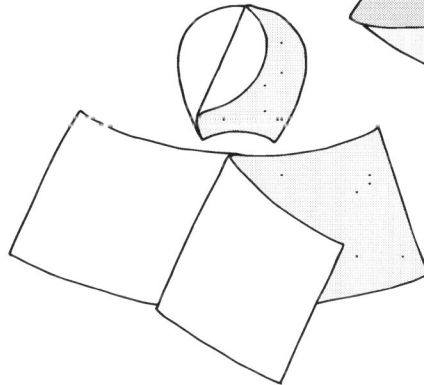

Step 19: Mark placement lines for the ruching and lace trim on the on the right sides of the bonnet brim and bonnet brim lining where indicated on the pattern.

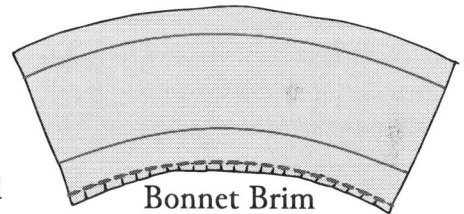

Step 20: Stay-stitch the back edge of the bonnet and bonnet lining and clip the curves.

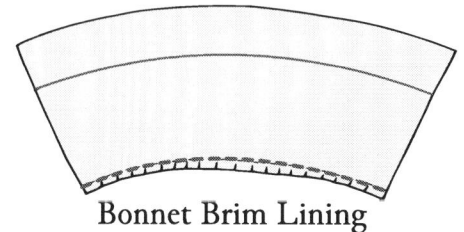

Bonnet Brim

Bonnet Brim Lining

Step 21: Finish the edges of the ruching with a narrow rolled hem OR cut 1/4-inch (6 mm) off one edge and serge the raw edges in a similar or complimentary color thread using a single needle on the serger.

Step 22: Sew three rows of gathering stitches along the ruching where indicated on the pattern.

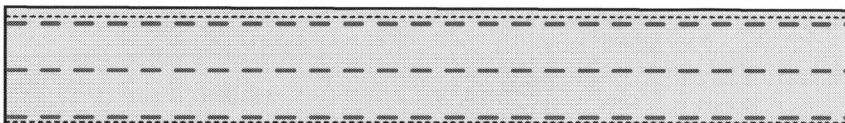

Step 23: Draw all three gathering threads together to create even ruching along the strip. Pin the strip on the bonnet brim where marked on the fabric arranging the fullness evenly. Top stitch along each side of the ruching and down the center to secure to the bonnet. Carefully remove the gathering stitches.

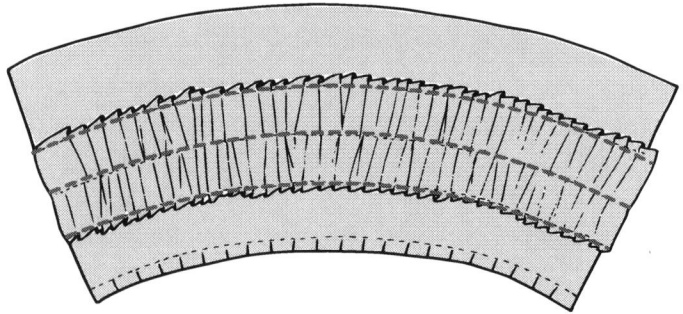

Step 24: Sew gathered lace along placement line of the bonnet brim lining. If using a different size lace, place the edge of the lace AT LEAST 1/4-inch (6 mm) FROM BRIM EDGE.

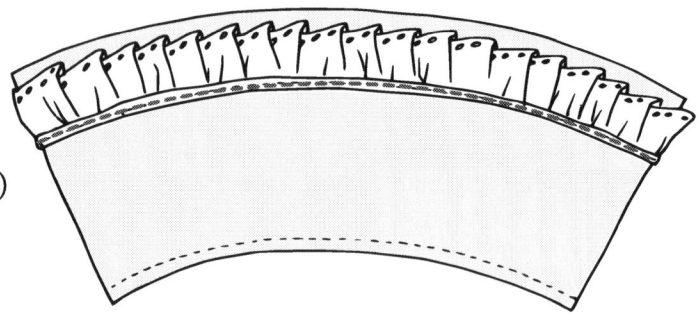

Step 25: Pin the bonnet back to the back edge of the bonnet brim, matching the center dots. Stitch. Press the seam allowance toward the bonnet brim and top stitch 1/8-inch (3 mm) from the seam through all the layers. Trim excess fabric. Repeat for the bonnet lining pieces.

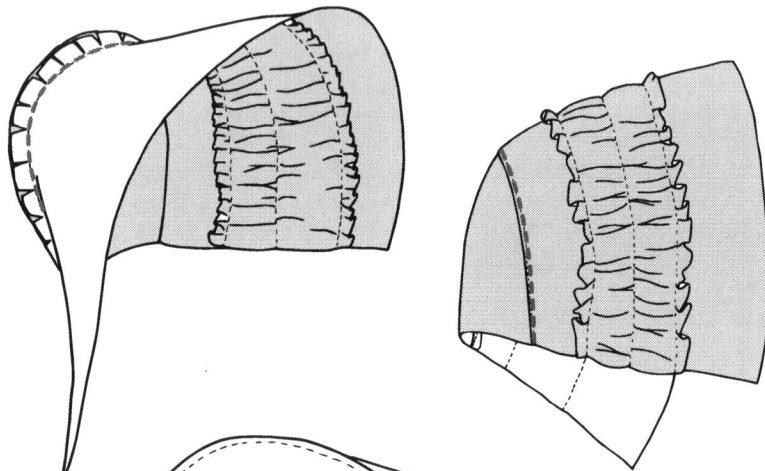

Step 26: Pin the bonnet and bonnet lining right sides together. Stitch, being careful not to catch the lace in seam along the brim. Leave a 2-1/2-inch opening along the bottom edge of the bonnet for turning. Clip the corners and curves and trim seam allowance to 1/8-inch (3 mm).

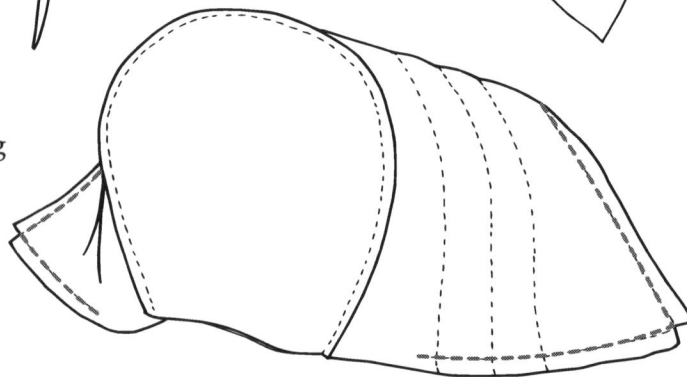

Step 27: Turn the bonnet right side out, squaring the corners with a blunt needle. Press, following the seam lines. Turn the seam allowances at the back opening in and whipstitch to close. Topstitch along the entire edge of the bonnet.

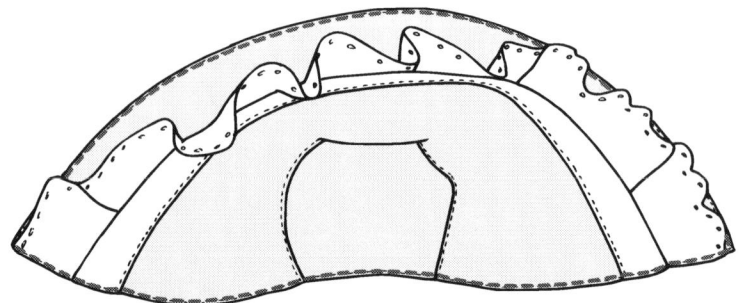

Step 28: With bonnet turned inside out, tack lining to bonnet fabric along the curved seam of the back piece to prevent lining from shifting.

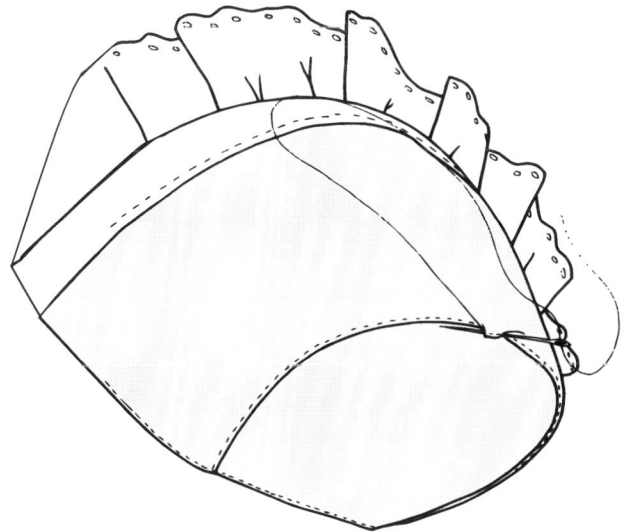

Step 29: Turn the bonnet right side out. Fold one end of a 12 inch (30 cm) long piece of 5/8-inch (16 mm) wide ribbon as shown. Attach one on each side of the bonnet where indicated on the pattern.

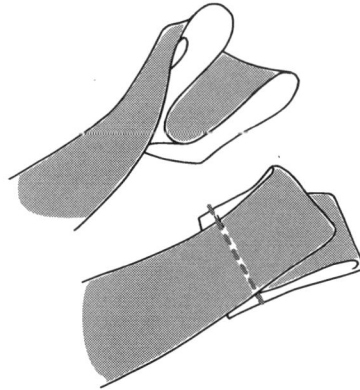

View A Jacket and Bonnet

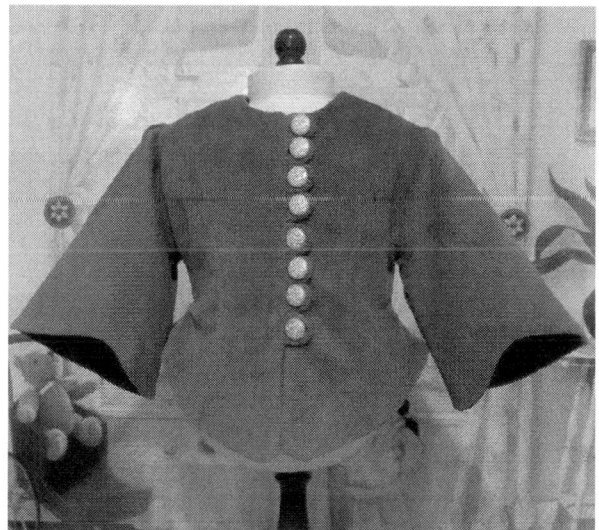

View B Jacket

Pattern Pieces

Cutting Layout for 45-inch (1.14 m) wide Fabric
11 Pieces

24 ~ 1850s View A & B Jacket Back
25 ~ 1850s View A & B Jacket Side Back
26 ~ 1850s View A & B Jacket Front
27 ~ 1850s View A & B Jacket Side Front
28 ~ 1850s View A Sleeve
29 ~ 1850s View B Sleeve
30 ~ 1850s View A Tab Closure
31 ~ 1850s Bonnet Brim
32 ~ 1850s Bonnet Back
33 ~ 1850s Bonnet Ruching
34 ~ 1850s View B Bias Tubing

View A Jacket Back

View A
1850s Girls Jacket and Bonnet
Use pieces: 24, 25, 26, 27, 28, 30, 31, 32, and 33

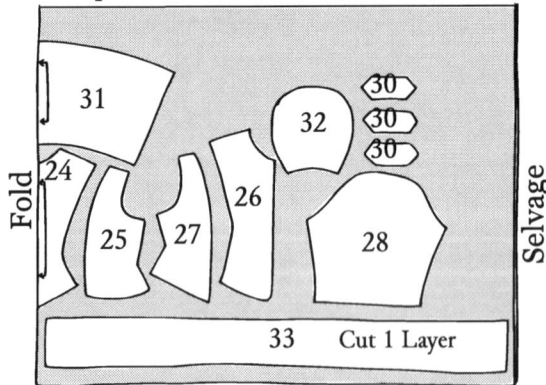

View A
1850s Girls Jacket and Bonnet Lining
Use pieces: 24, 25, 26, 27, 28, 30, 31, and 32

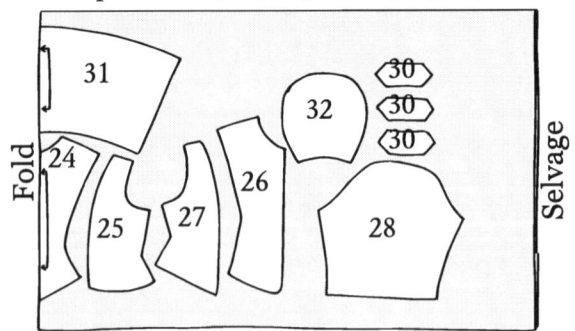

View B
1850s Girls Jacket and Bonnet
Use pieces: 24, 25, 26, 27, 29, 31, 32, and 34

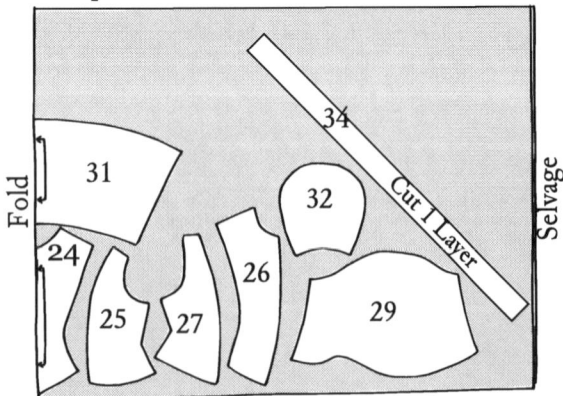

View B
1850s Girls Jacket and Bonnet Lining
Use pieces: 24, 25, 26, 27, 29, 31, and 32

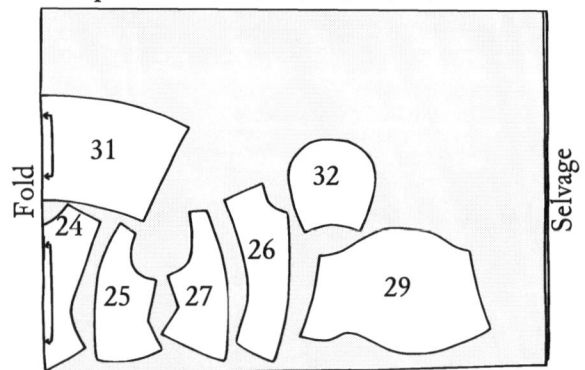

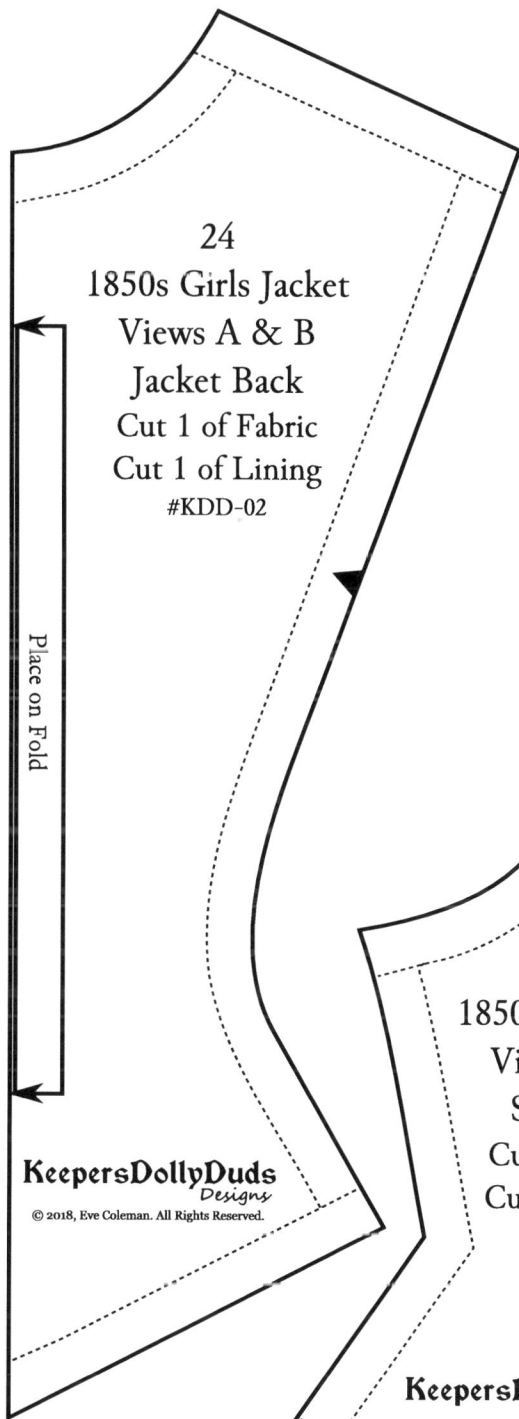

24
1850s Girls Jacket
Views A & B
Jacket Back
Cut 1 of Fabric
Cut 1 of Lining
#KDD-02

Place on Fold

KeepersDollyDuds
Designs
© 2018, Eve Coleman. All Rights Reserved.

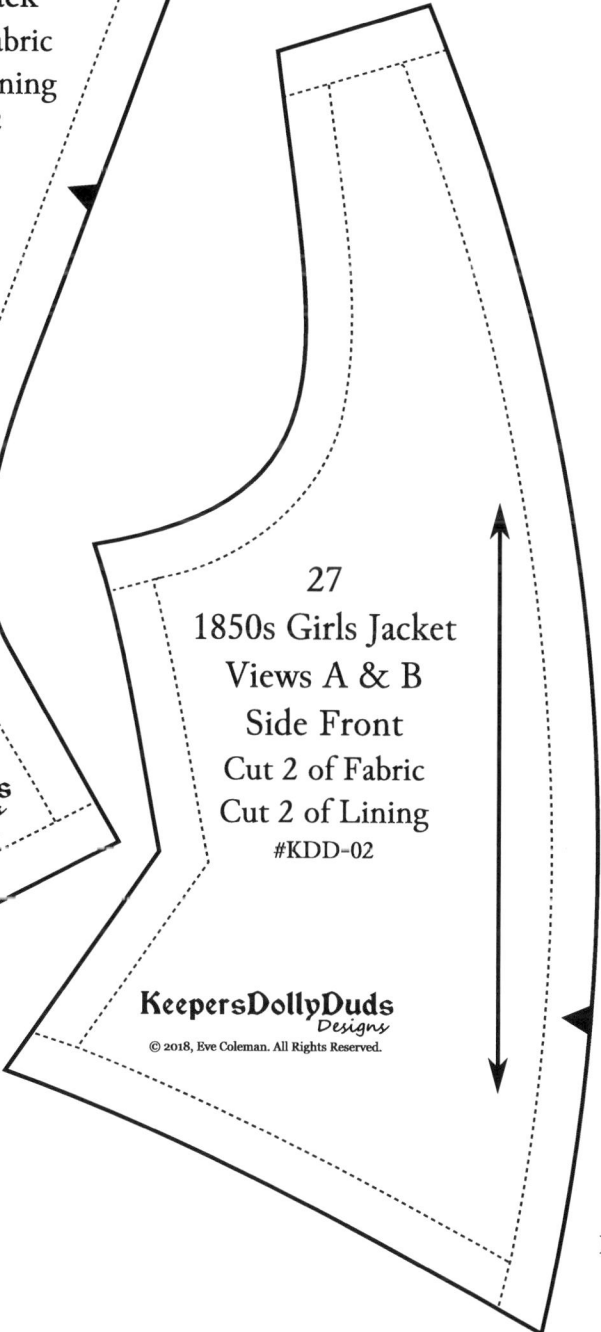

27
1850s Girls Jacket
Views A & B
Side Front
Cut 2 of Fabric
Cut 2 of Lining
#KDD-02

KeepersDollyDuds
Designs
© 2018, Eve Coleman. All Rights Reserved.

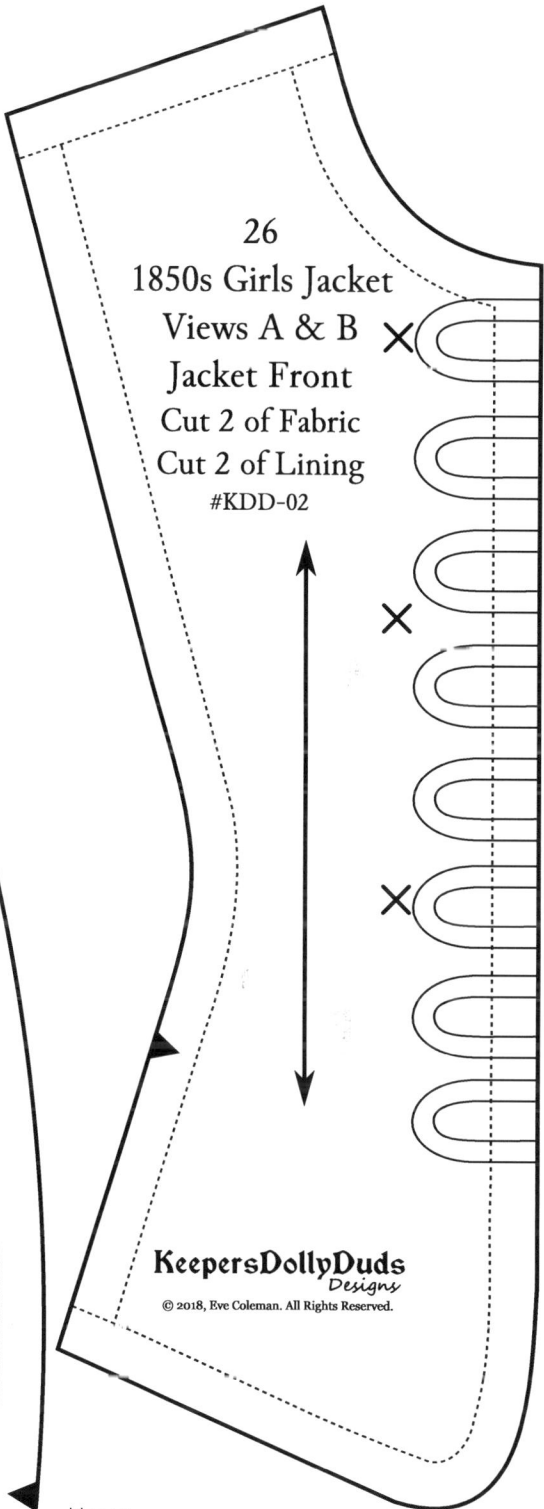

26
1850s Girls Jacket
Views A & B
Jacket Front
Cut 2 of Fabric
Cut 2 of Lining
#KDD-02

KeepersDollyDuds
Designs
© 2018, Eve Coleman. All Rights Reserved.

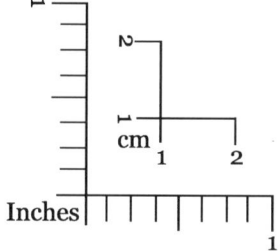

1

2

1

cm   1   2

Inches

1

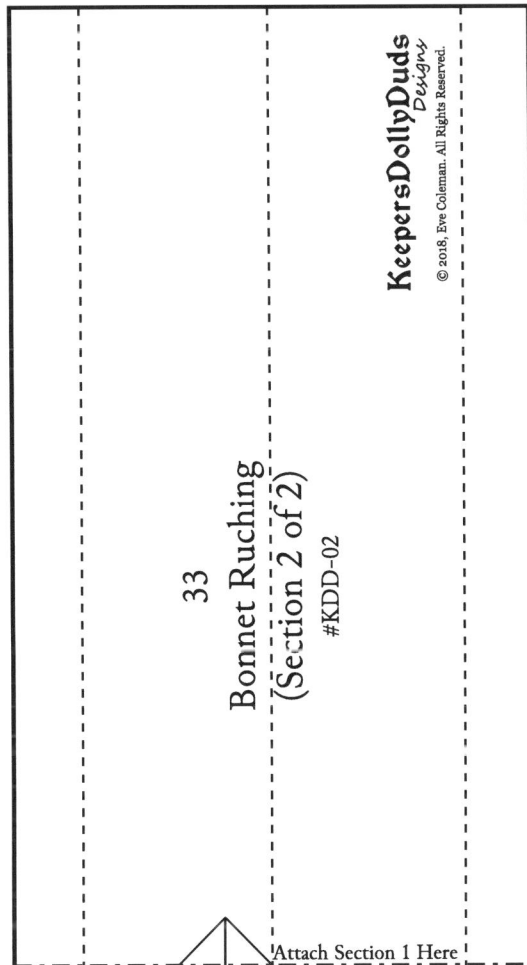

33
Bonnet Ruching
(Section 2 of 2)
#KDD-02

Attach Section 1 Here

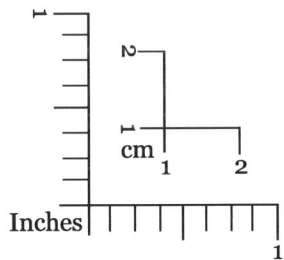

1
2
1
cm   1   2
Inches   1

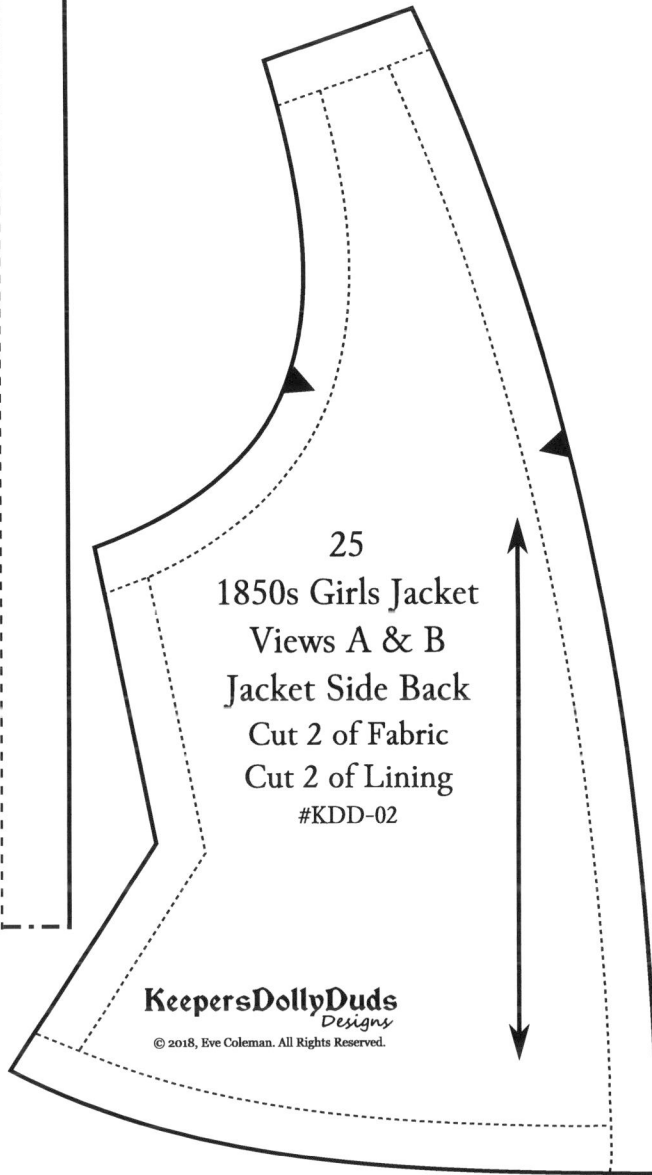

25
1850s Girls Jacket
Views A & B
Jacket Side Back
Cut 2 of Fabric
Cut 2 of Lining
#KDD-02

KeepersDollyDuds
Designs
© 2018, Eve Coleman. All Rights Reserved.

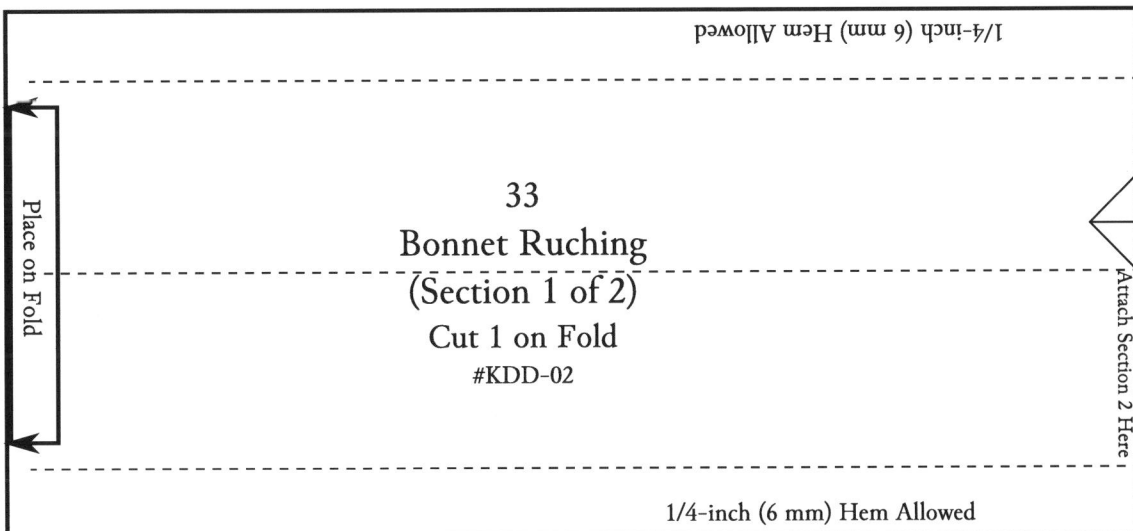

1/4-inch (6 mm) Hem Allowed

33
Bonnet Ruching
(Section 1 of 2)
Cut 1 on Fold
#KDD-02

Place on Fold

Attach Section 2 Here

1/4-inch (6 mm) Hem Allowed

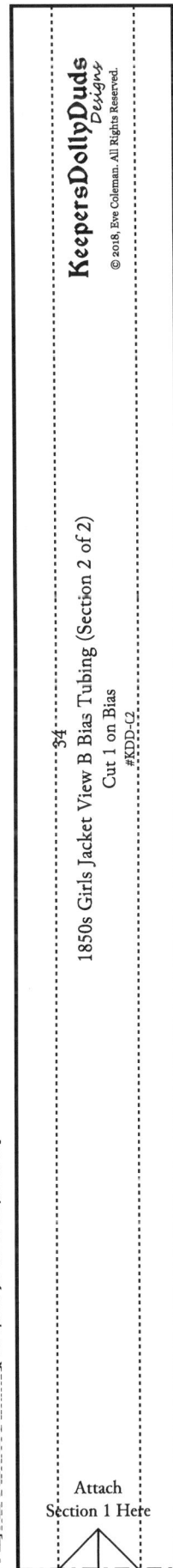

34

1850s Girls Jacket View B Bias Tubing (Section 2 of 2)
Cut 1 on Bias
#KDD-C2

Attach
Section 1 Here

28

1850s Girls Jacket
View A
Jacket Sleeve
Cut 2 of Fabric
Cut 2 of Lining
#KDD-02

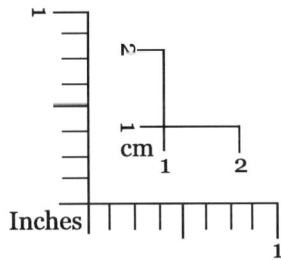

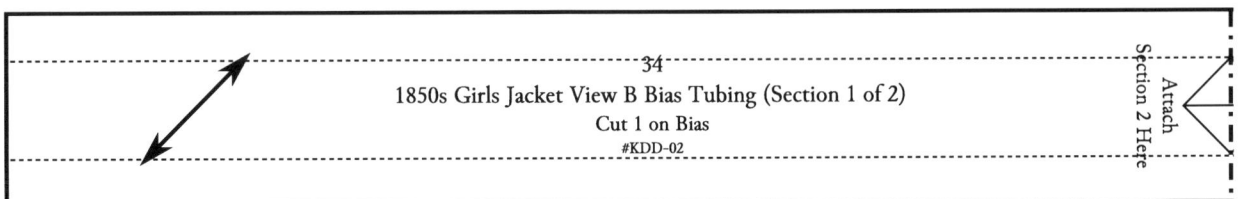

Gather

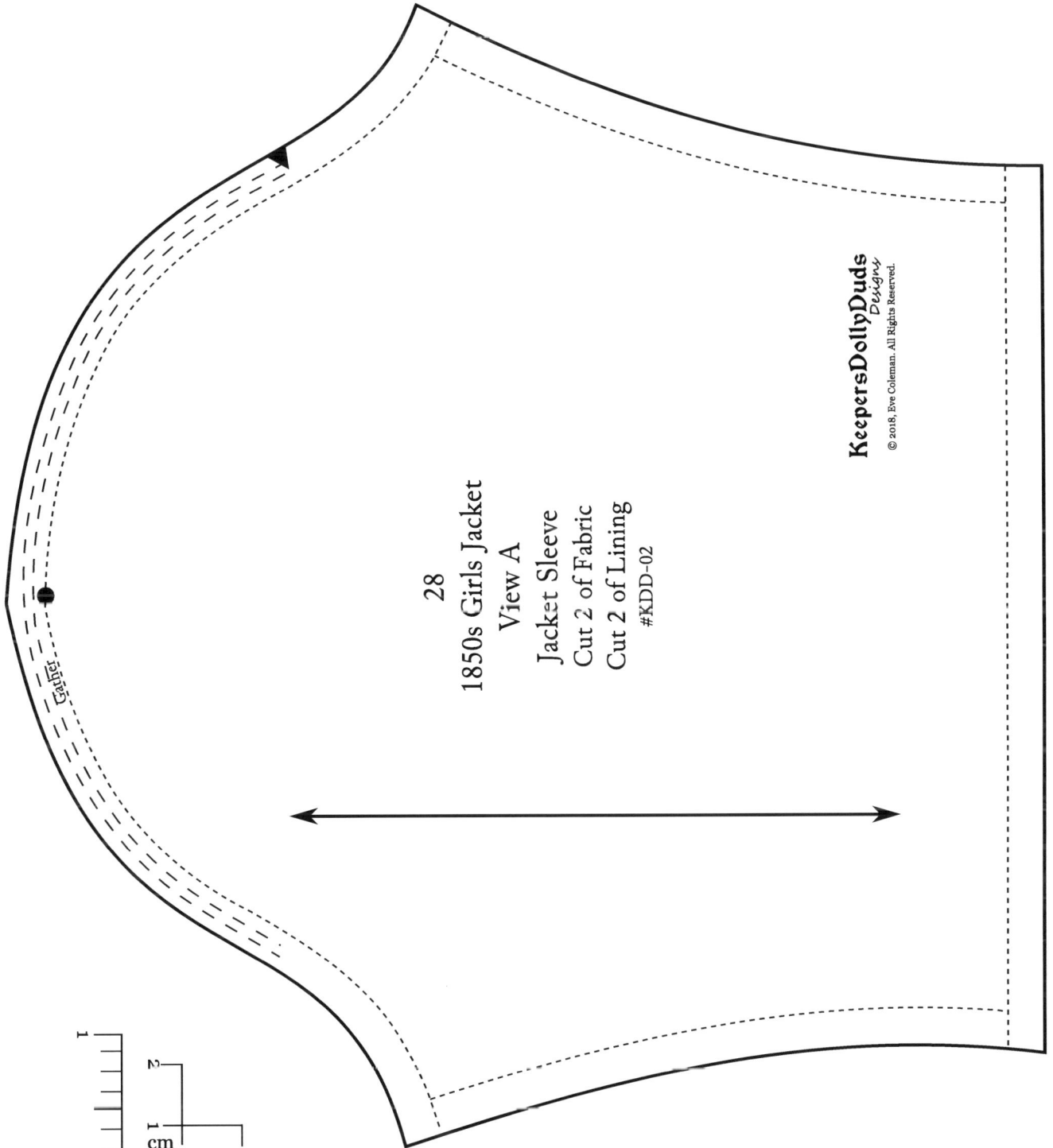

1

2

cm
1   2

Inches   1

34

1850s Girls Jacket View B Bias Tubing (Section 1 of 2)
Cut 1 on Bias
#KDD-02

Attach
Section 2 Here

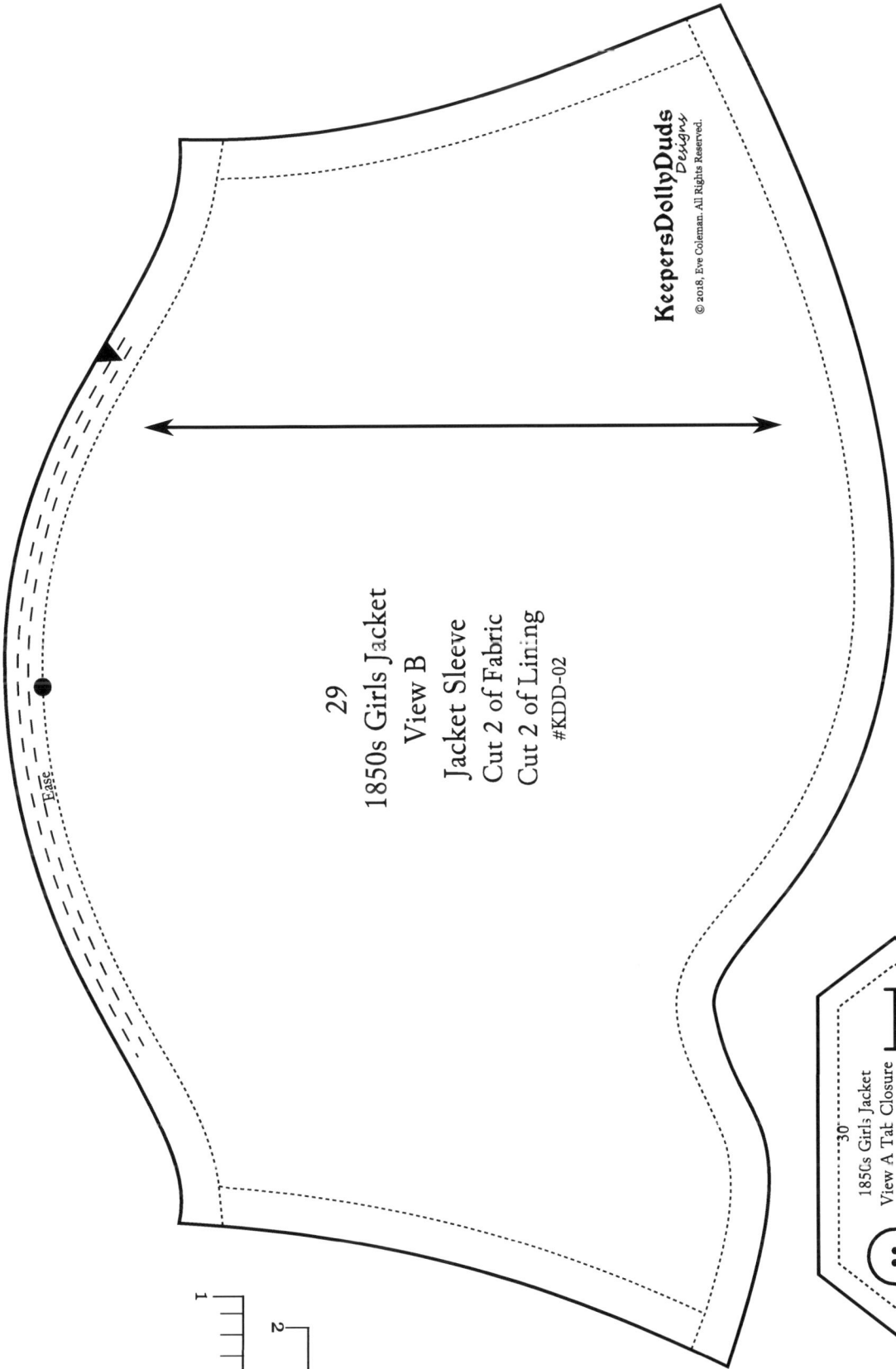

29
1850s Girls Jacket
View B
Jacket Sleeve
Cut 2 of Fabric
Cut 2 of Lining
#KDD-02

Ease

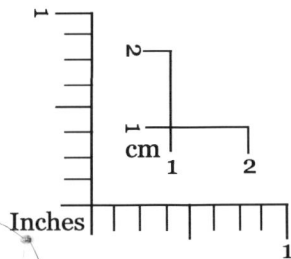

1850s Girls Jacket
View A Tab Closure
Cut 3 of Fabric
Cut 3 of Lining
KeepersDollyDuds
© 2018, Eve Coleman. All Rights Reserved.

1
2
1
cm   1   2
Inches   1

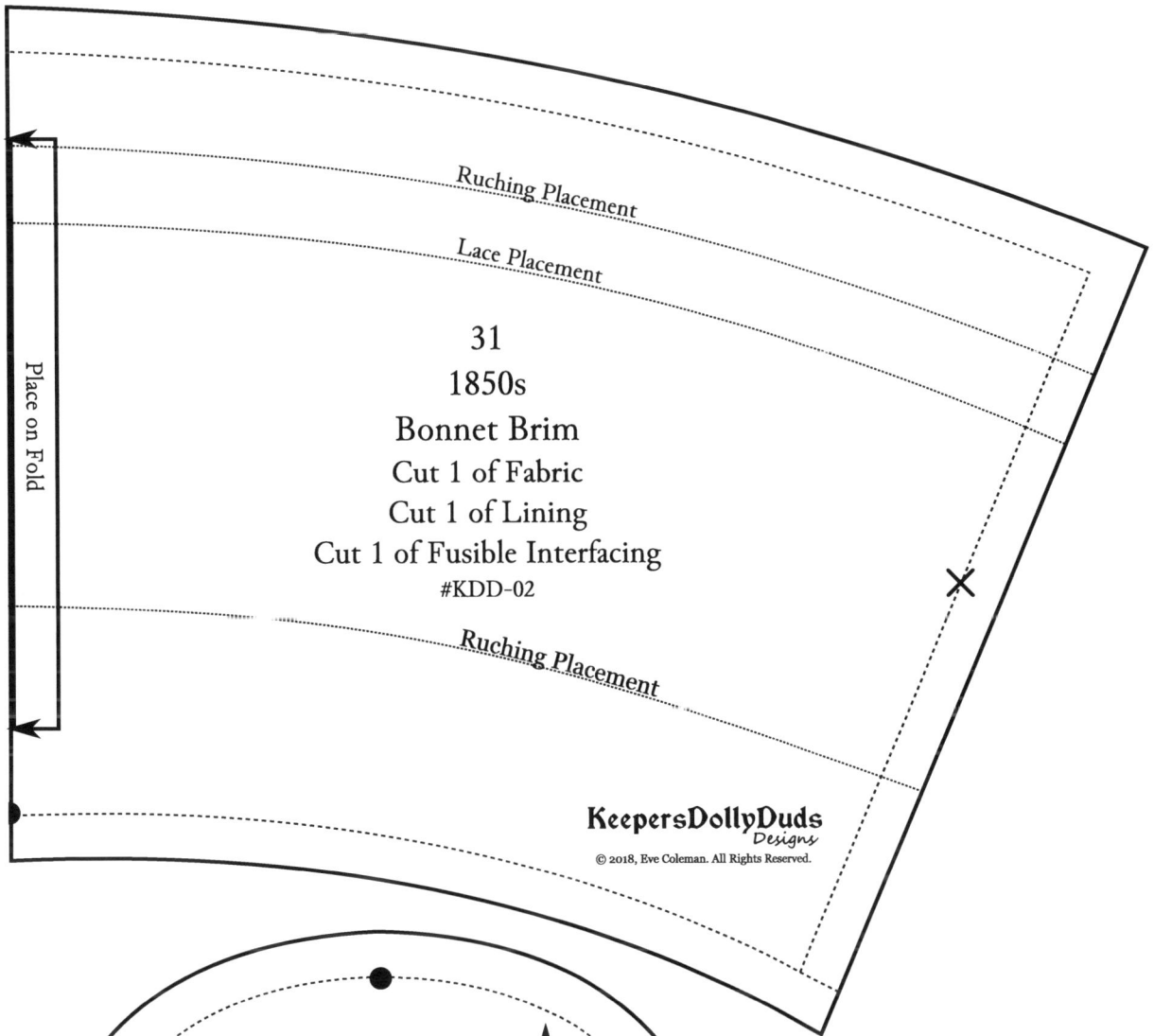

Ruching Placement

Lace Placement

Place on Fold

31
1850s
Bonnet Brim
Cut 1 of Fabric
Cut 1 of Lining
Cut 1 of Fusible Interfacing
#KDD-02

Ruching Placement

KeepersDollyDuds
Designs
© 2018, Eve Coleman. All Rights Reserved.

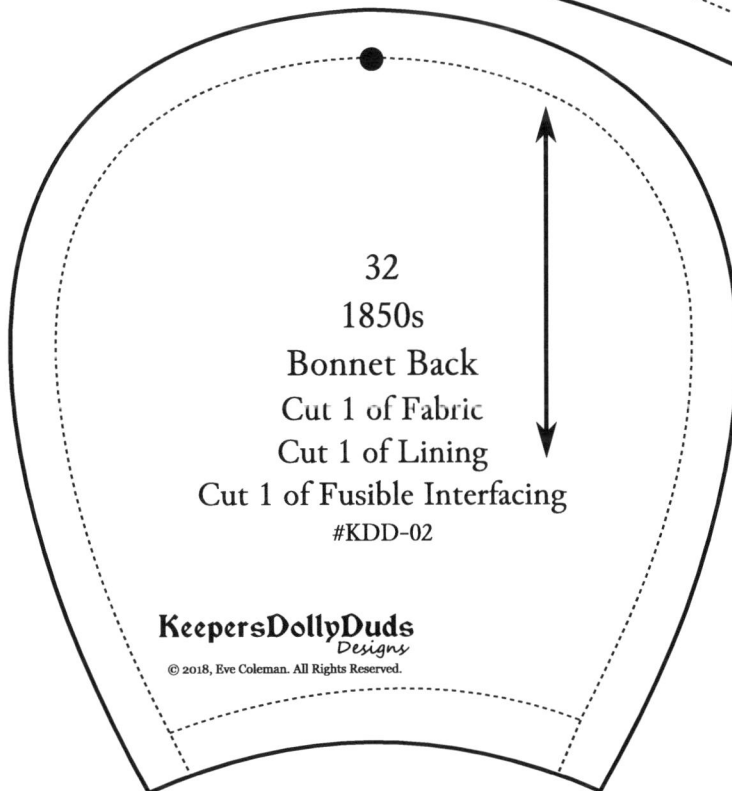

32
1850s
Bonnet Back
Cut 1 of Fabric
Cut 1 of Lining
Cut 1 of Fusible Interfacing
#KDD-02

KeepersDollyDuds
Designs
© 2018, Eve Coleman. All Rights Reserved.

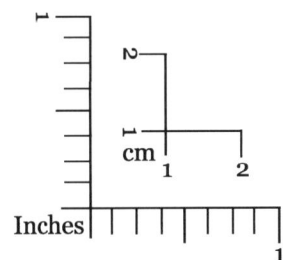

Civil War Dress and Apron

Materials List

#KDD-12

Suggested Fabrics: *Dress, Dress Contrast, and Apron* in light weight cotton, homespun, cotton blends, linen, muslin, batiste, or silk. Not suitable for knits.

Fabric Yardage:

Dress ~ 1/2 yard (0.5 m) 45-inch wide fabric
Dress Contrast ~ 1/4 yard (0.25 m) 45-inch wide fabric
Apron ~ 1/3 yard (0.33 m) 45-inch wide fabric

Notions:

___Thread

Dress

___1/3 yard 1/2-inch (12 mm) wide lace
___Seven small decorative buttons
___Three small snaps OR 3-inches of
    1/2-inch (12 mm) wide hook and
    loop tape OR three 3/8-inch (9 mm)
    buttons

Apron

___One yard 1/2-inch wide (12 mm) lace
___4-inches 1-inch wide lace
___Three small decorative buttons

Civil War Dress

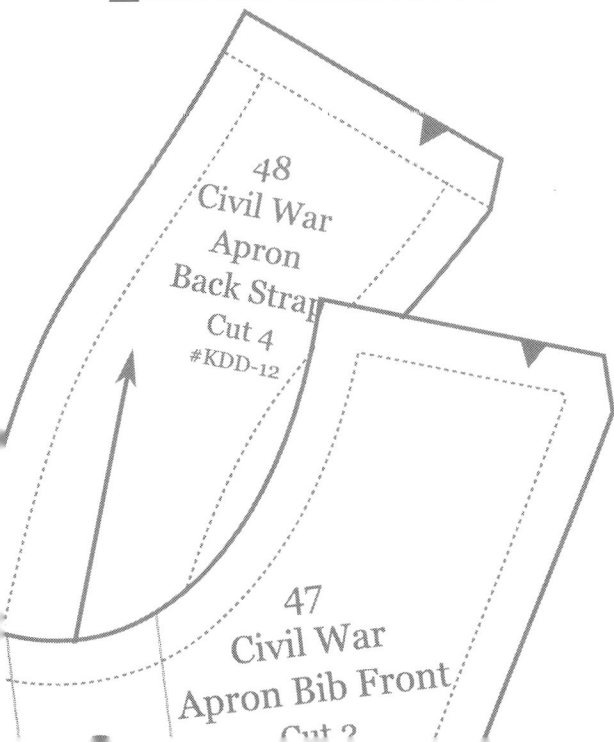

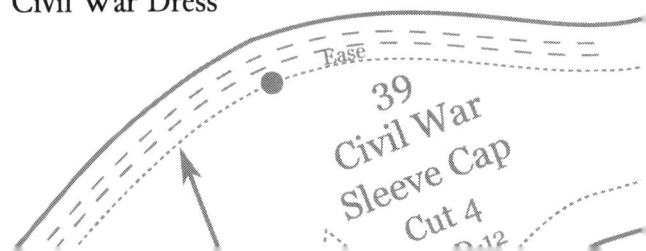

Civil War Dress Bodice

Step 1: Turn the sides of the placket under along the foldlines and press to crease. Pin the placket to the center of the bodice front and stitch in place close to the edges.

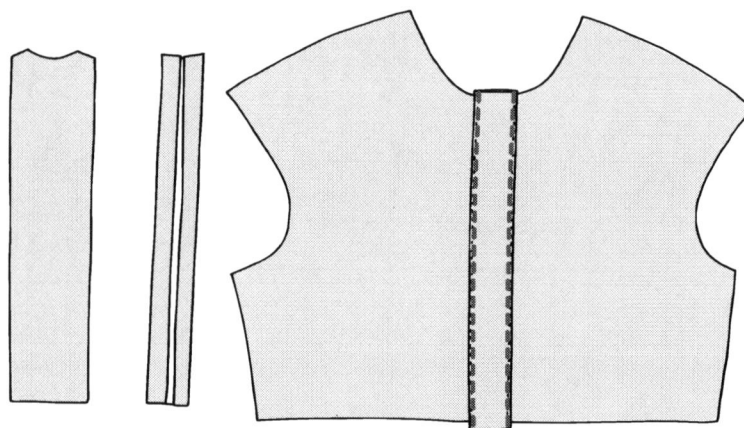

Step 2: With the right sides together, pin the bodice backs to the bodice front along the shoulder. Stitch and finish the seam allowances if desired. Press the seam allowances toward the back. For slimmer dolls, sew darts on the bodice back.

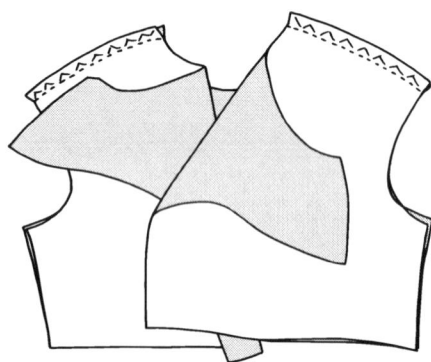

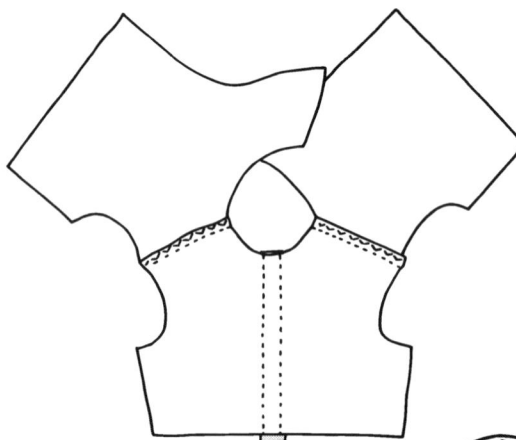

Step 3: With the right sides together, pin the back facing to the bodice front facing along the shoulders. Stitch and finish the seam allowance if desired. Press the seam allowance toward the front facing. Finish the outside edge of the facing.

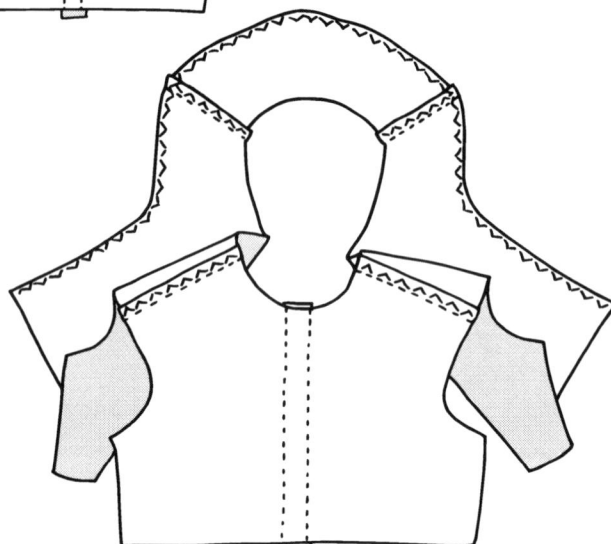

Collar

Step 4: With the decorative edge facing the collar, pin lace along the outer edge of the right side of two collar pieces. With the right sides together, pin the remaining two collar pieces over the collar pieces with the lace. Stitch along the outer edge of each collar. Notch the curves and trim the seam allowances to 1/8-inch (3 mm). Turn right side out and press, following the seamline.

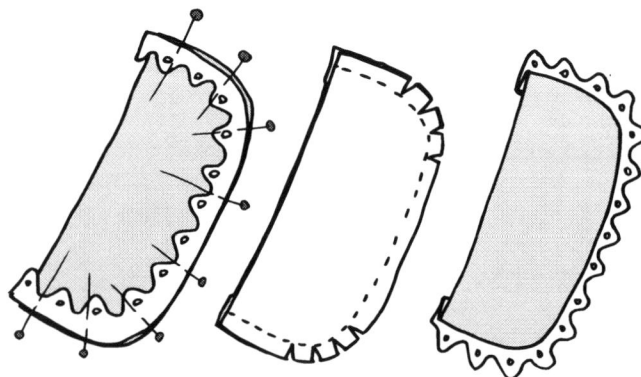

Step 5: Pin the collar to the right side of the bodice neckline, matching the dots. Bring the bodice facing over the collar and pin along the neckline, taking care to align the shoulder seams. Stitch. Clip the curves and turn right side out, squaring the corners with a blunt needle. Understitch the neckline along the collar. Press, following the seamline and along the back fold lines.

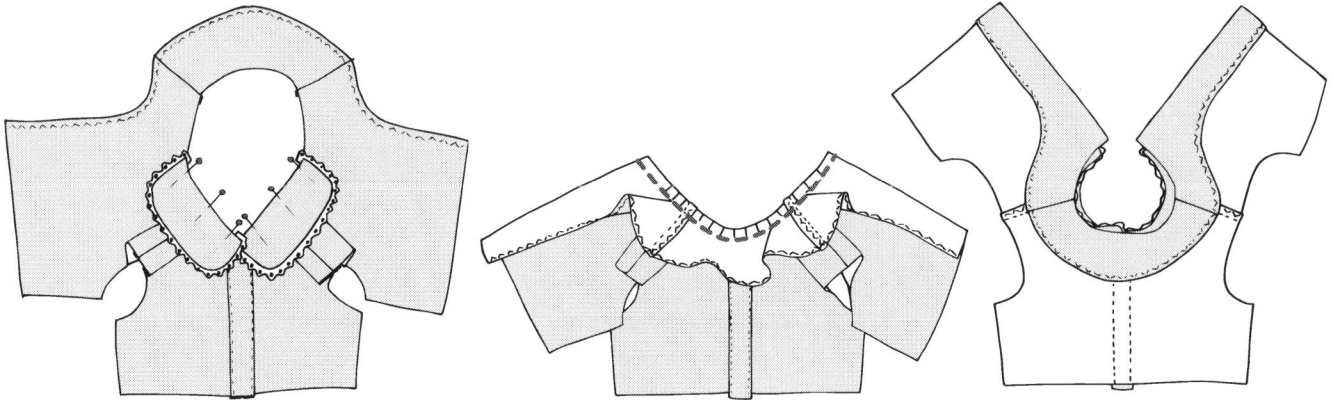

Sleeve Caps and Sleeves

Step 6: Pin two sets of sleeve caps right sides together along the bottom edge. For a sharp corner in the center, reduce the stitch length on your machine. This will allow you to clip the corner closer to the stitching without it fraying. Clip the corners and curves being sure to clip as close to the seamline in the center corner as possible without clipping the stitching line. Trim the seam allowance to 1/8-inch (3 mm) and turn right side out. Press, following the seam lines. Sew two rows of gathering stitches along the top edge where indicated on the pattern.

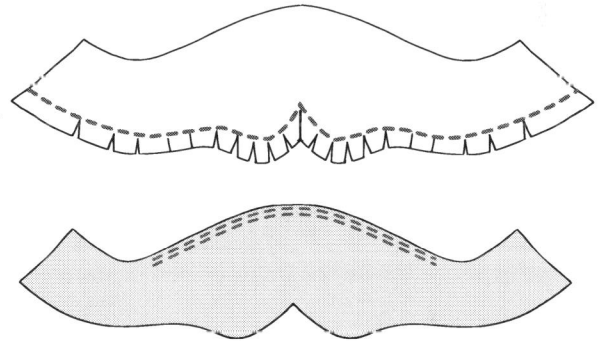

Step 7: Cut a slit on each sleeve along the placket cutting line. Spread each slit apart and, with the right sides together, pin one edge of a placket along each of the slits as shown. The seam allowance of the slits will follow the seam allowance of the placket forming a wide "V" shape. The point of each "V" should fall just inside the placket seam allowance. Stitch in place.

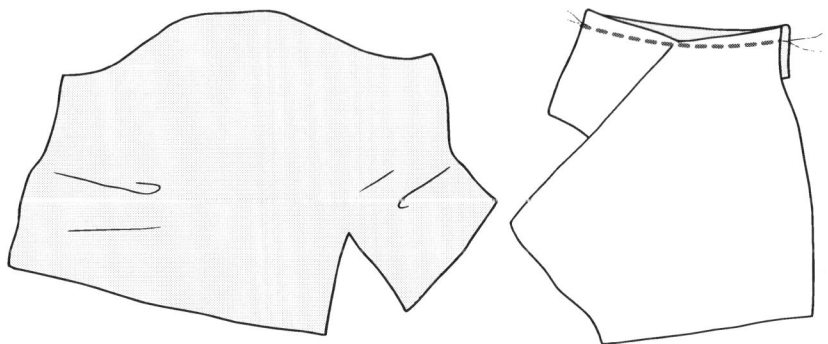

Step 8: Press the seam allowance toward placket and fold the opposite side of the placket under to bind the raw edge. Pin along the seamline and topstitch along the folded edge to secure.

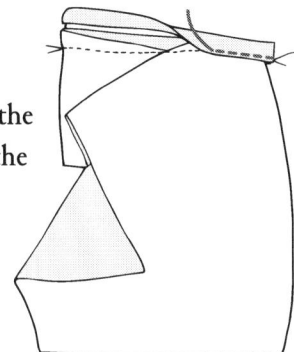

Step 9: Sew gathering stitches along the top edges of the sleeves.

Step 10: With the right sides together, pin the sleeve caps to the armscyes, matching the notches. Pin the sleeves over the sleeve caps right sides together and matching the notches. Draw up the gathering stitches to fit, distributing the fullness evenly along the armscye. Stitch. Clip the curves up to the seamlines. Finish the seam allowances, if desired. Press the seam allowances toward the bodice.

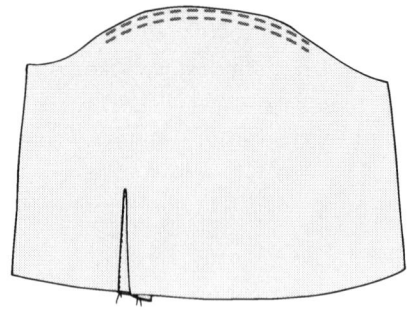

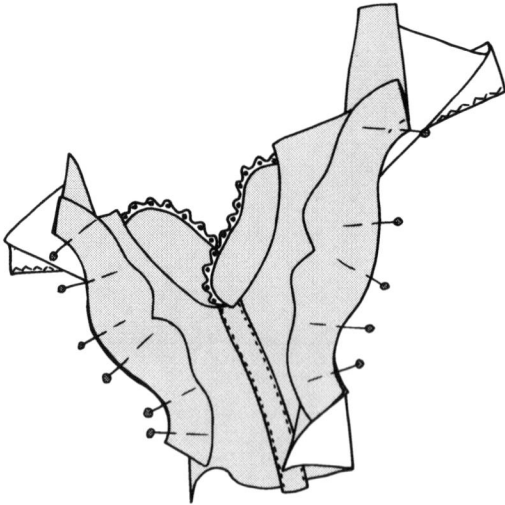

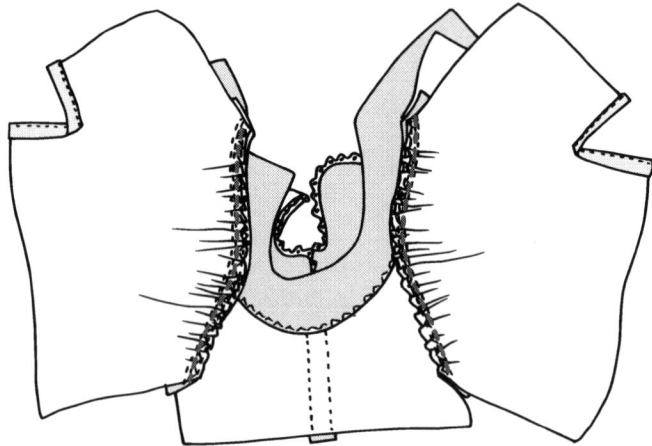

Step 11: Fold the ties along the foldline right sides together. Using a 1/8- inch (3 mm) seam allowance, stitch where indicated on the pattern. Clip the corners and turn right side out, squaring the corners with a blunt needle. Press following the seamline.

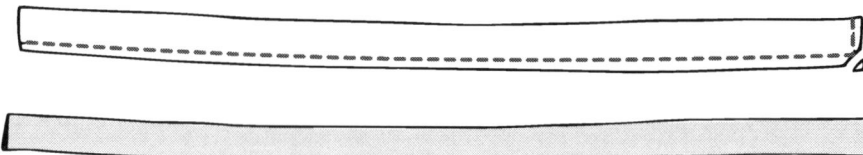

Step 12: With the seam side facing down, pin the ties to the bodice front where indicated on the pattern. Baste to secure. Finish the side seam allowances of the bodice and sleeves, if desired.

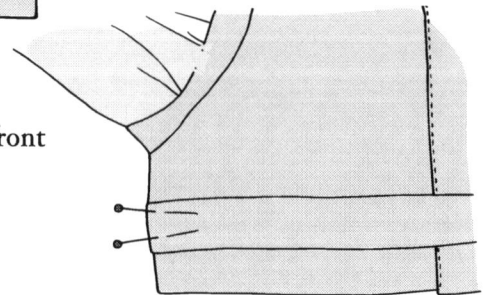

Step 13: With right sides together, sew the side seams of the sleeves, sleeve caps and bodice. Press the seams open and turn right side out. Sew gathering stitches along the lower edge of the sleeve.

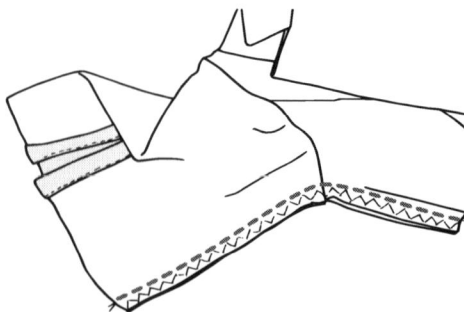

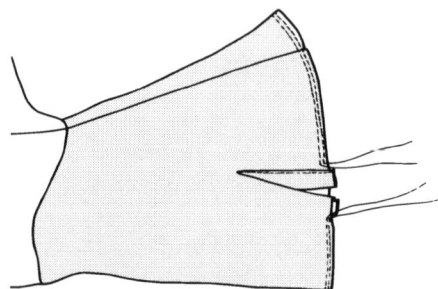

Step 14: Fold cuffs in half lengthwise, wrong side out. Turn up a 1/4-inch (6 mm) seam allowance on one side and press. With a 1/4-inch (6 mm) seam allowance, stitch each end of the cuffs. Turn right side out and press, squaring the corners with a blunt needle.

Step 15: Turn the front side of the placket under and pin in place. With right sides together, pin the cuff to the sleeve, lining up the placket edges with the edges of the cuff. Draw up the gathering stitches to fit, distributing the fullness evenly along the cuff. Stitch in place. Bring the other side of the cuff over the seam allowance and stitch in place along the seamline.

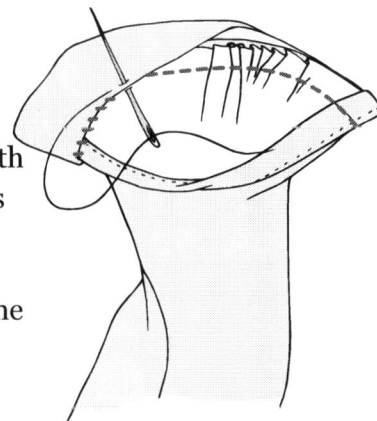

Peplum and Skirt

Step 16: With the right sides together, pin two sets of peplum pieces together along the outside edges. Stitch. Clip the corners and curves and trim the seam allowances to 1/8-inch. Turn right side out squaring the corners with a blunt needle. Press, following the seamline.

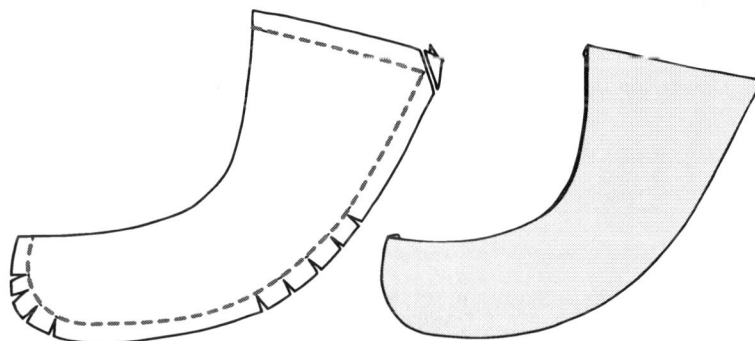

Step 17: With the right sides together, pin the peplum pieces to the bottom edge of the bodice where indicated on the pattern.

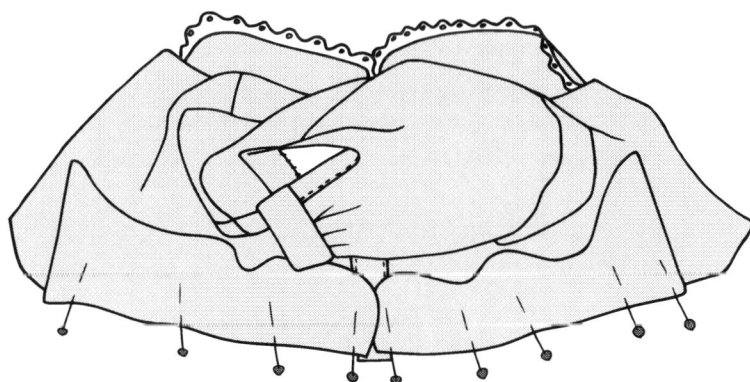

Dress Skirting

Step 18: Finish the back edges of the skirting. Sew two rows of gathering stitches along the top where indicated on the pattern.

Step 19: With the right sides together, sew the back edges of the skirt together from the dot to the bottom edge. Press the seam allowances open from the top edge to the bottom edge.

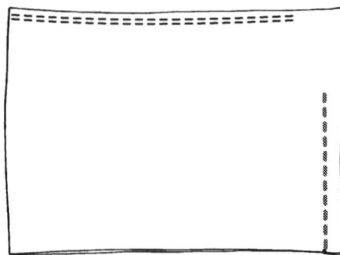

Step 20: With the right sides together, pin the skirting over the peplum on the bodice, aligning the folded edges of the skirting with the fold lines on the bodice back. Draw up the gathers to fit, distributing the fullness evenly along the waistline. Unfold the bodice back facings and fold them wrong side out along the fold line over the gathered edge of the skirting. Pin to secure. Stitch all the layers together and finish the edges if desired. Turn right side out and press the seam allowance toward the bodice.

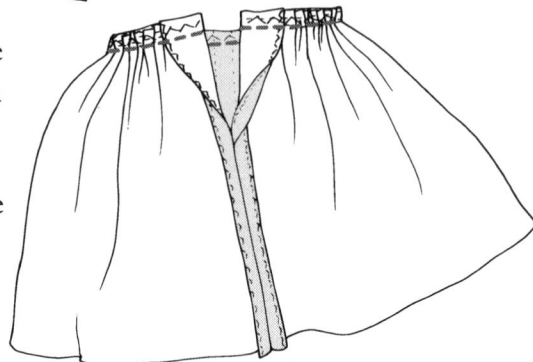

Step 21: Finish the bottom edge of the skirting. Turn up a 1/2-inch (12 mm) hem. Press and pin in place. Machine or hand stitch to secure.

Step 22: Make buttonholes on the proper left and attach buttons on the proper right where indicated on the pattern. Snaps or hook and loop tape may be used instead of buttons.

Step 23: Sew buttons to the back ends of the cuffs where indicated on the pattern. Make button loops on the front ends where indicated on the pattern, following the instructions below.

To make the button loop, use a single strand of button thread to make a loop that loosely fits the diameter of the button. Tack the loop in place at each end to secure. Do not cut the thread.

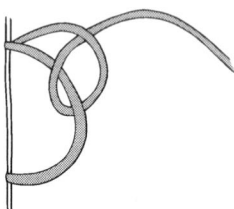

Starting at the end that the thread is attached, make a blanket stitch on the thread loop. Tighten the stitch snugly around the loop.

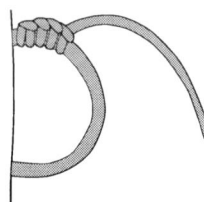

Continue adding stitches until the loop is completely covered.

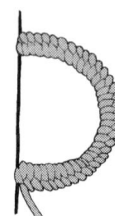

Tack the end of the thread at the end of the loop and draw it through the fabric to hide. Trim off the extra thread.

Step 24: Attach 5 small decorative buttons along the front placket where indicated on the pattern.

Apron

Step 25: Pin lace along the center front of the apron bib front. Stitch down the center front to secure.

Step 26: With the right sides together, pin the apron back strap to the apron bib front matching the notches at the shoulder lines. Stitch. Press the seam allowances open. Repeat for the lining.

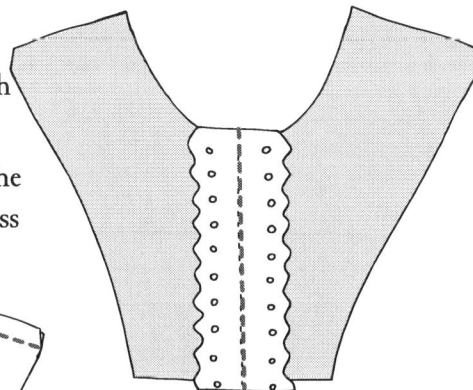

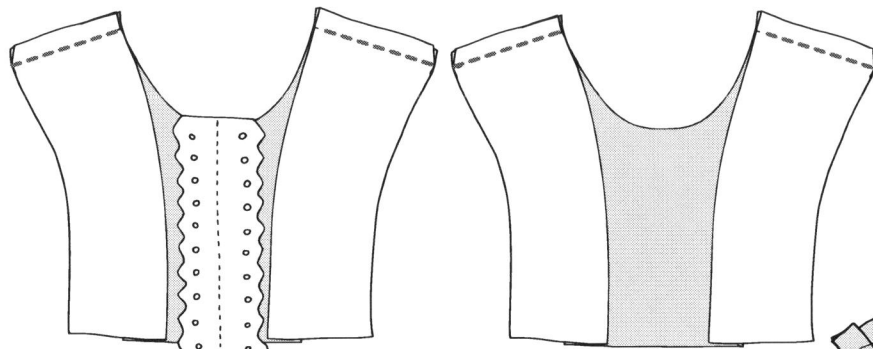

Step 27: Fold the bretelles right side out along the fold lines. Press flat. Pin the bretelles along the side edges of the apron front.

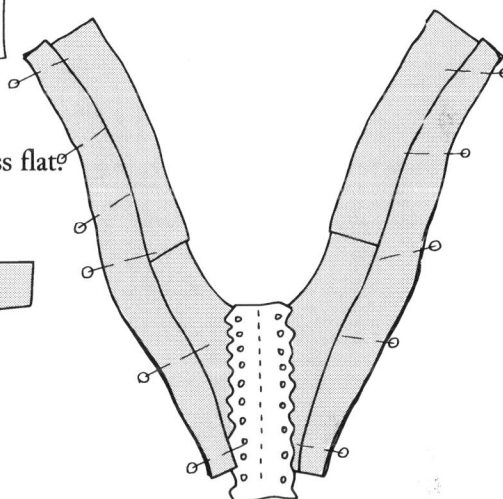

Step 28: Lay the apron bib lining over the top of the apron and bretelles. Pin in place along the inside and outside edges. Stitch, leaving the front and back ends open. Clip the curves and trim the seam allowances to 1/8-inch (3 mm). Turn right side out and press, following the seam lines.

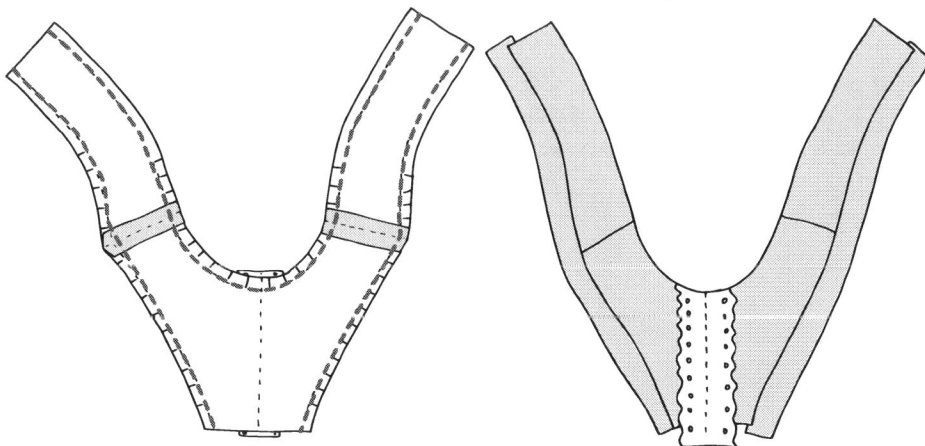

Ties

Step 29: Make a narrow hem on the long sides of both the ties.

Step 30: With the right sides together, fold the bottom end of each tie in half. Pin and stitch to secure. Finger press the seams open and turn right side out, pushing the point out with a blunt needle. Press flat.

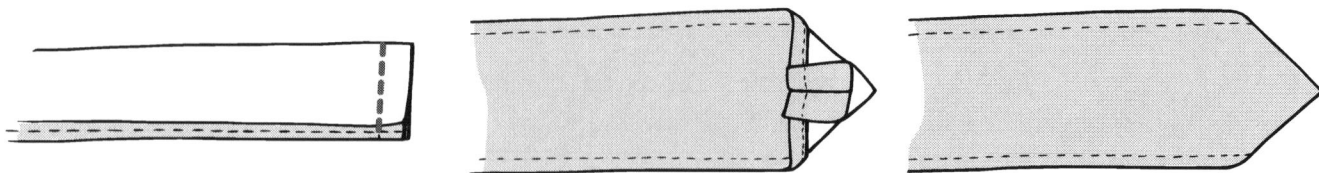

Step 31: With the right sides together, fold the top end of each tie in half. Stitch from the dot to the the end to form pleats. Press the pleats flat with the center fold line following the seam line.

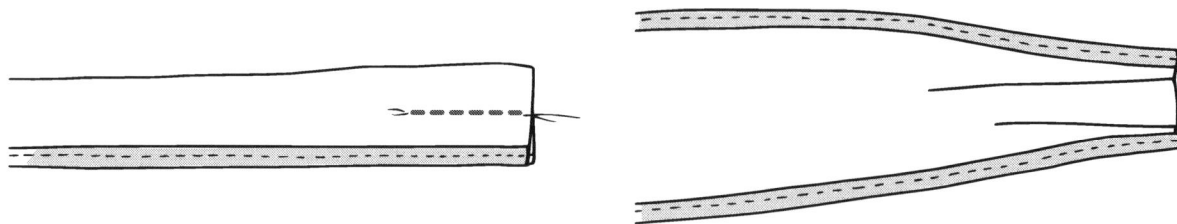

Step 32: Pin lace along the outside edge of the apron skirting with the decorative edge facing the apron. Stitch. Finish the seam allowance, if desired.

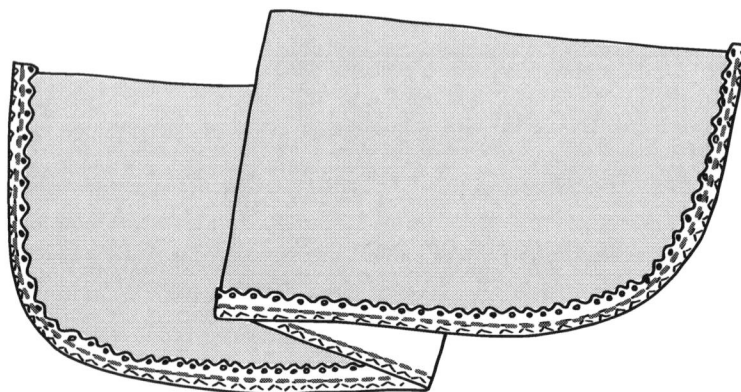

Step 33: Press the seam allowance toward the apron. Topstitch close to the edge of the apron to secure the seam allowance. Sew two rows of gathering stitches along the top edge of the apron skirting.

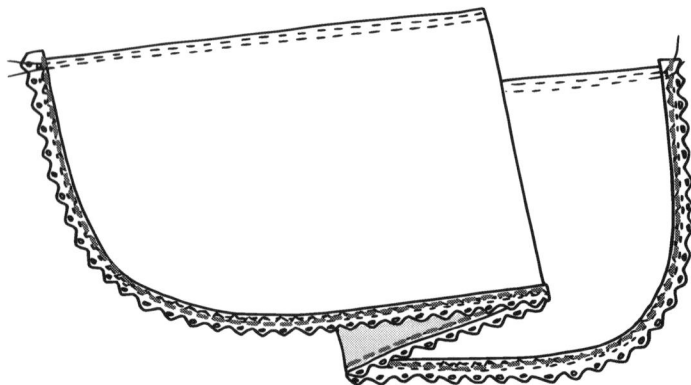

Step 34: Pin the apron bib and back straps to the waistband right sides together where indicated on the pattern. With the right sides together, pin the waistband lining over the waistband, apron bib, and backstraps. Stitch.

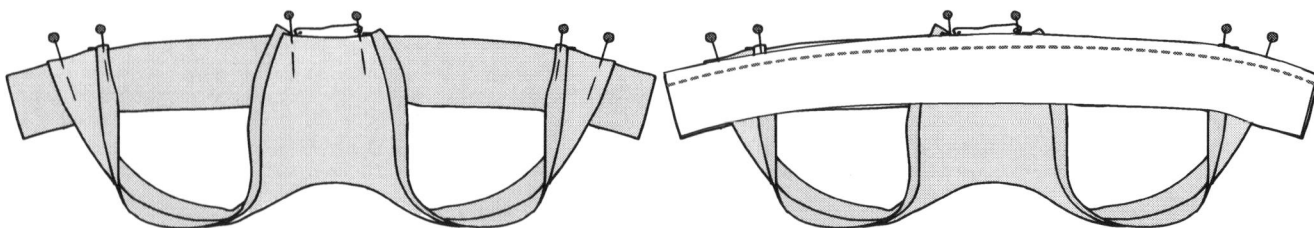

Step 35: With the right sides together, pin the apron skirt to the bottom edge of the waistband. Draw up the gathering stitches to fit, distributing the fullness evenly along the waistband. Stitch in place.

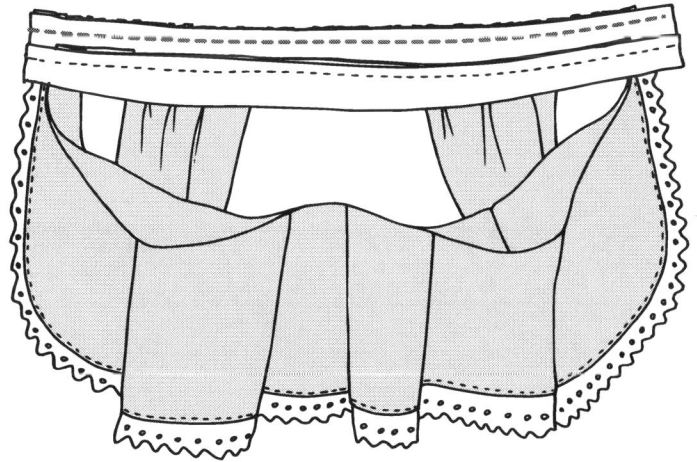

Step 36: Spread the apron bib and skirt open. With the right sides together, pin the pleated edged of a tie to each side of the waistband, making sure the ends stay between the seam allowances on the waistband. Fold the waistband lining over the top of the ties and pin in place. Stitch the ends and clip the corners.

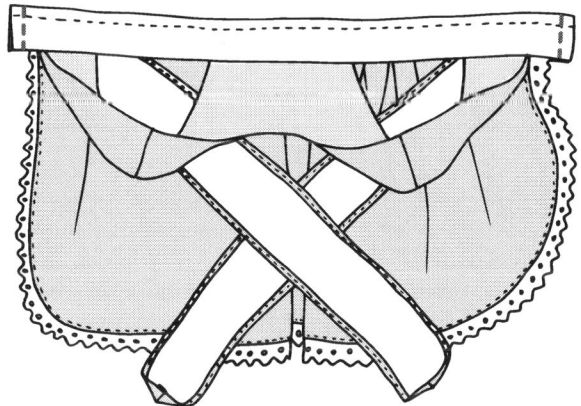

Step 37: Turn the waistband right side out, squaring the corners with a blunt needle. Press, the top edge following the seam line. Turn the bottom edge under and pin along the seamline of the apron skirt. Handstitch in place. Finish the front of the apron bib with three decorative buttons as indicated on the pattern.

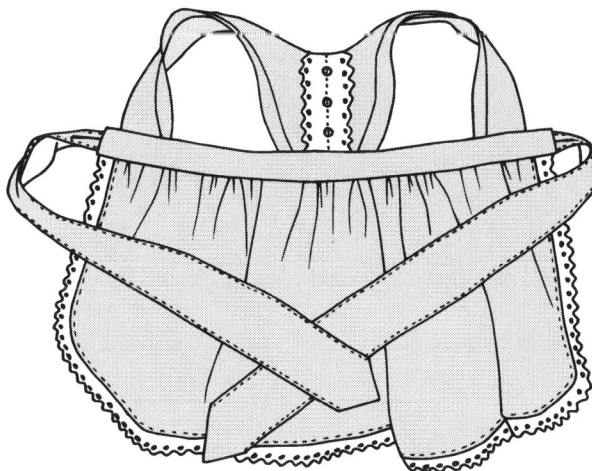

Cutting Layout for 45-inch (1.14 m) wide Fabric
18 Pieces

35 ~ Civil War Dress Bodice Front
36 ~ Civil War Dress Bodice Back
37 ~ Civil War Dress Front Placket
38 ~ Civil War Dress Collar
39 ~ Civil War Dress Sleeve Cap
40 ~ Civil War Dress Front Facing
41 ~ Civil War Dress Peplum
42 ~ Civil War Dress Sleeve
43 ~ Civil War Dress Sleeve Placket
44 ~ Civil War Dress Sleeve Cuff
45 ~ Civil War Dress Side Ties
46 ~ Civil War Dress Skirting
47 ~ Civil War Apron Bib
48 ~ Civil War Apron Back Strap
49 ~ Civil War Apron Bretelles
50 ~ Civil War Apron Waistband
51 ~ Civil War Apron Ties
52 ~ Civil War Apron Skirting

Civil War Dress
Use pieces: 35, 36, 37, 39, 40, 41, 45, and 46

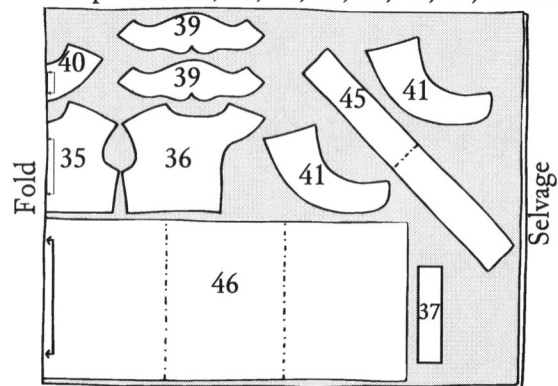

Civil War Dress Contrast
Use pieces: 38, 42, 43, and 44

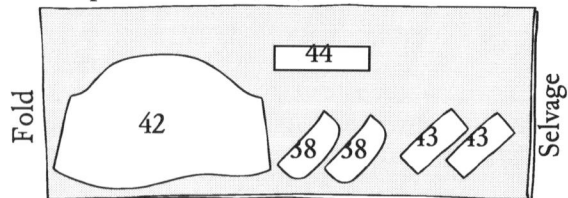

Civil War Apron
Use pieces: 47, 48, 49, 50, 51, and 52

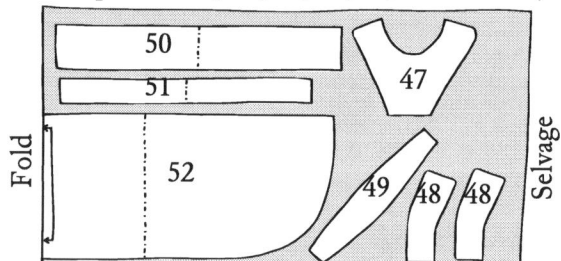

Civil War Dress

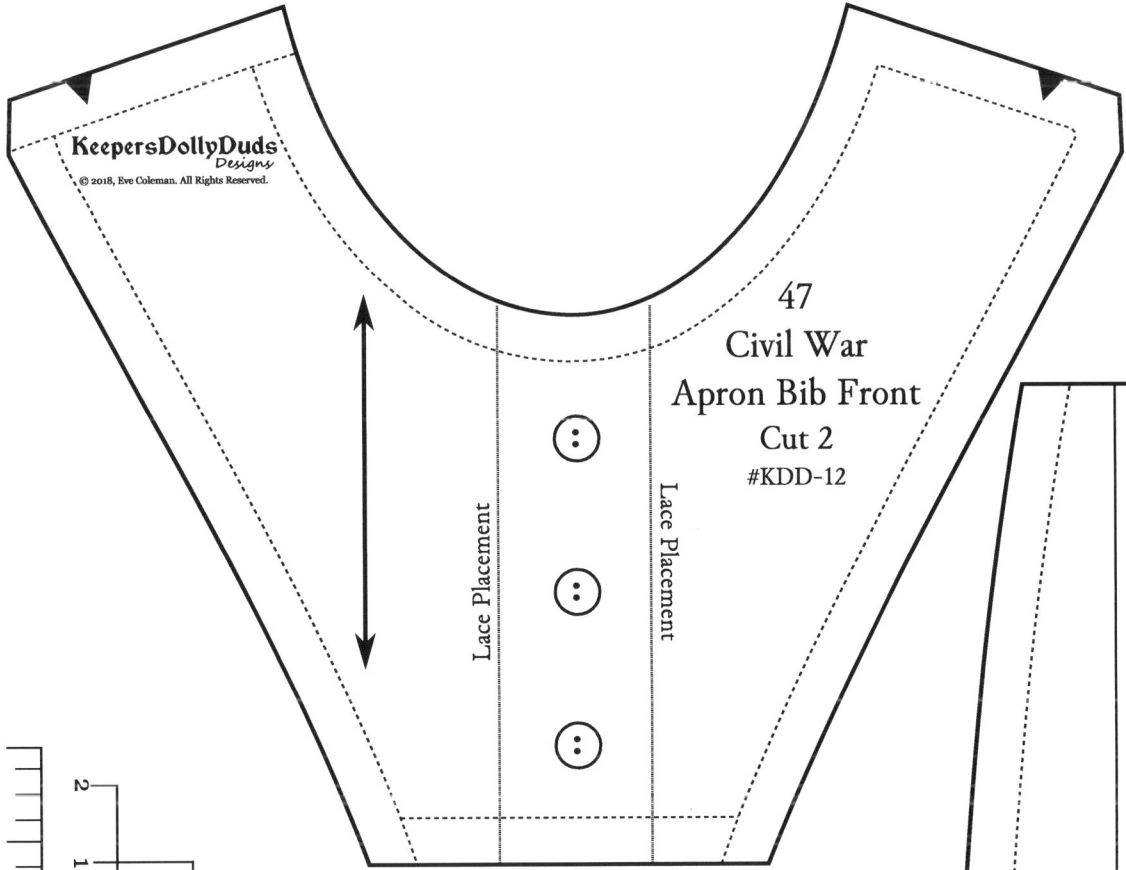

47
Civil War
Apron Bib Front
Cut 2
#KDD-12

Lace Placement

Lace Placement

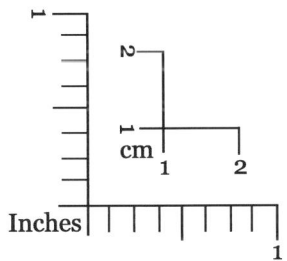

1
1
2
2
1
cm 1 2
Inches 1

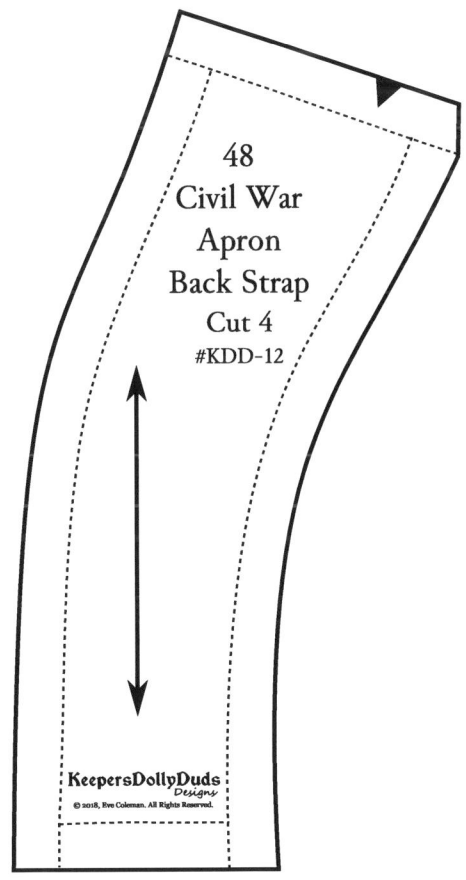

48
Civil War
Apron
Back Strap
Cut 4
#KDD-12

KeepersDollyDuds
Designs
© 2018, Eve Coleman. All Rights Reserved.

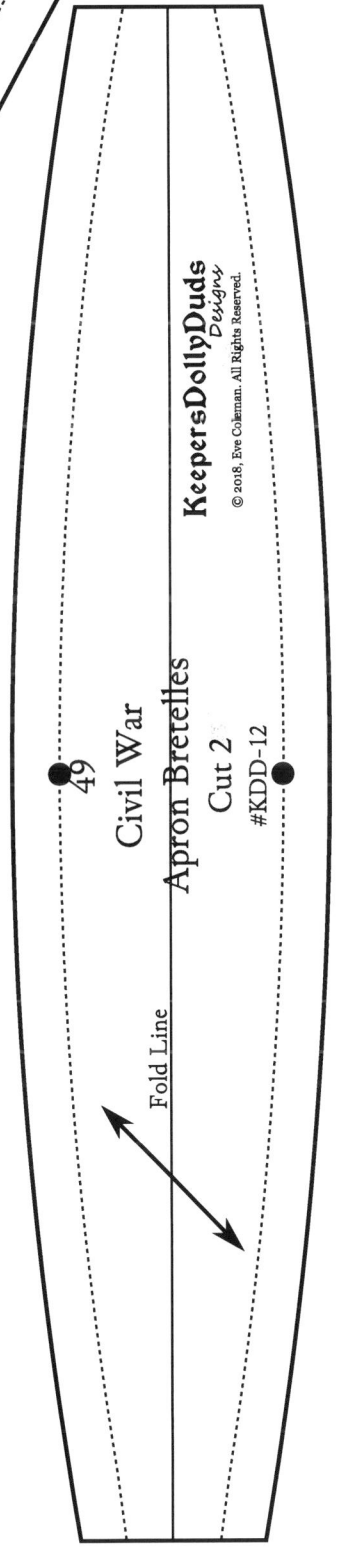

49
Civil War
Apron Bretelles
Cut 2
#KDD-12

Fold Line

KeepersDollyDuds
Designs
© 2018, Eve Coleman. All Rights Reserved.

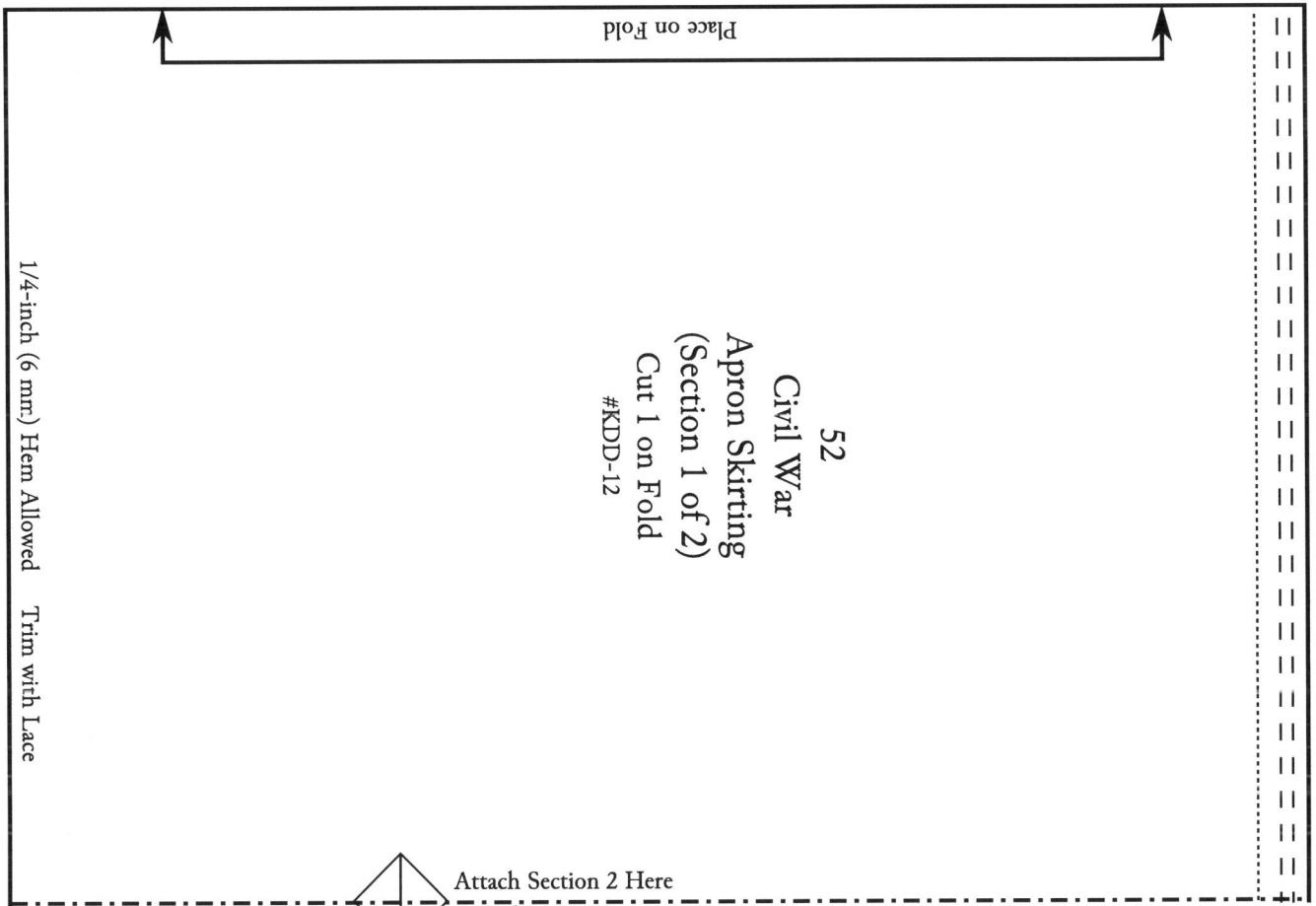

Place on Fold

52
Civil War
Apron Skirting
(Section 1 of 2)
Cut 1 on Fold
#KDD-12

1/4-inch (6 mm) Hem Allowed   Trim with Lace

Attach Section 2 Here

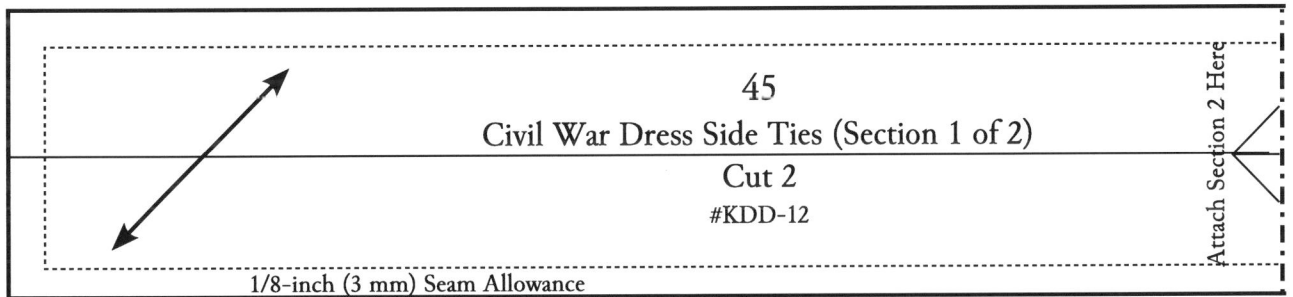

45
Civil War Dress Side Ties (Section 1 of 2)
Cut 2
#KDD-12

Attach Section 2 Here

1/8-inch (3 mm) Seam Allowance

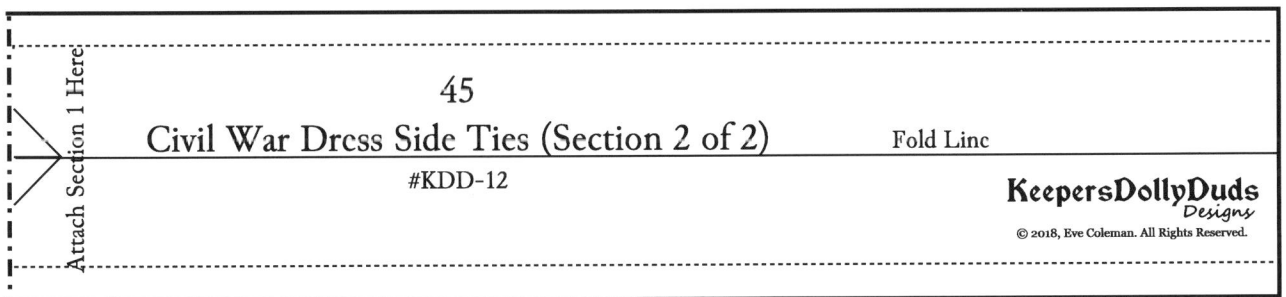

Attach Section 1 Here

45
Civil War Dress Side Ties (Section 2 of 2)
#KDD-12

Fold Line

KeepersDollyDuds
Designs
© 2018, Eve Coleman. All Rights Reserved.

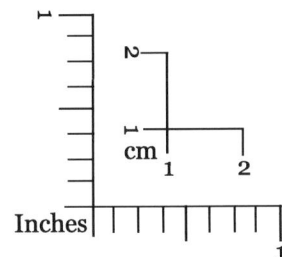

~ Page 91 ~

Attach Section 1 Here

52
Civil War Apron Skirting
(Section 2 of 2)
#KD-12

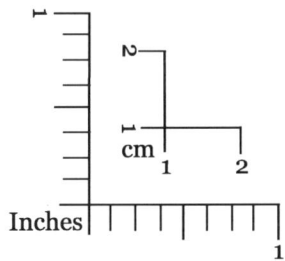

1

2

1

cm 1   2

Inches   1

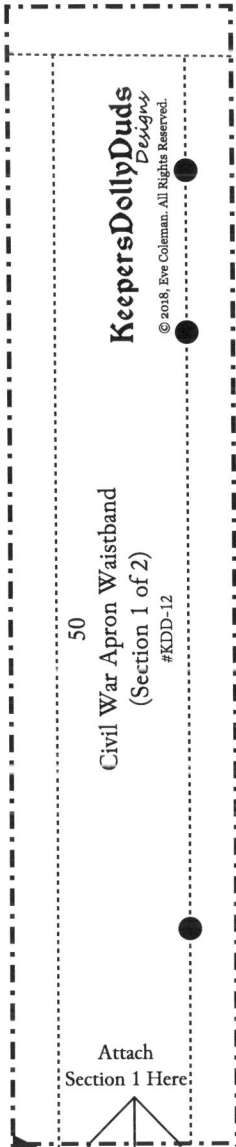

50

Civil War Apron Waistband
(Section 1 of 2)
#KDD-12

Attach Section 2 Here

Attach
Section 1 Here

Attach
Section 2 Here

50

Civil War Apron Waistband
(Section 1 of 2)
Cut 2
#KDD-12

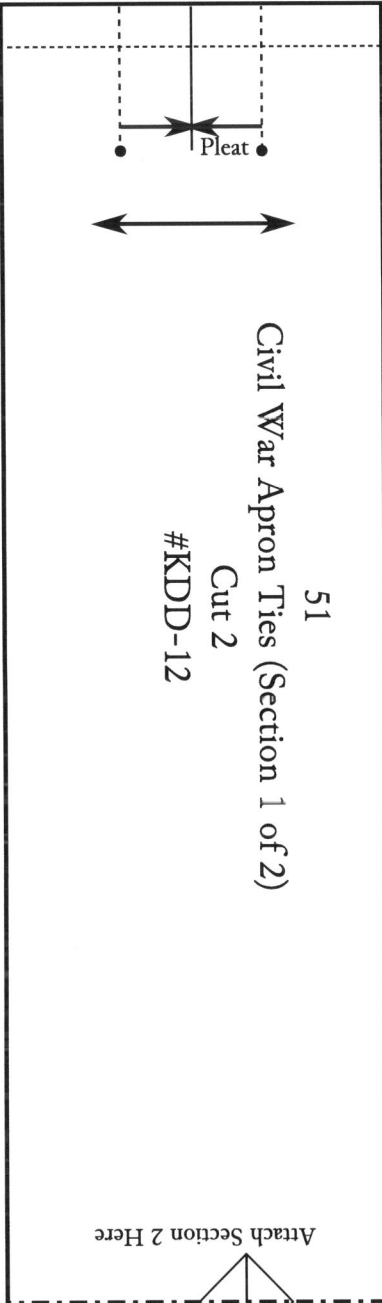

Pleat

51

Civil War Apron Ties (Section 1 of 2)
Cut 2
#KDD-12

Attach Section 2 Here

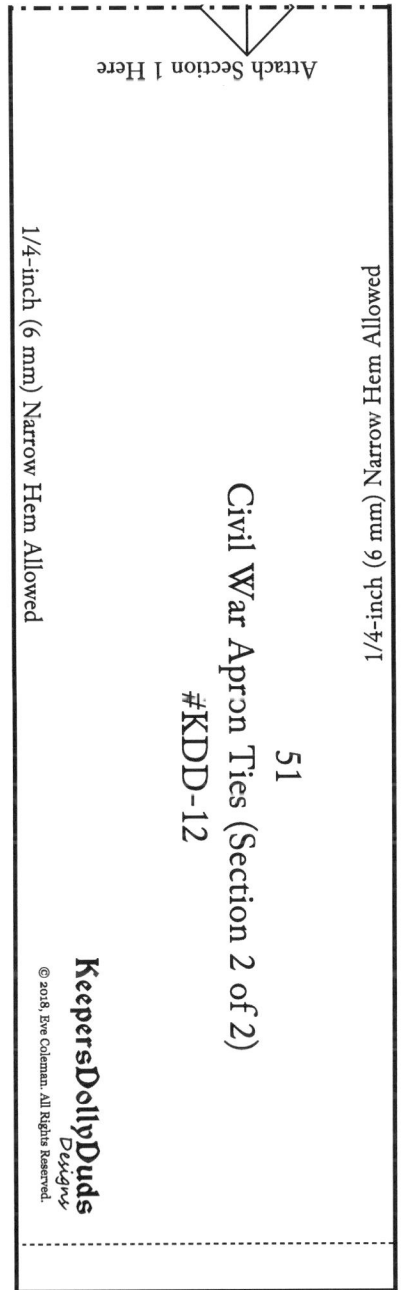

Attach Section 1 Here

1/4-inch (6 mm) Narrow Hem Allowed

1/4-inch (6 mm) Narrow Hem Allowed

51

Civil War Apron Ties (Section 2 of 2)
#KDD-12

44

Civil War Dress
Sleeve Cuff

Cut 2
#KDD-12

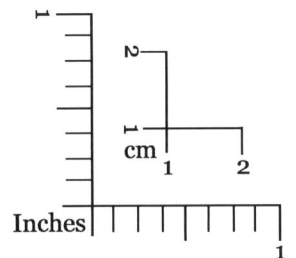

1
2
1 cm
1 2
Inches
1

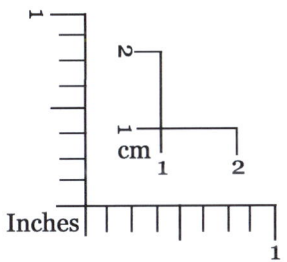

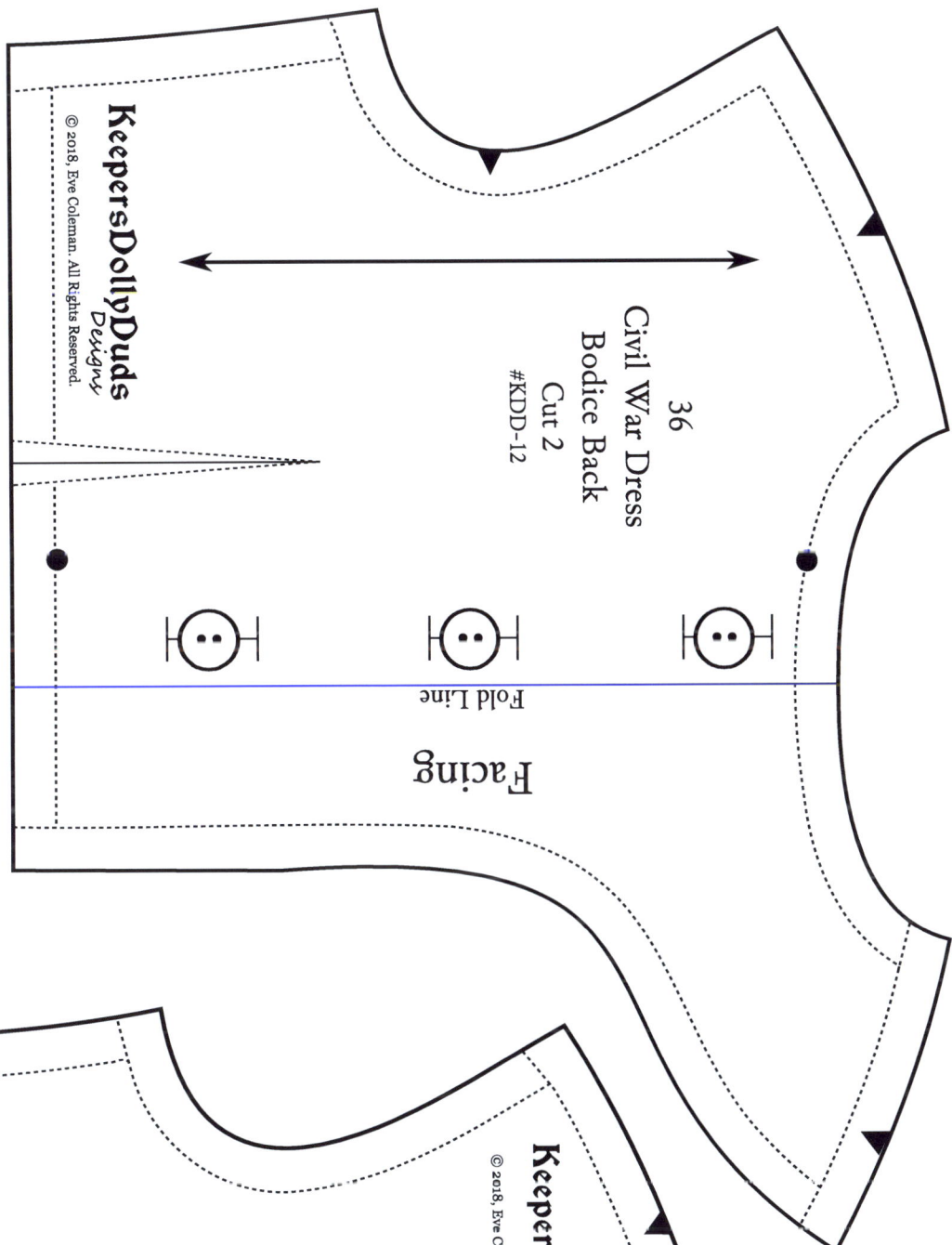

Civil War Dress
Bodice Back
Cut 2
#KDD-12

36

KeepersDollyDuds
Designs
© 2018, Eve Coleman. All Rights Reserved.

Facing

Fold Line

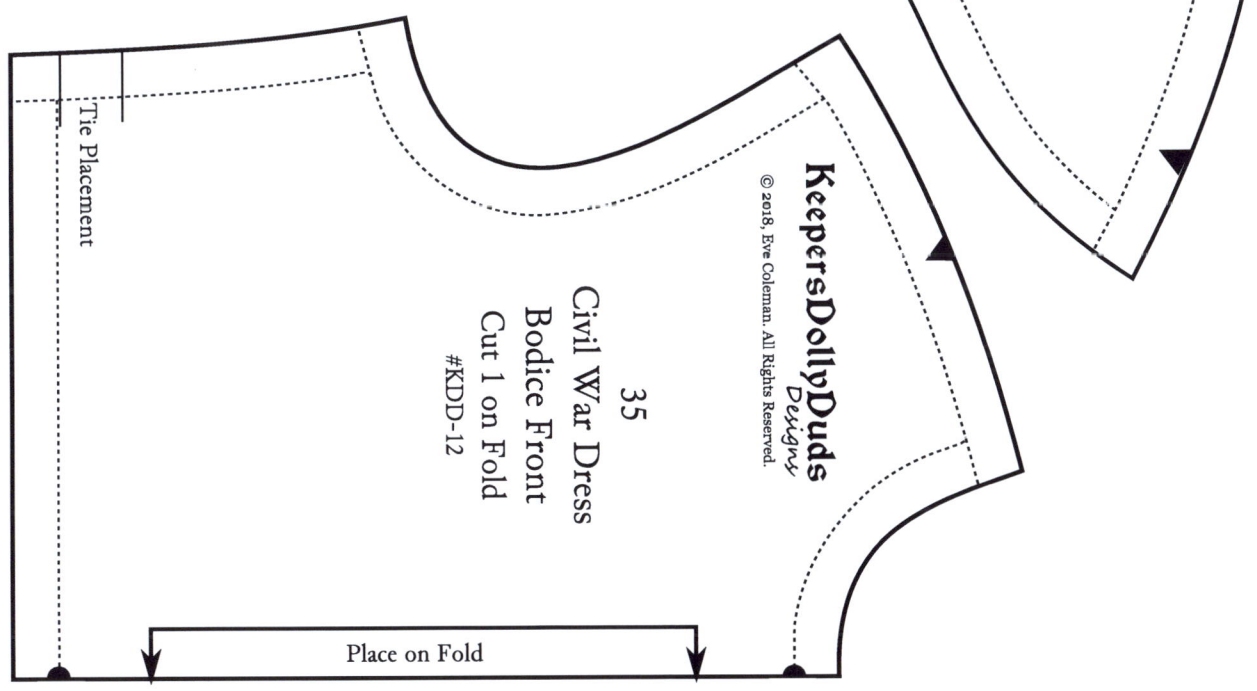

Civil War Dress
Bodice Front
Cut 1 on Fold
#KDD-12

35

KeepersDollyDuds
Designs
© 2018, Eve Coleman. All Rights Reserved.

Tie Placement

Place on Fold

40

KeepersDollyDuds
Designs
© 2018, Eve Coleman. All Rights Reserved.

Civil War Dress
Front Facing
Cut 1 on Fold
#KDD-12

Place on Fold

43
Civil War Dress
Sleeve Placket
Cut 2
#KDD-12

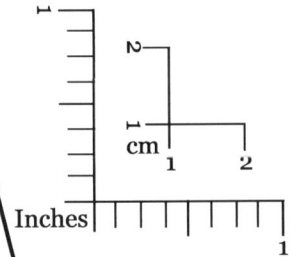

1

2

1
cm   1   2

Inches   1

37 Civil War Dress Front Placket Cut 1 #KDD-12

Fold Line

Fold Line

KeepersDollyDuds
Designs
© 2018, Eve Coleman. All Rights Reserved.

41
Civil War Dress
Peplum
Cut 4
#KDD-12

© 2018, Eve Coleman. All Rights Reserved.
KeepersDollyDuds
Designs

38
Civil War Dress
Collar
Cut 4
#KDD-12

KeepersDollyDuds
Designs
© 2018, Eve Coleman. All Rights Reserved.

KeepersDollyDuds
Designs
© 2018, Eve Coleman. All Rights Reserved.

Ease

39
Civil War Dress
Sleeve Cap
Cut 4
#KDD-12

Inches

cm

1   2

1   2

1

1

2

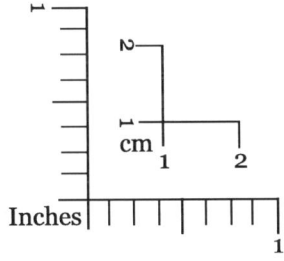

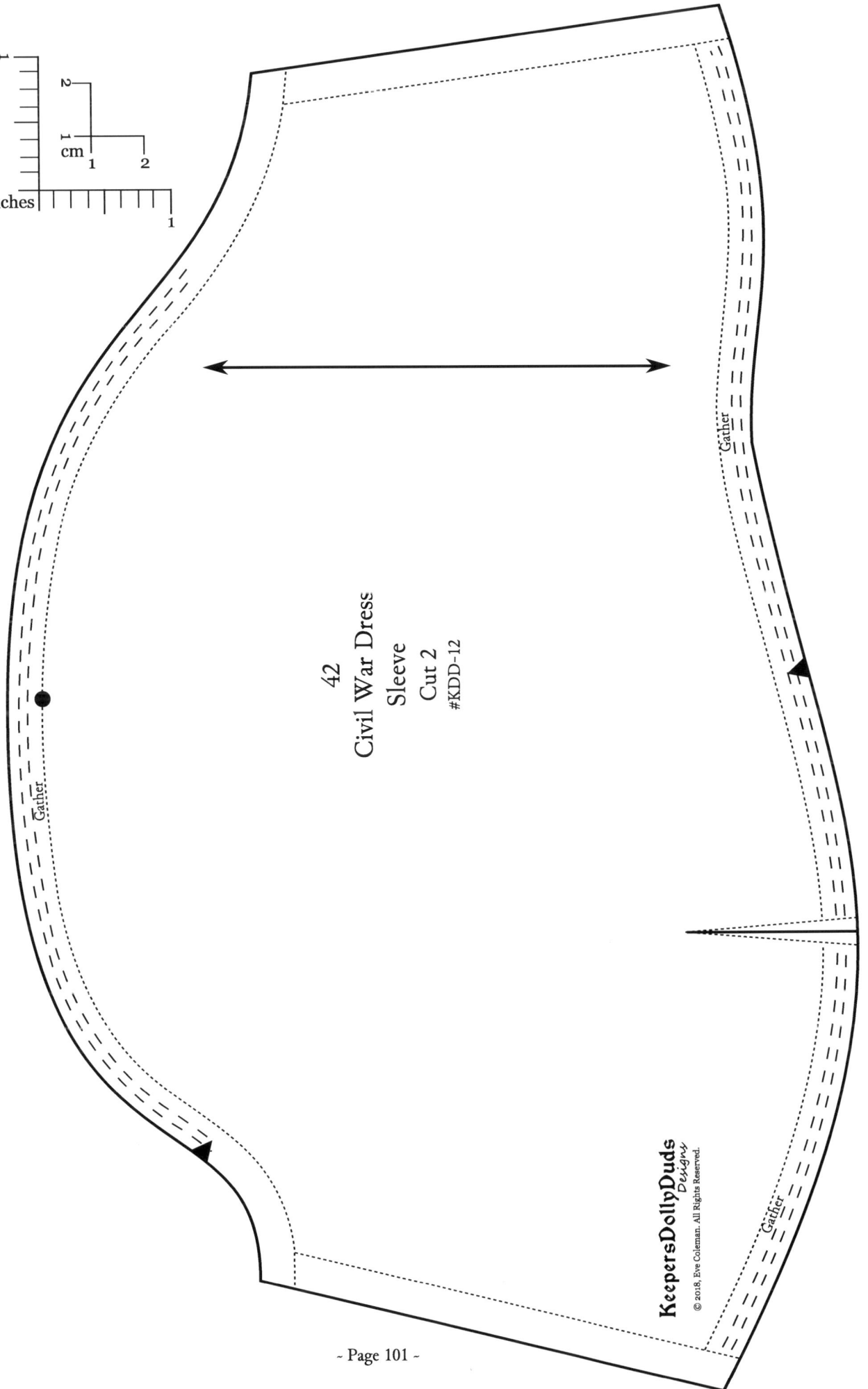

42
Civil War Dress
Sleeve
Cut 2
#KDD-12

Gather

Gather

Gather

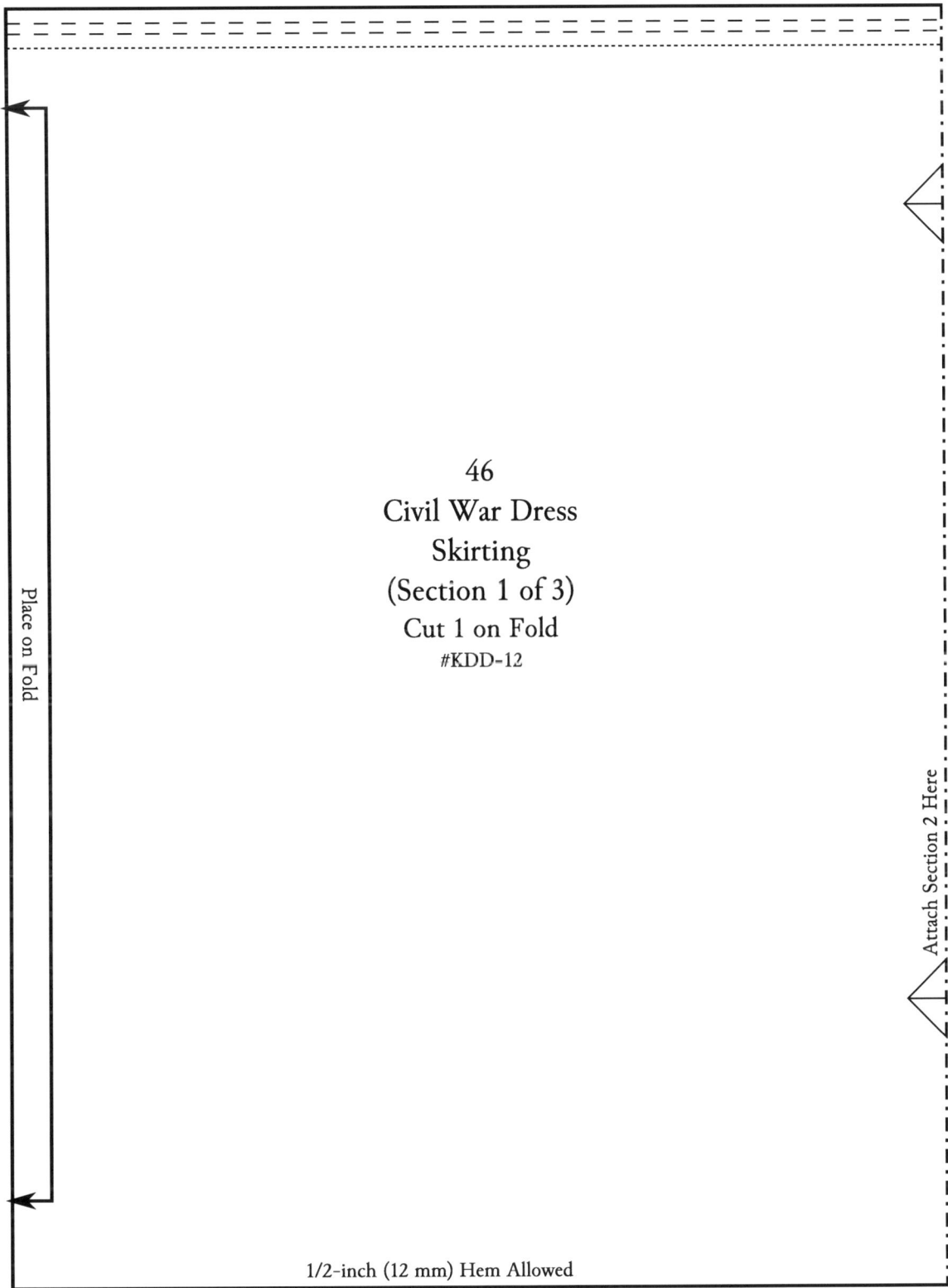

Place on Fold

46
Civil War Dress
Skirting
(Section 1 of 3)
Cut 1 on Fold
#KDD-12

Attach Section 2 Here

1/2-inch (12 mm) Hem Allowed

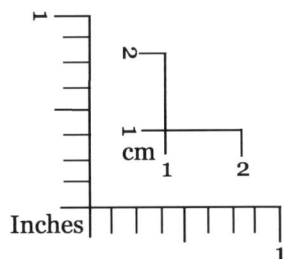

Inches

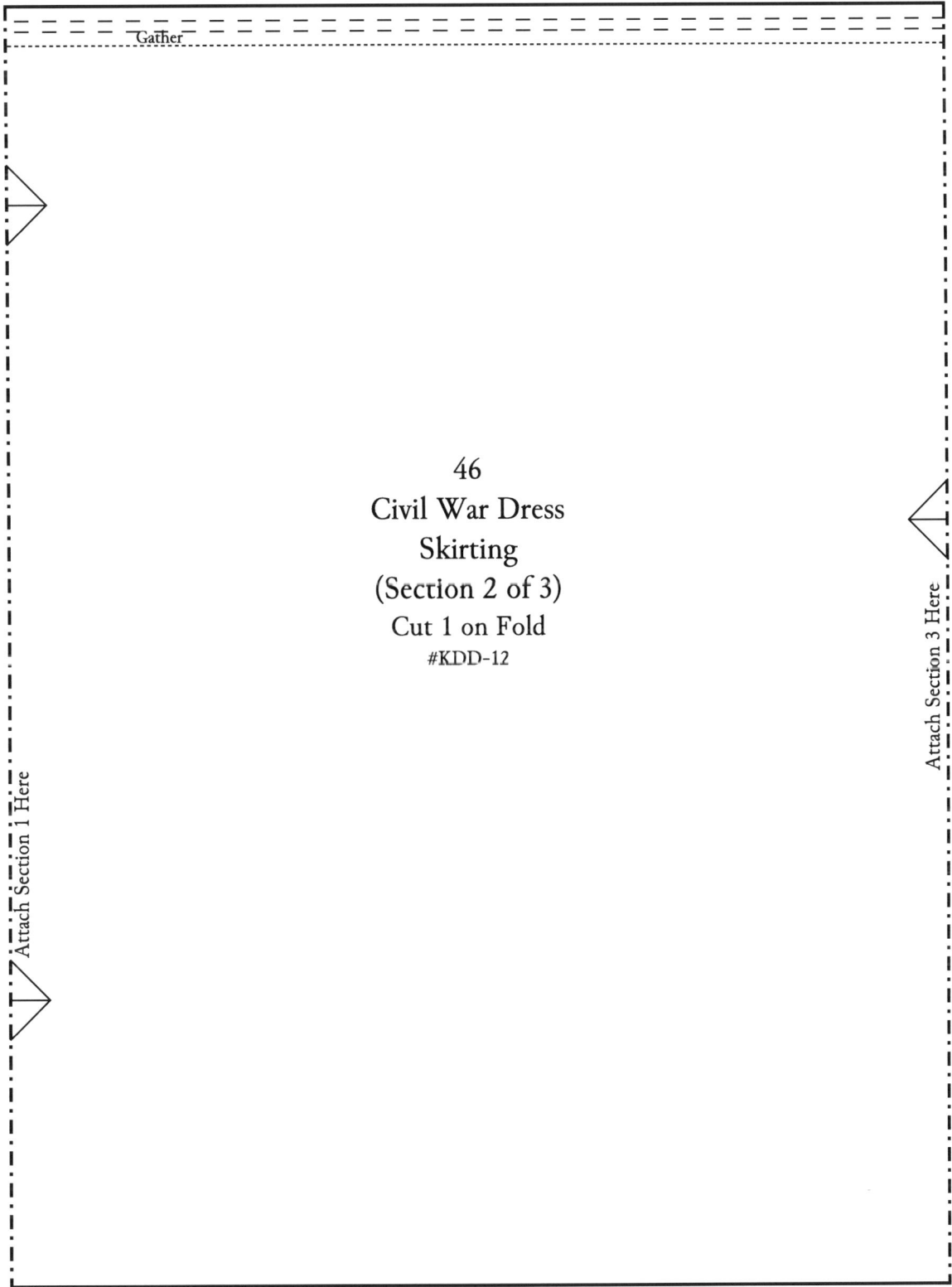

Gather

Attach Section 1 Here

Attach Section 3 Here

46
Civil War Dress
Skirting
(Section 2 of 3)
Cut 1 on Fold
#KDD-12

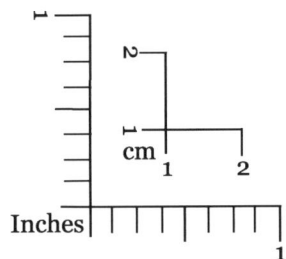

Inches

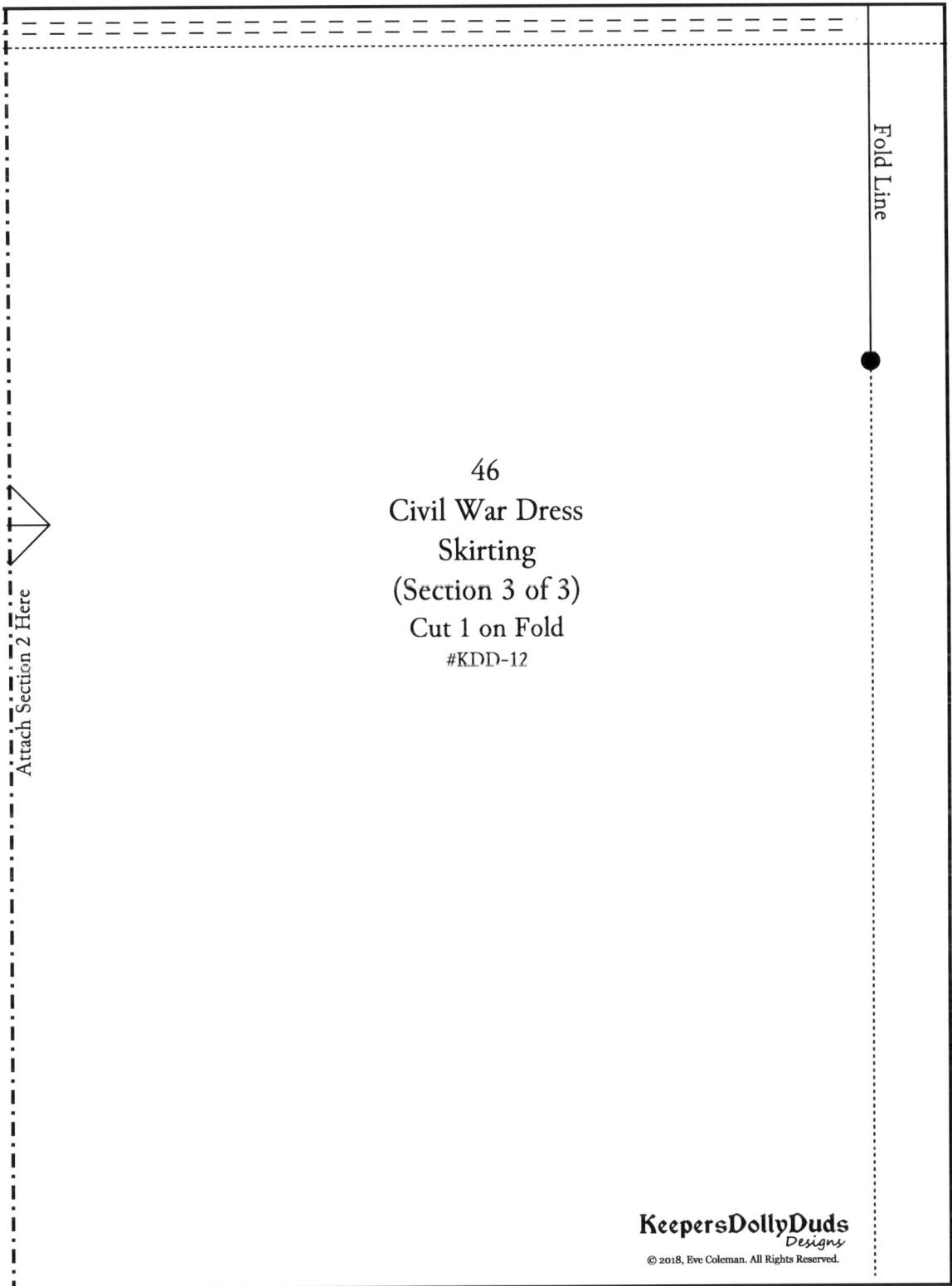

Fold Line

Attach Section 2 Here

46
Civil War Dress
Skirting
(Section 3 of 3)
Cut 1 on Fold
#KDD-12

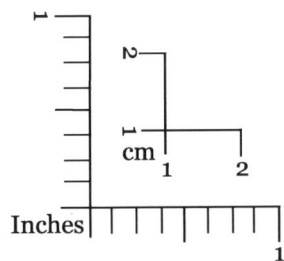

cm

Inches

Prairie Ruffles

Materials List

#KDD-03

Suggested Fabrics: *Pinafore* in light weight cotton, homespun, cotton blends, linen, muslin, batiste. Not suitable for knits. *Dress* in cotton, homespun, cotton blends, light weight wool, linen. Not suitable for knits.

Fabric Yardage:

Pinafore ~ 1/2 yard (0.5 m) 45-inch wide fabric
Dress ~ 1/2 yard (0.5 m) 45-inch wide fabric

Notions:

__Thread
Pinafore
__Two 3/8-inch (9 mm) buttons OR
  snaps for the back closure
__Six 1/4-inch (6 mm) buttons for the
  front placket
Dress
__Seven 3/8-inch (9 mm) buttons OR
  snaps for the back closure

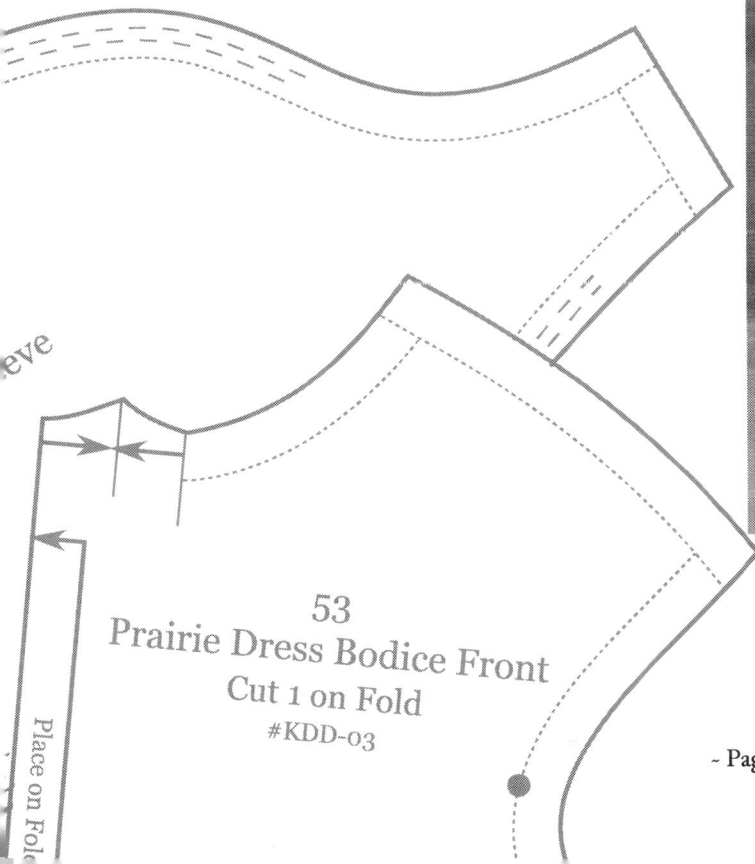

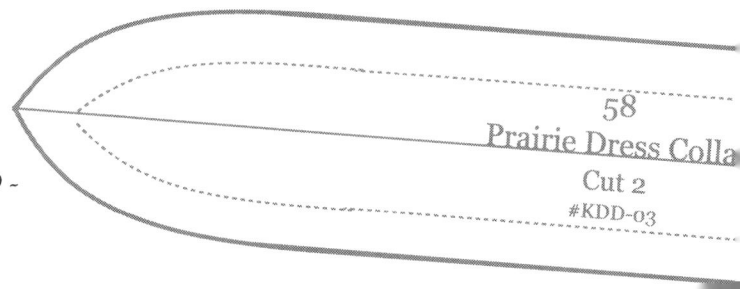

53
Prairie Dress Bodice Front
Cut 1 on Fold
#KDD-03

Place on Fold

eve

58
Prairie Dress Colla
Cut 2
#KDD-03

Dress and Bodice

Step 1: Fold the dress bodice front in half with the right sides together. Stitch the pleat at the neckline where indicated on the pattern. Open the pleat and line up the fold line with the seam. Press the pleat at the neckline only. Baste across the top edge of the pleat to secure. Finish the shoulder seam allowances if desired.

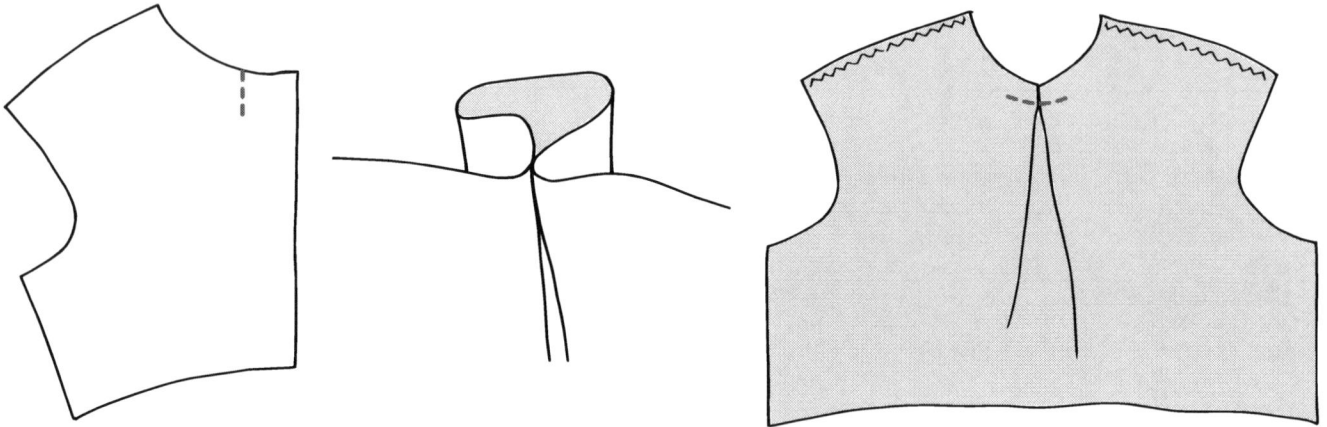

Step 2: Sew darts on the bodice back and press toward center back. Finish the shoulder seam allowances if desired.

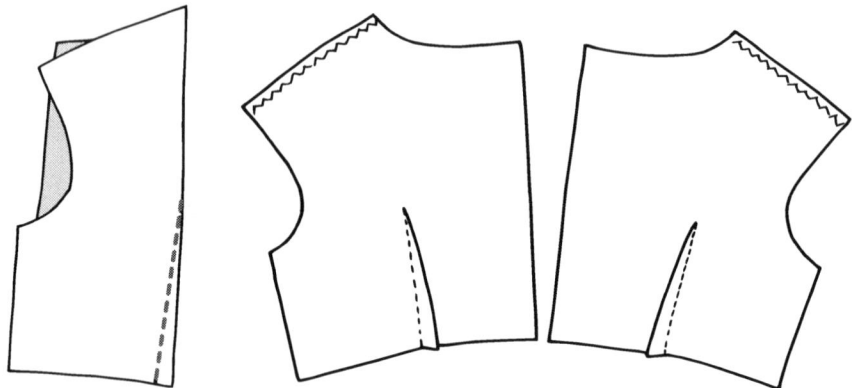

Step 3: Pin the dress bodice front and dress bodice back pieces right sides together at the shoulders. Stitch. Press the seam allowances open. Staystitch the neckline and clip the curve.

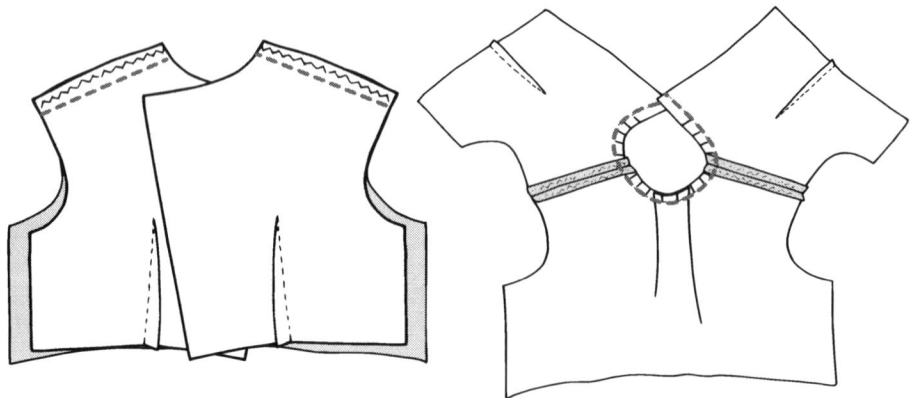

Dress Sleeves

Step 4: Make a narrow rolled hem along the straight edge of each shoulder ruffle. On the curved edges, sew two rows of gathering stitches.

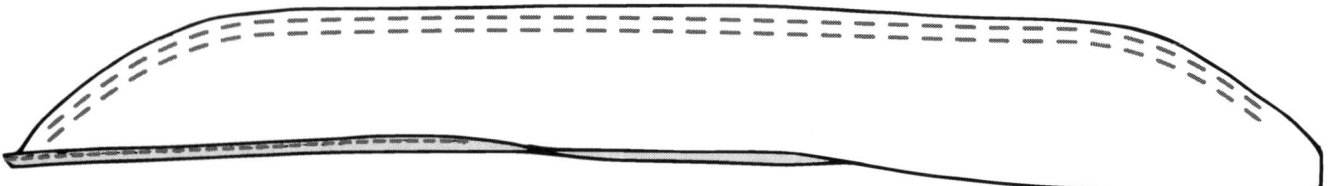

Step 5: Draw up the gathering stitches to create the ruffle. With right sides together, pin the ruffle to the armscye matching the center notch to the shoulder seam and the ends of the ruffle to the dots. Arrange the gathers evenly around the armscye. Pin or baste in place.

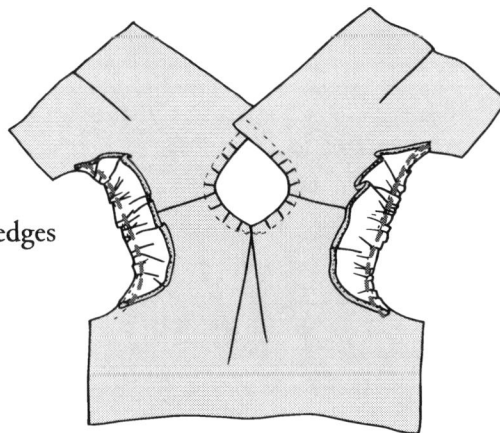

Step 6: Sew two rows of gathering stitches on the top and bottom edges of each sleeve where indicated on the pattern.

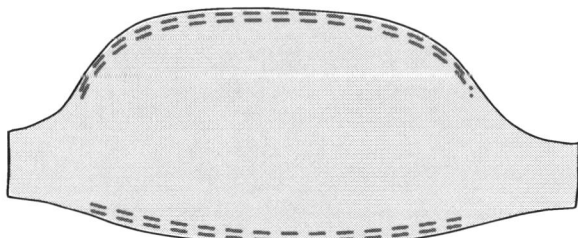

Step 7: With the right sides together, pin the lower edge of each sleeve to a sleeve band drawing up the gathering stitches and arranging the fullness evenly along the bands. Stitch. Trim the seam allowances to 1/8-inch (3 mm).

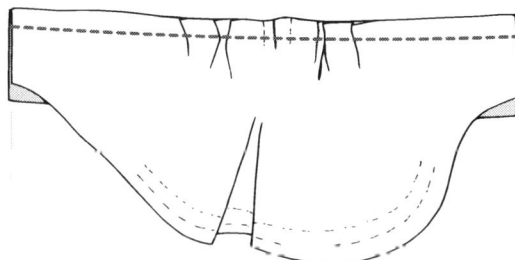

Step 8: With the right sides together, pin the sleeves to the armscyes over the ruffles, matching the double notches. Draw up the gathering stitches to fit, arranging the fullness evenly. Stitch. Clip the curves and finish the seam allowances, if desired. Press the seam allowances toward the bodice.

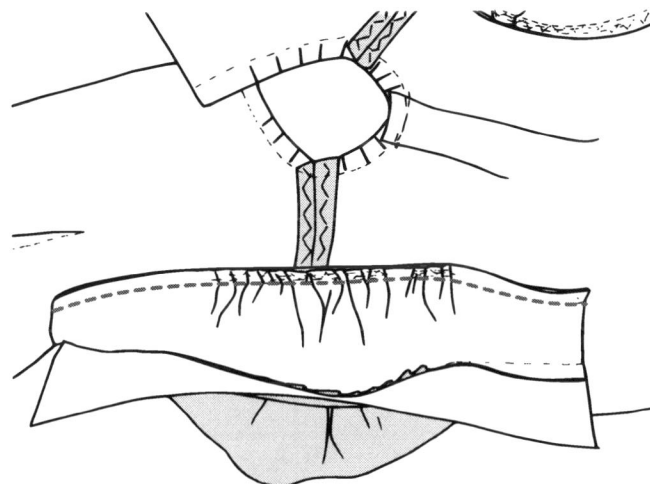

Step 9: Fold the ties along the foldline right sides together. Using a 1/8 inch (3 mm) seam allowance, stitch where indicated on the pattern. Clip the corners and turn right side out, squaring the corners with a blunt needle. Press along the seamline.

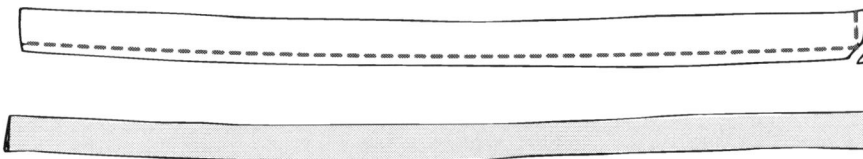

Step 10: With the seam side facing down, pin the open end of a tie to each side of the bodice front where indicated on the pattern. Baste to secure. Finish the side seam allowances, if desired.

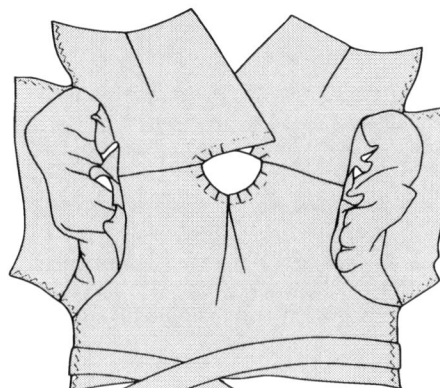

Step 11: Sew the side seams of the sleeves and bodice right sides together, taking care to line up the bottom edges of the sleeves and bodice and the seam allowances on the armscyes. Press the seam allowances open.

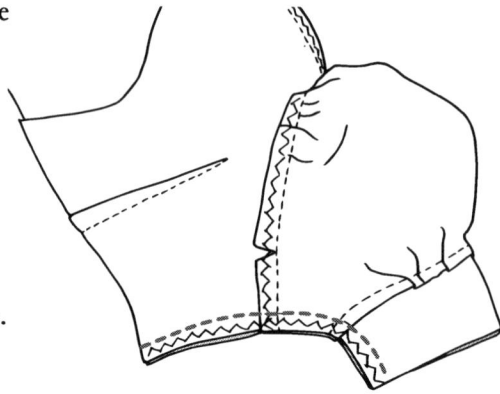

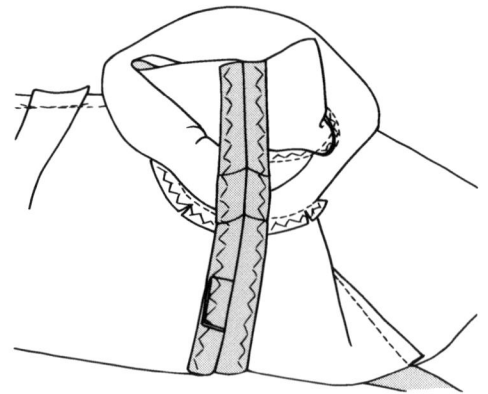

Step 12: Turn the sleeve bands under along the seam allowance and then again along the fold line. Pin the folded edge along the seamline and whipstitch to secure.

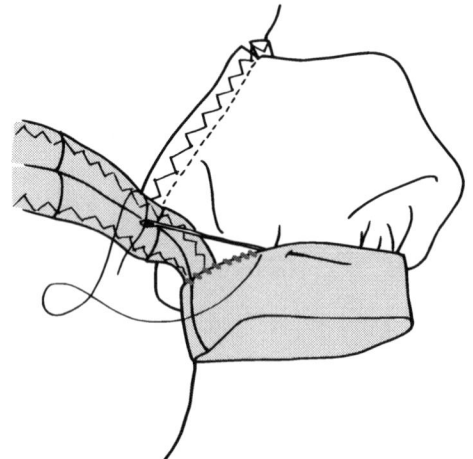

Dress Skirting

Step 13: Sew two rows of gathering stitches on the top edge of the skirting where indicated on the pattern.

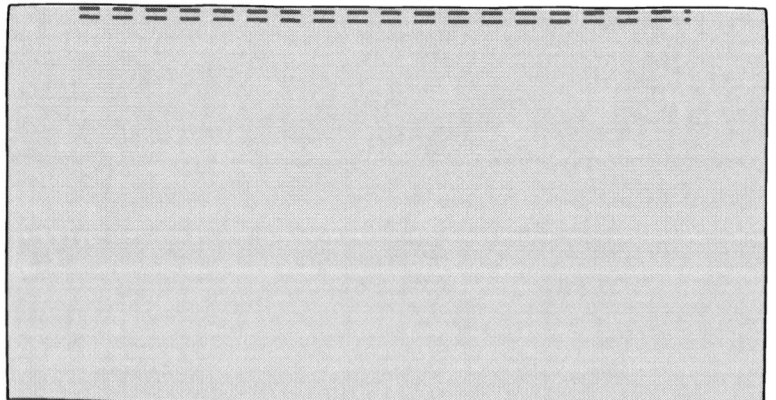

Step 14: Pin the skirting to the bottom edge of the bodice with the right sides together. Draw up the gathering stitches to fit and arrange the fullness evenly along the bodice. Stitch. Finish the seam allowances along the waistline and back edges, if desired.

Collar

Step 15: Fold the collar in half along the fold line with the right side out. Press.

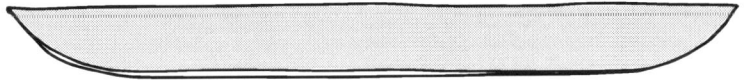

Step 16: Pin the collar to the neckline, matching the center notch on the collar to the center front of the bodice. Ease the neckline around the curve of the collar on each end. Fold the top back edges of the bodice over the ends of the collar. Stitch. Finish the neckline edge, if desired.

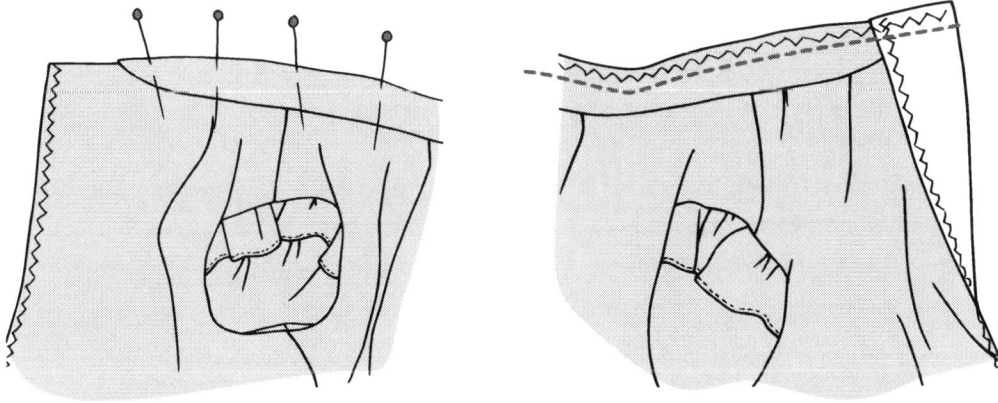

Step 17: Turn the top back edge right side out, squaring the corners with a blunt needle. Press the collar seam allowance toward the bodice and the bodice back along the fold line to create a facing.

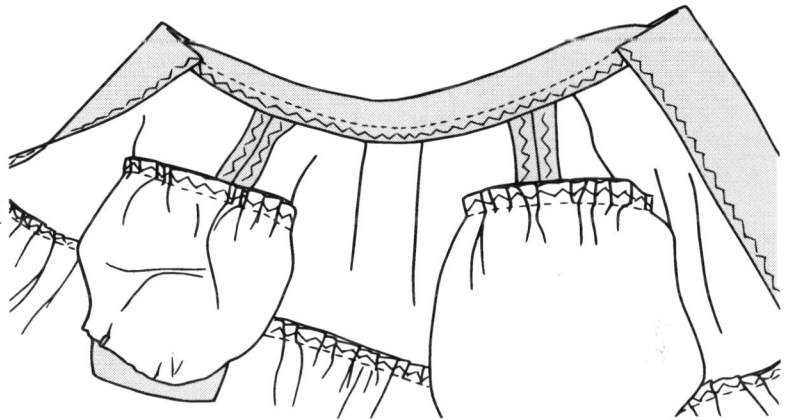

Finishing the Dress

Step 18: With the right sides together, turn each back facing under at the bottom edge along the fold line. Pin in place. Stitch across the facing 1/2-inch (12 mm) from the bottom edge. Finish the bottom edge of the skirting. Turn the facing right side out, squaring the corners with a blunt needle. Press a 1/2- inch (12 mm) hem under along the bottom edge of the skirting and pin in place. Stitch the hem by machine or by hand.

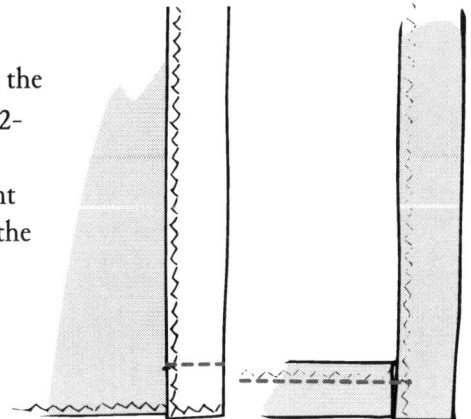

Step 19: Tack the facing in place at the waistline. Make button holes on proper left and sew buttons on proper right where indicated on the pattern.

Pinafore

Step 20: Pin the bodice front to the bodice back pieces right sides together along the shoulders. Stitch. Press the seam allowances open. Repeat for the bodice lining pieces.

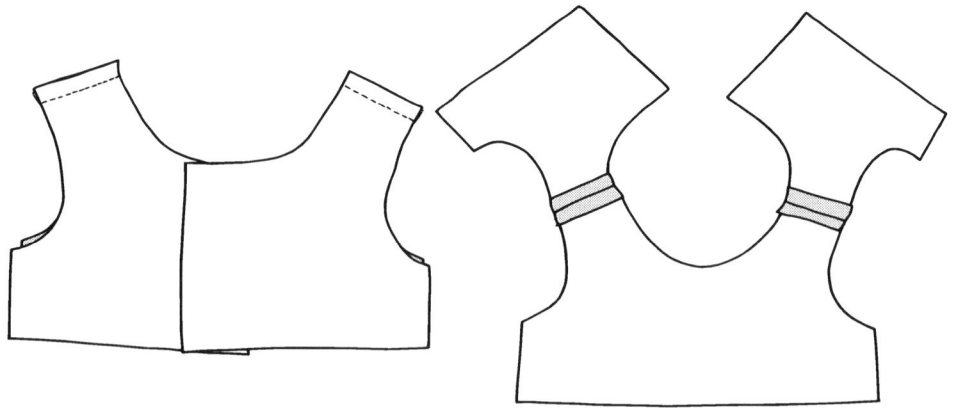

Step 21: Pin the bodice and bodice lining right sides together. Stitch around the armscyes and along the back edges of the bodice. Clip curves along armscye and trim seam allowance to 1/8-inch (3 mm). Turn right side out and press, following the seamlines.

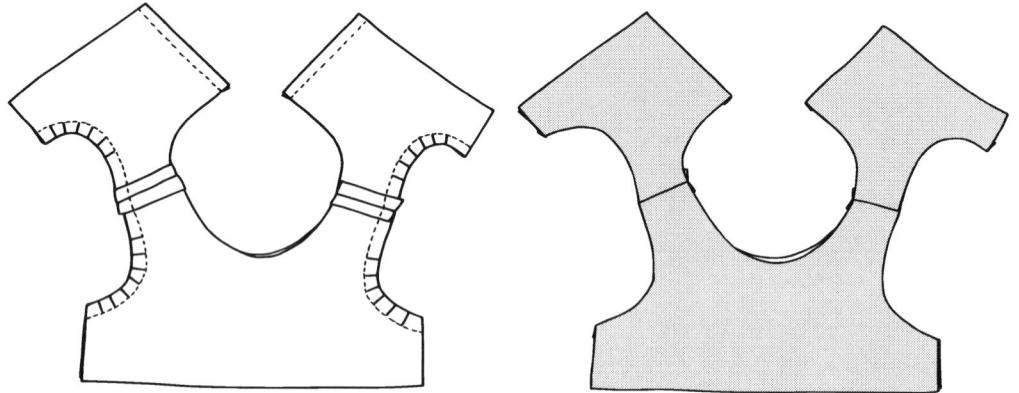

Step 22: Sew each of the side seams of the bodice and bodice lining together as shown in the illustration. Press the seam allowances open and fold sides back down.

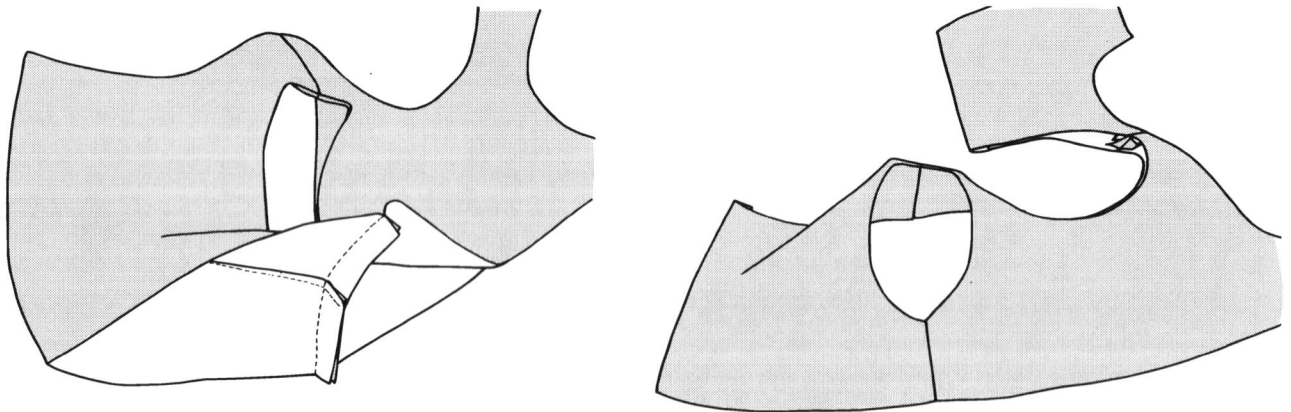

Pinafore Skirting

Step 23: Finish the bottom and side edges of the skirting.

Finishing the Pinafore

Step 24: With the right sides together, turn each back facing under at the bottom edge along the fold line. Pin in place. Stitch across the facing 3/4-inch (19 mm) from the bottom edge. Finish the bottom edge of the skirting. Turn the facing right side out, squaring the corners with a blunt needle. Press a 3/4-inch (19 mm) hem under along the bottom edge of the skirting and pin in place. Stitch the hem by machine or by hand.

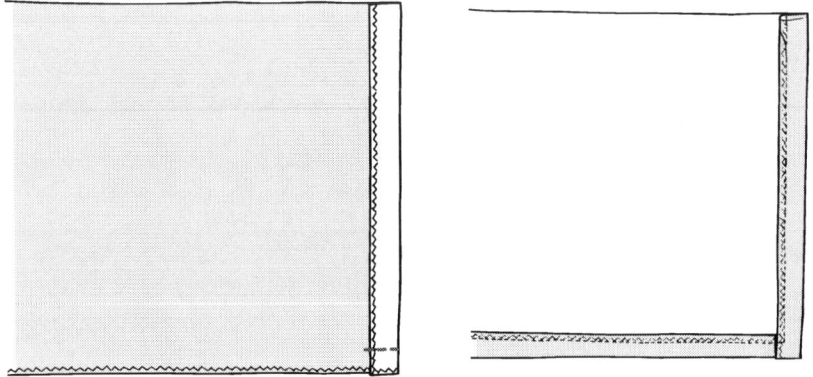

Step 25: Sew two rows of gathering stitches along the top edge of the pinafore skirting where indicated on the pattern.

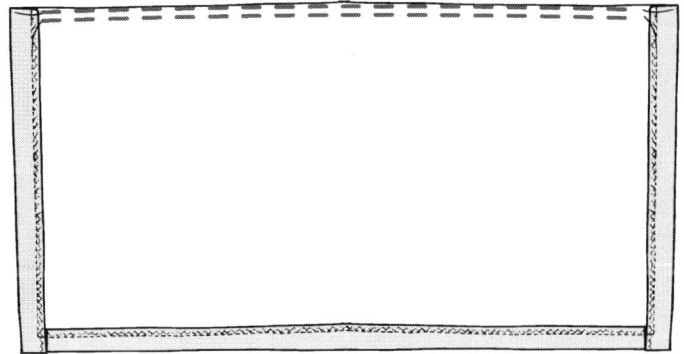

Step 26: Pin the pinafore skirting to the pinafore bodice between the dots and matching the center notches. Draw up the gathering stitches to fit, leaved the section between the center dots ungathered. This is where the front placket will be attached. Arrange the fullness of the skirting evenly along the lower edge of bodice. Stitch, being careful not to catch bodice lining into seam. Trim the seam allowance to 1/8-inch (3 mm). Press the seam allowance toward the bodice, being careful not to crush the gathers.

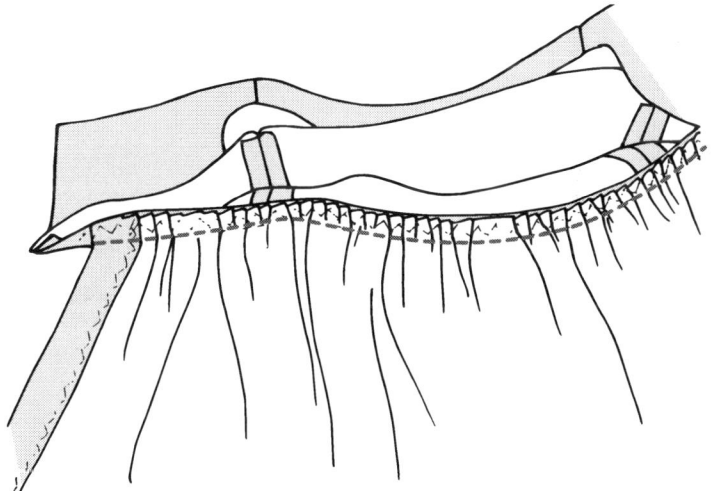

Step 27: Turn the lower edge of the bodice lining under along the seam allowance. Whipstitch the lining to the skirting along the seamline.

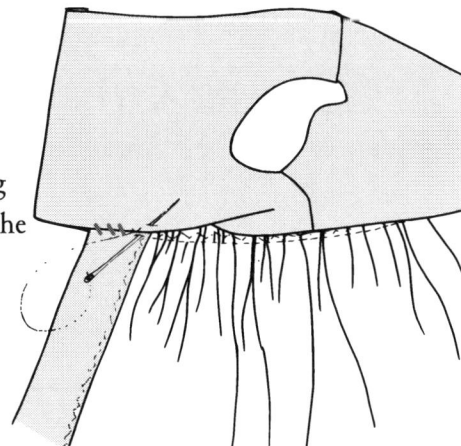

Pinafore Ruffles and Placket

Step 28: Make a narrow rolled hem along the straight edge of each pinafore ruffles. On the curved edges, sew two rows of gathering stitches.

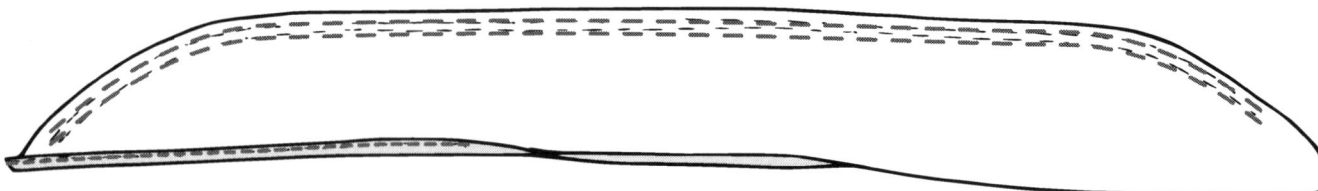

Step 29: With the right sides up, pin the ruffles to the neckline of the pinafore, matching the dots. Draw up the gathering stitches to fit and arrange the fullness evenly along the neckline. Stitch.

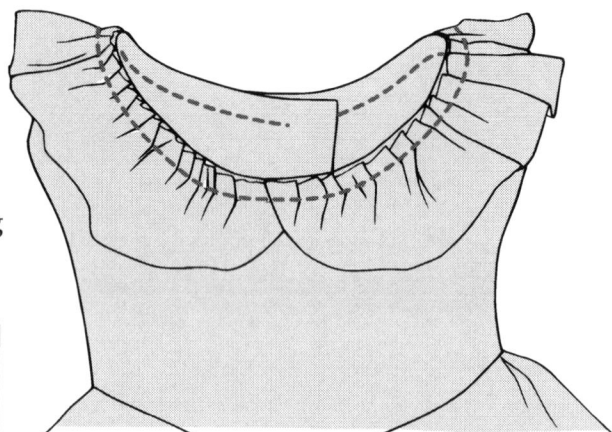

Step 30: Fold the two bottom corners of the placket under so that they meet in the center as shown. Press. Fold each side of the placket under along the fold lines. Press. Turn up the bottom point to form two neat corners. Press.

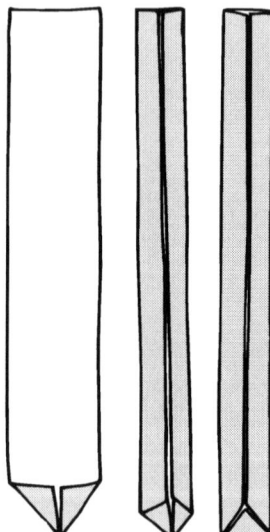

Step 31: Pin the placket to the bodice and skirt front where indicated on the pattern. Topstitch along the sides and bottom end to secure.

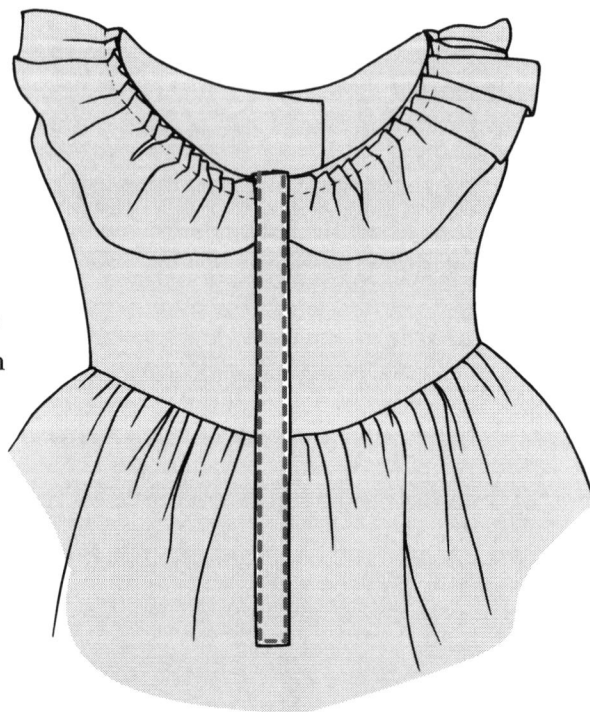

Step 32: Fold the binding strip in half lengthwise, right side out. Press. Leaving at least a 1/4-inch (6 mm) overhang, line up the raw edges of the binding strip with the raw edges of bodice neckline. Sew the binding strip to the neckline.

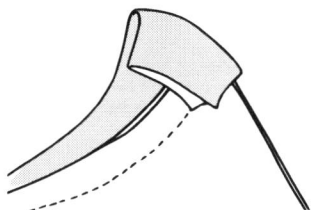

Step 33: Trim the raw edges of the neckline make a nice even edge and trim the ends of the binding strip to 1/4 inch (6 mm). Wrap the folded edges of the binding strip over the raw edges of the neckline. Pin, then hand stitch in place, making sure to sew in the tucked ends of the binding strip.

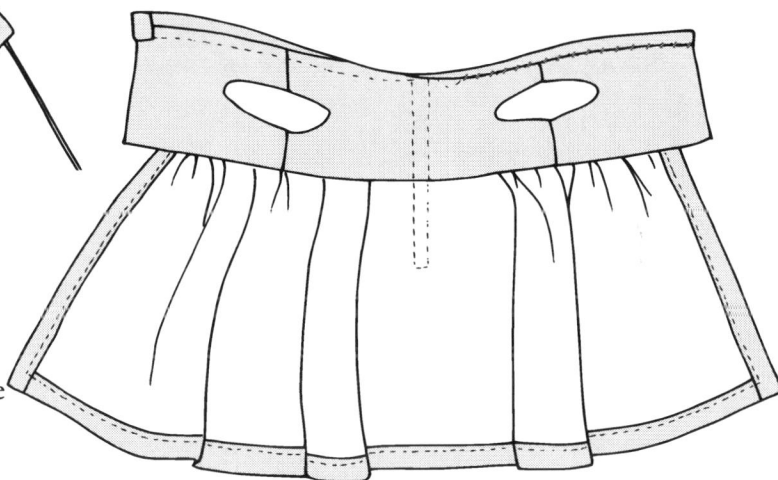

Finishing the Pinafore

Step 34: On the back of the pinafore, make button holes on the proper left and sew buttons on the proper right where indicated on the pattern. Sew six small buttons along the placket where indicated on the pattern.

Pattern Pieces

Cutting Layout for 45-inch (1.14 m) wide Fabric
14 Pieces

53 ~ Prairie Dress Bodice Front
54 ~ Prairie Dress Bodice Back
55 ~ Prairie Dress Sleeve Ruffle
56 ~ Prairie Dress Sleeve
57 ~ Prairie Dress Sleeve Band
58 ~ Prairie Dress Collar
59 ~ Prairie Dress Skirting
60 ~ Prairie Dress Tie
61 ~ Prairie Pinafore Bodice Front
62 ~ Prairie Pinafore Bodice Back
63 ~ Prairie Pinafore Ruffle
64 ~ Prairie Pinafore Placket
65 ~ Prairie Pinafore Skirting
66 ~ Prairie Pinafore Bias Binding

Prairie Ruffles Dress
Use pieces: 53, 54, 55, 56, 57, 58, 59 and 60

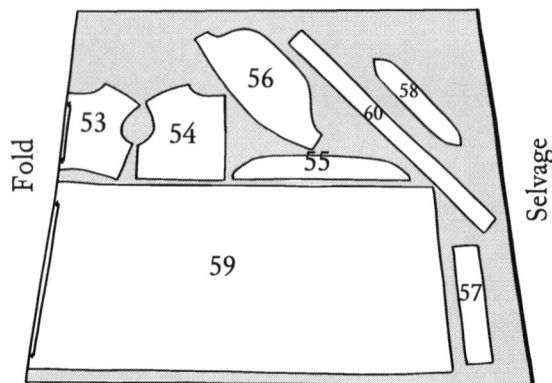

Prairie Ruffles Pinafore
Use pieces: 61, 62, 63, 64, 65, and 66

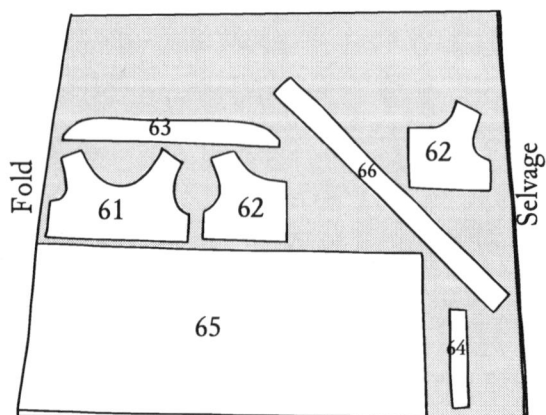

Facing

Fold Line

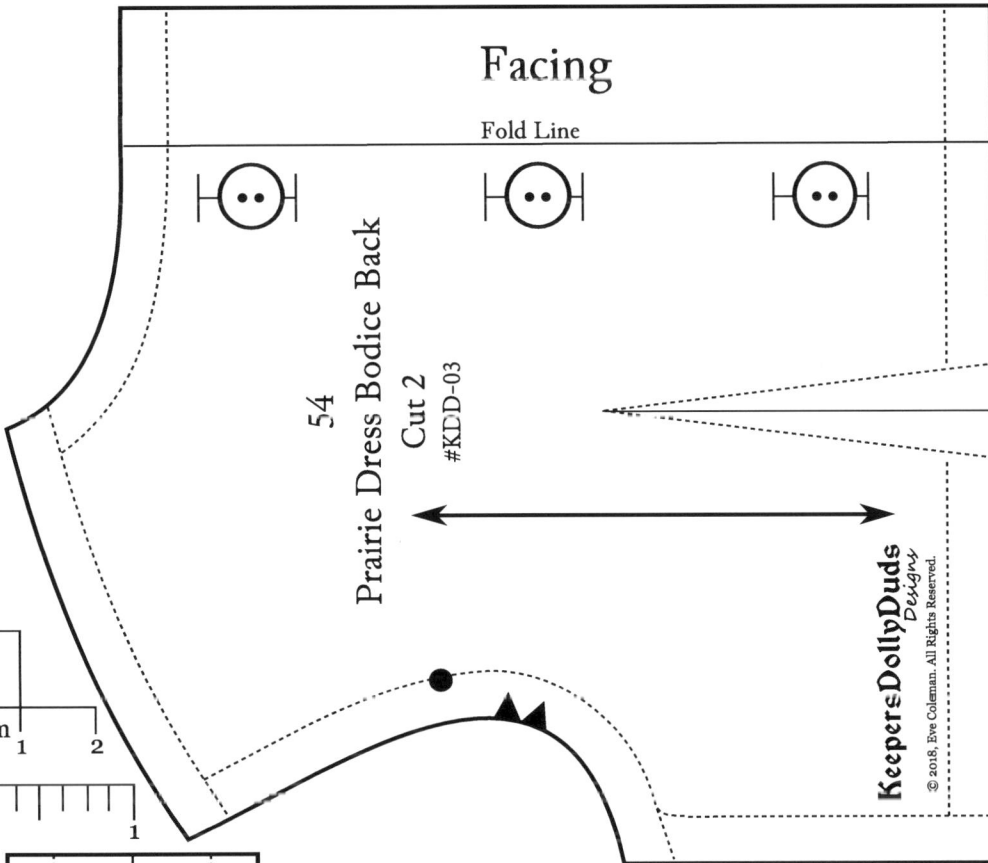

Prairie Dress Bodice Back
54
Cut 2
#KDD-03

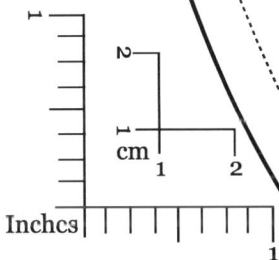

1

2

cm 1   2

Inches   1

Prairie Dress Sleeve Ruffle
55
Cut 2
#KDD-03

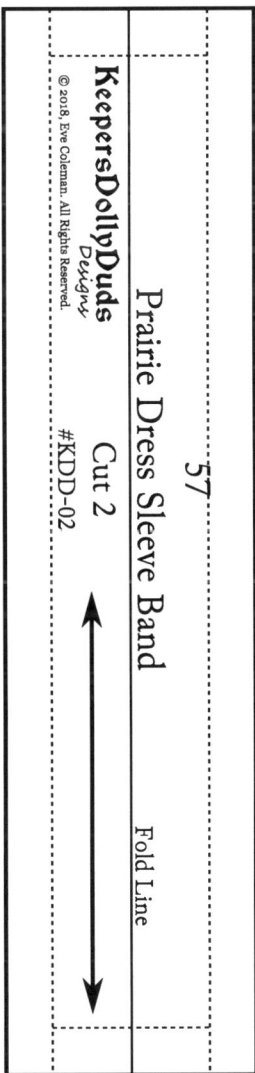

Prairie Dress Sleeve Band
57
Cut 2
#KDD-02

Fold Line

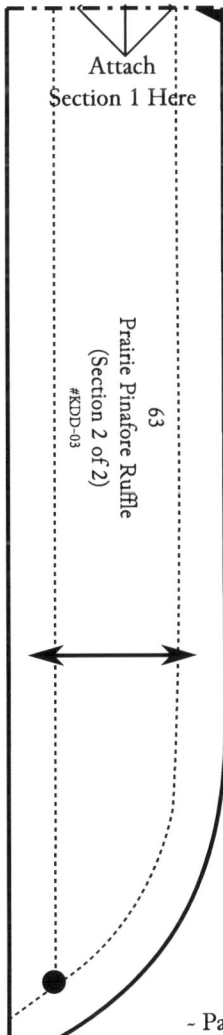

Attach
Section 1 Here

63
Prairie Pinafore Ruffle
(Section 2 of 2)
#KDD-03

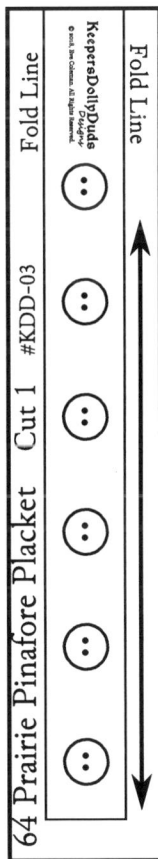

Fold Line

64 Prairie Pinafore Placket   Cut 1   #KDD-03

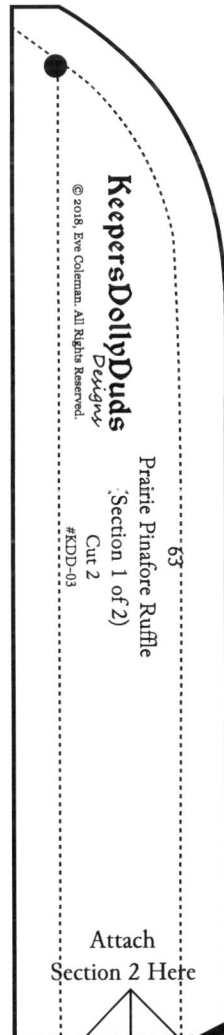

63
Prairie Pinafore Ruffle
(Section 1 of 2)
Cut 2
#KDD-03

Attach
Section 2 Here

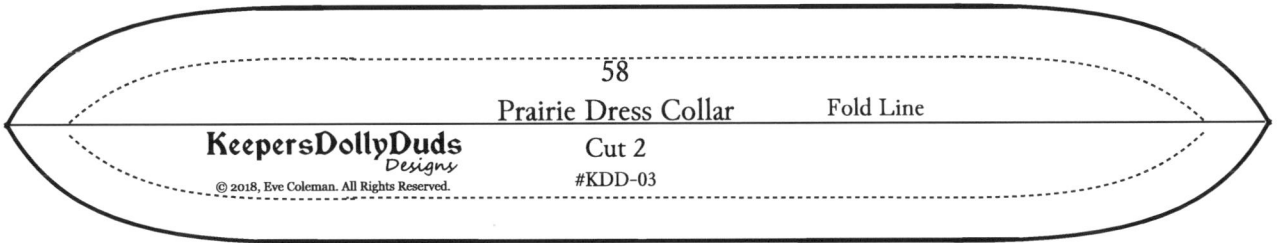

58
Prairie Dress Collar

Fold Line

KeepersDollyDuds Designs
© 2018, Eve Coleman. All Rights Reserved.

Cut 2
#KDD-03

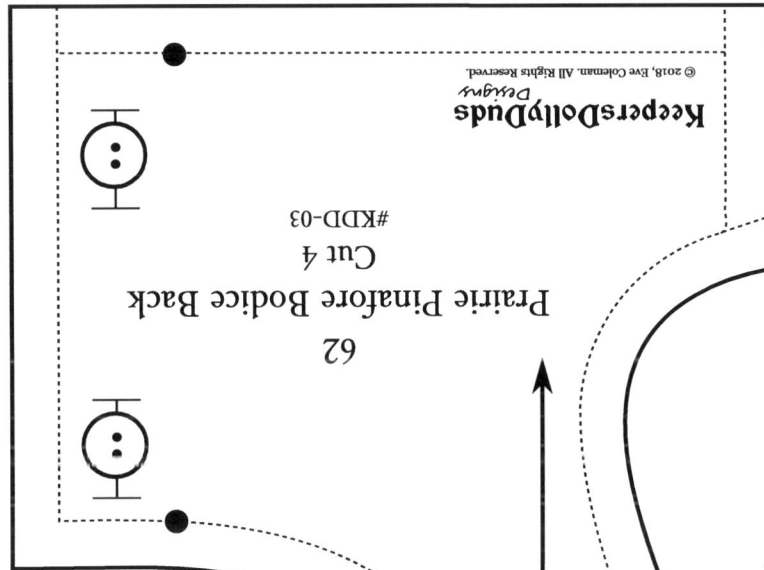

62
Prairie Pinafore Bodice Back
Cut 4
#KDD-03

KeepersDollyDuds Designs
© 2018, Eve Coleman. All Rights Reserved.

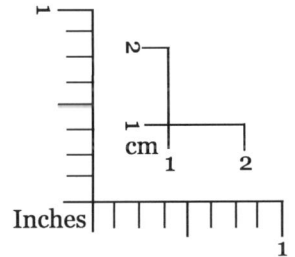

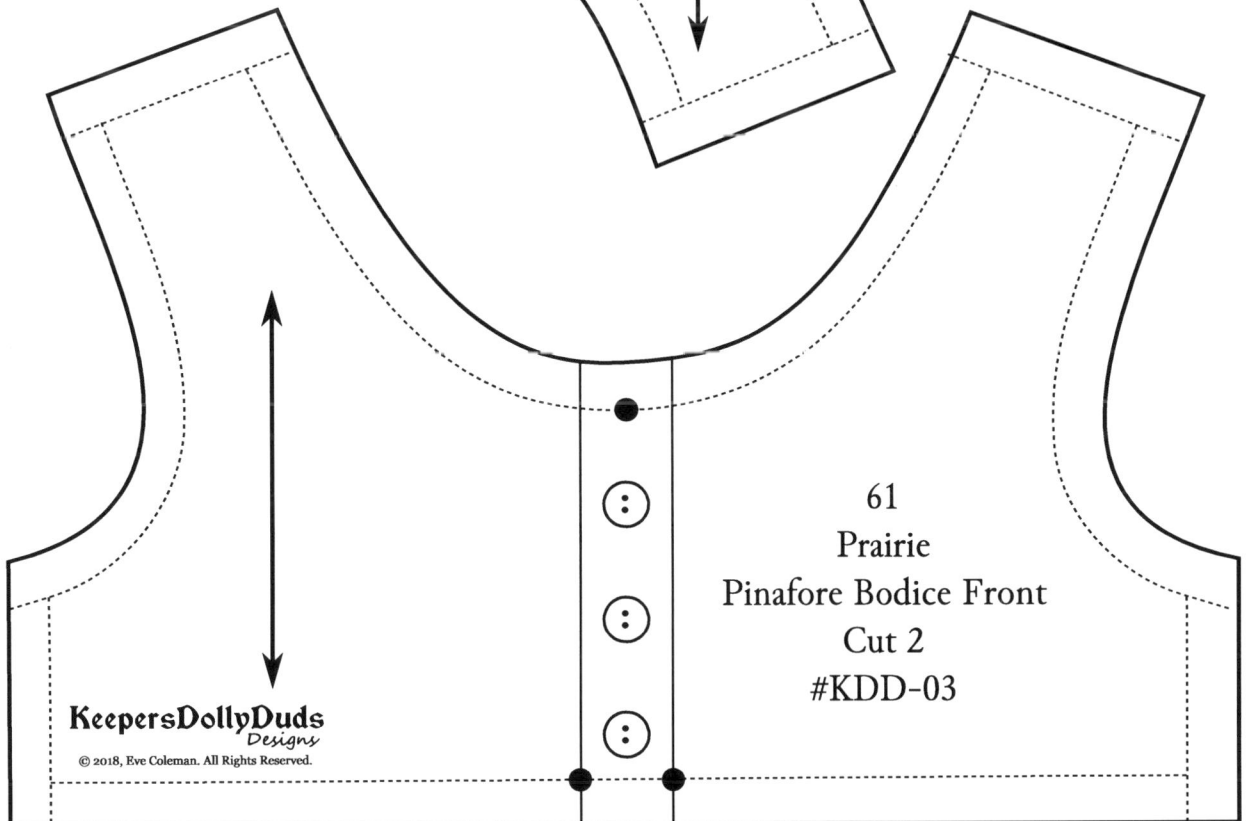

61
Prairie
Pinafore Bodice Front
Cut 2
#KDD-03

KeepersDollyDuds Designs
© 2018, Eve Coleman. All Rights Reserved.

56
Prairie Dress Sleeve
Cut 1
#KDD-03

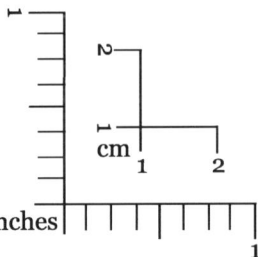

Gather

Gather

53
Prairie Dress Bodice Front
Cut 1 on Fold
#KDD-03

Place on Fold

Tie Placement

1

2

1

cm   1   2

Inches

1

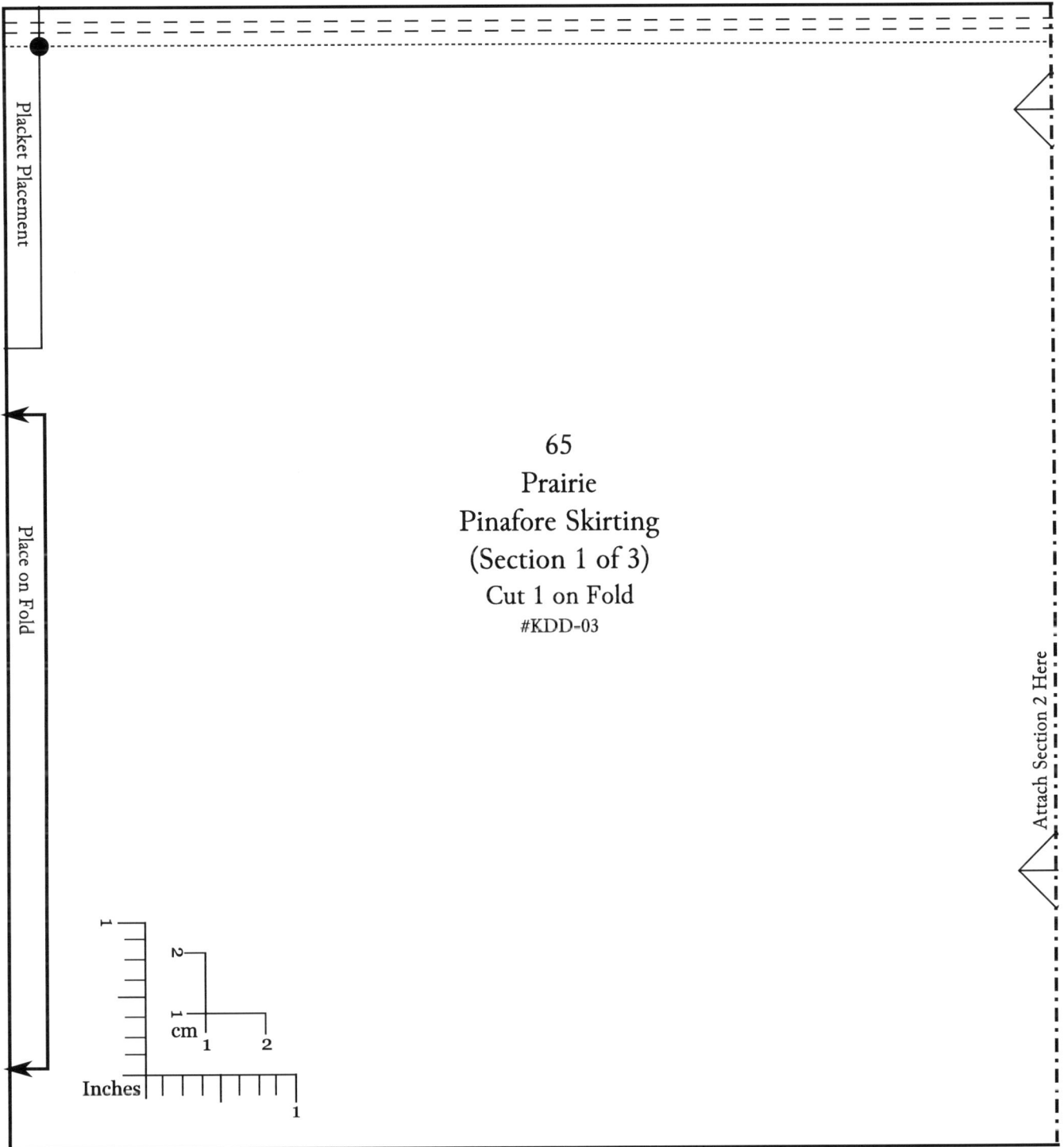

Placket Placement

Place on Fold

65
Prairie
Pinafore Skirting
(Section 1 of 3)
Cut 1 on Fold
#KDD-03

Attach Section 2 Here

1
1
2
1
cm 1   2
Inches   1

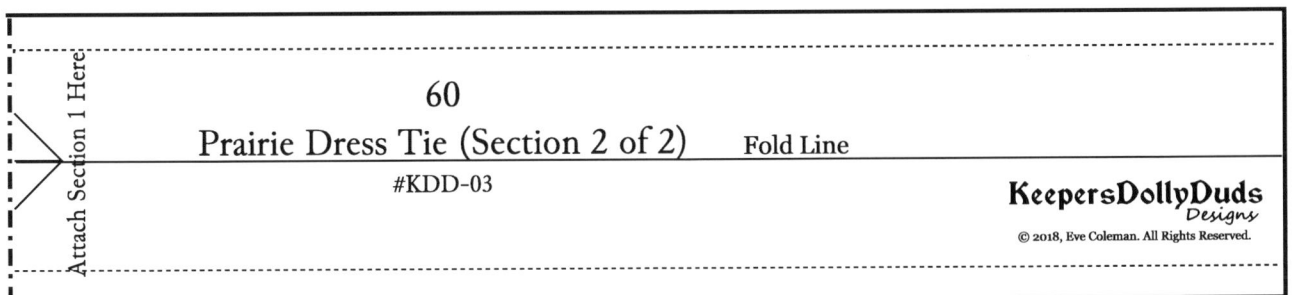

Attach Section 1 Here

60
Prairie Dress Tie (Section 2 of 2)   Fold Line
#KDD-03

KeepersDollyDuds
Designs
© 2018, Eve Coleman. All Rights Reserved.

Gather

1
2
1
cm   1   2
Inches   1

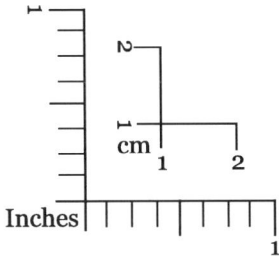

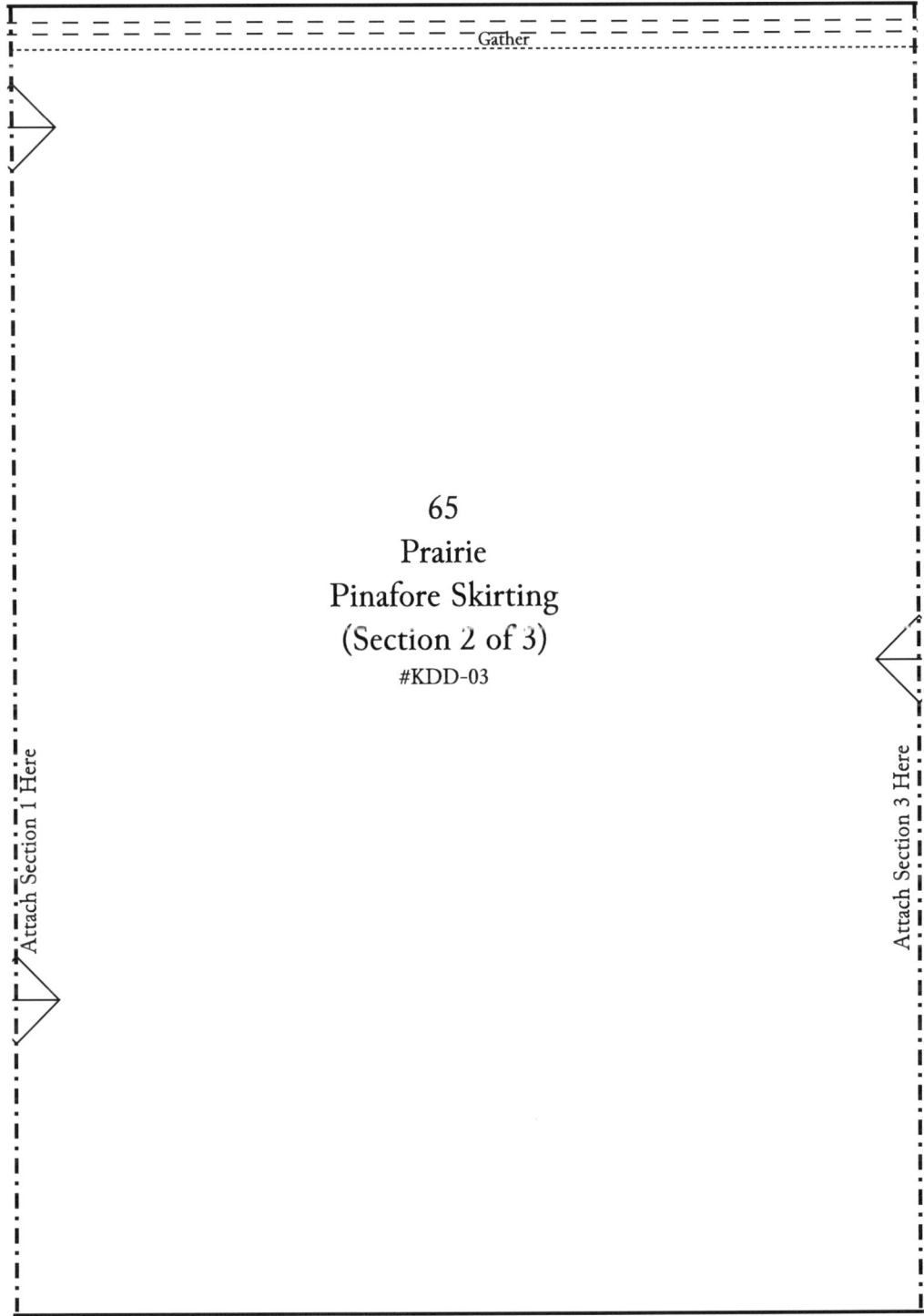

65
Prairie
Pinafore Skirting
(Section 2 of 3)
#KDD-03

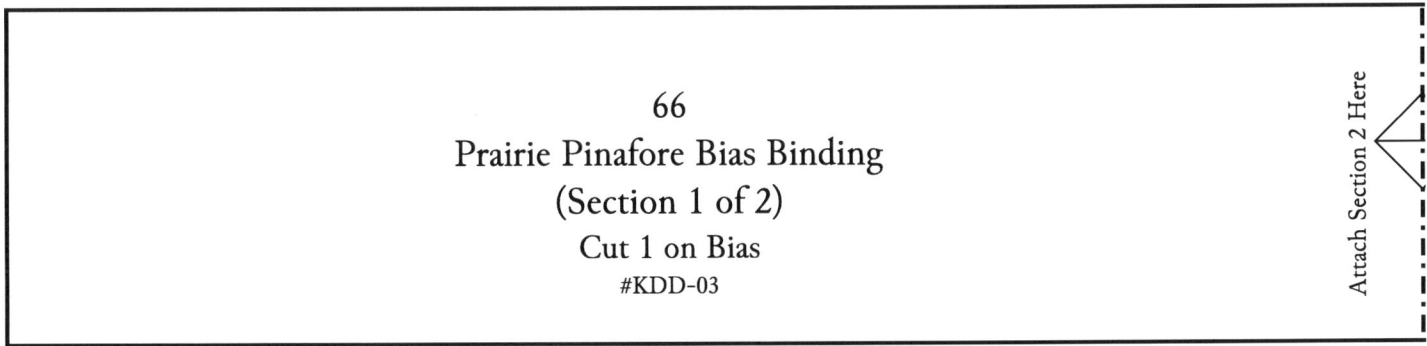

Attach Section 1 Here

Attach Section 3 Here

66
Prairie Pinafore Bias Binding
(Section 1 of 2)
Cut 1 on Bias
#KDD-03

Attach Section 2 Here

Inches

1

2

1

cm 1 2

1

Attach Section 2 Here

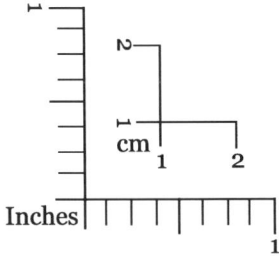

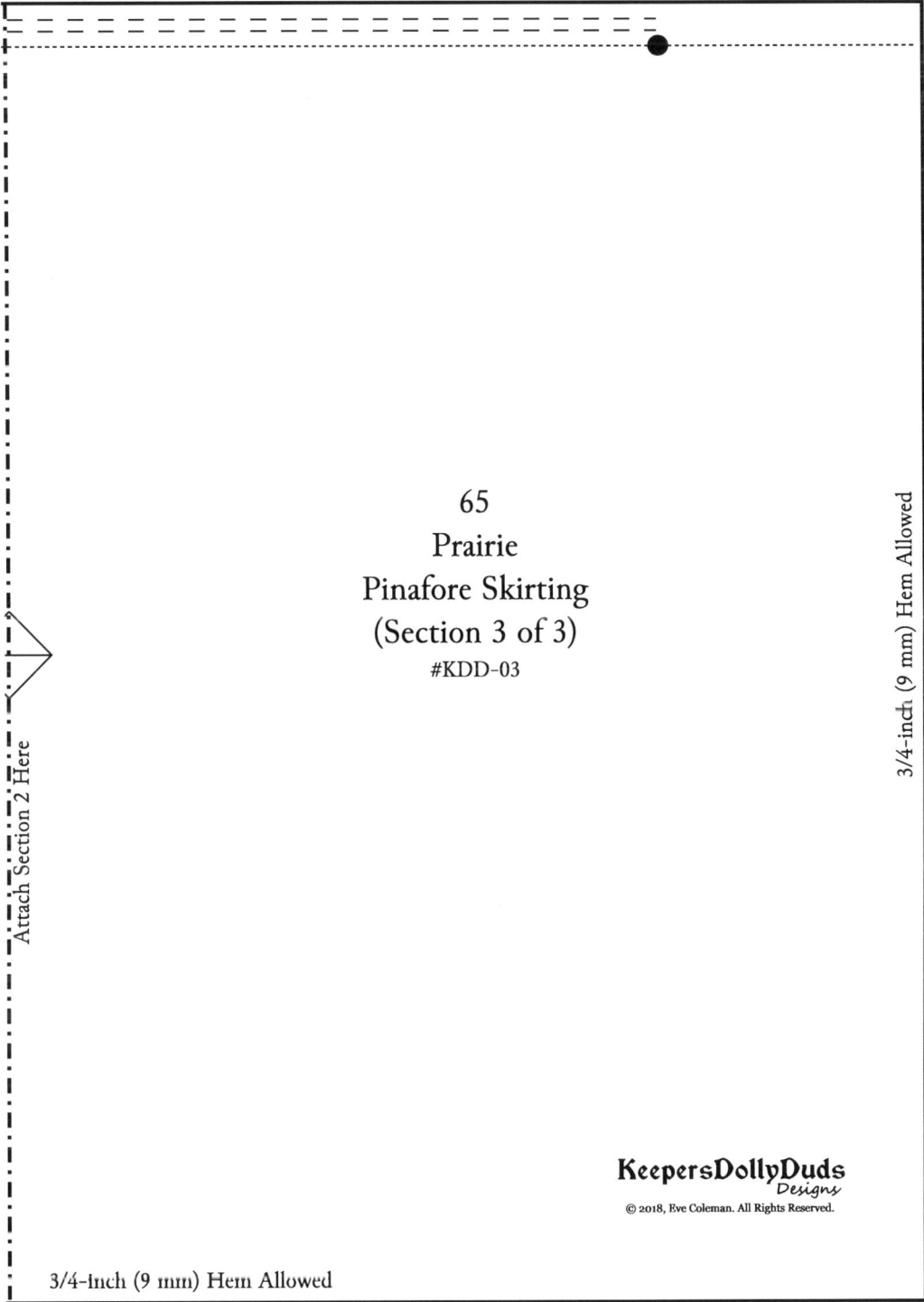

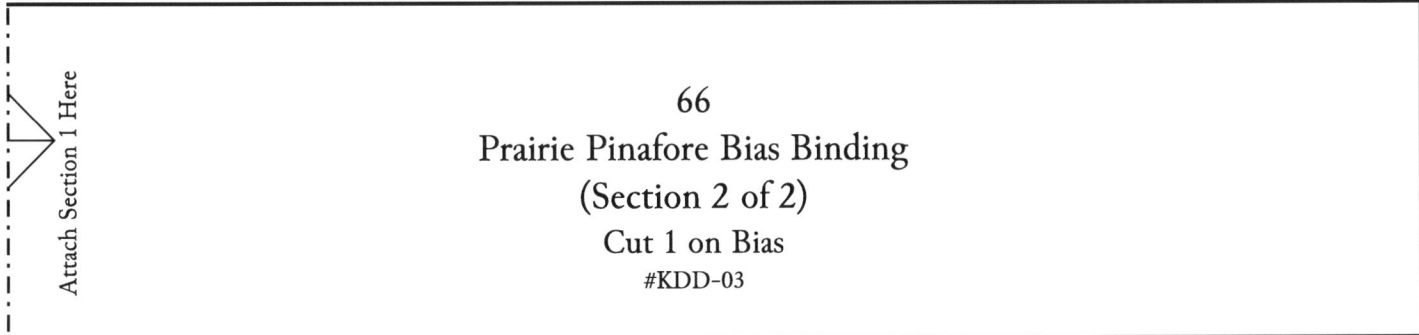

65
Prairie
Pinafore Skirting
(Section 3 of 3)
#KDD-03

KeepersDollyDuds
Designs
© 2018, Eve Coleman. All Rights Reserved.

Attach Section 1 Here

66
Prairie Pinafore Bias Binding
(Section 2 of 2)
Cut 1 on Bias
#KDD-03

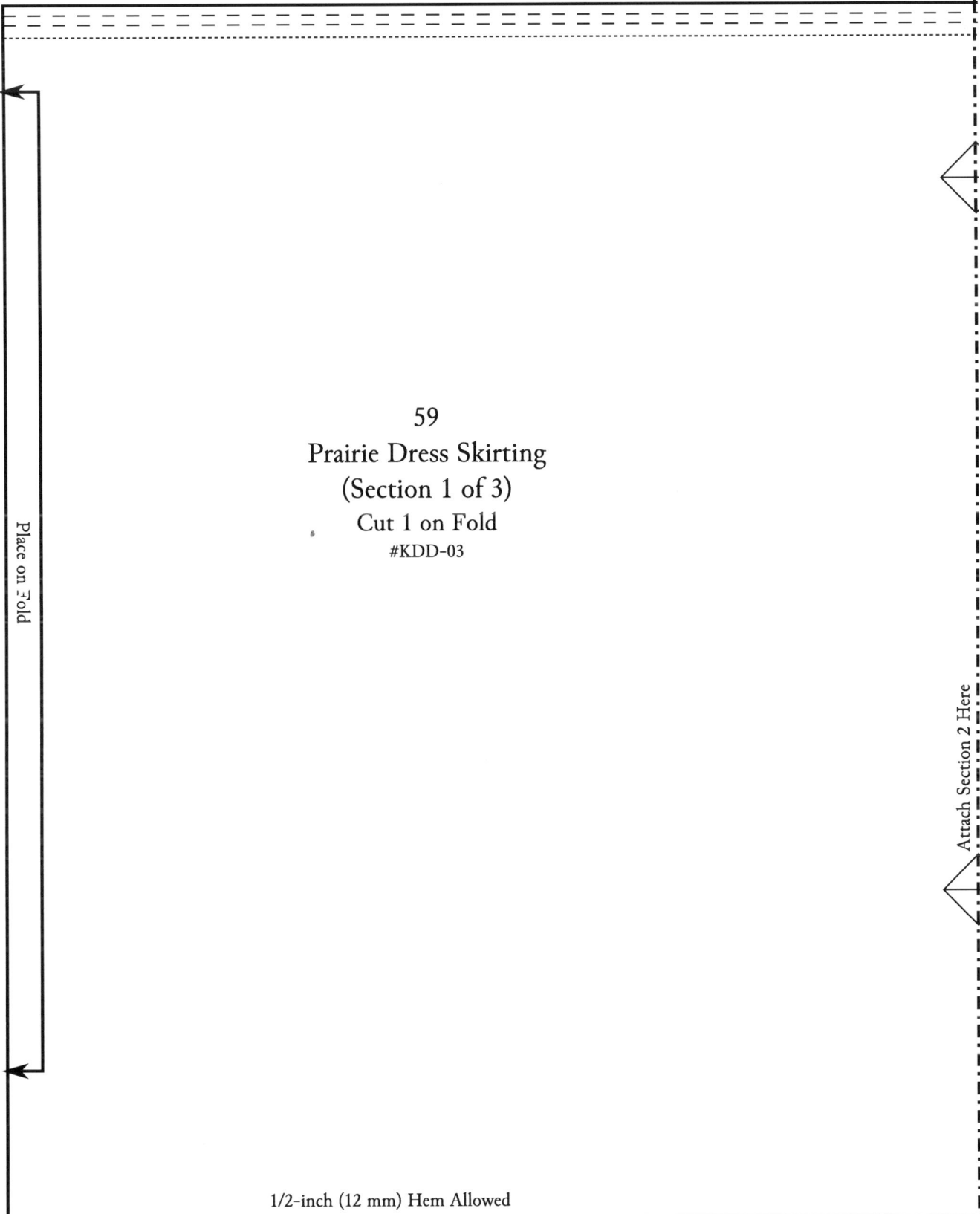

59
Prairie Dress Skirting
(Section 1 of 3)
Cut 1 on Fold
#KDD-03

Place on Fold

Attach Section 2 Here

1/2-inch (12 mm) Hem Allowed

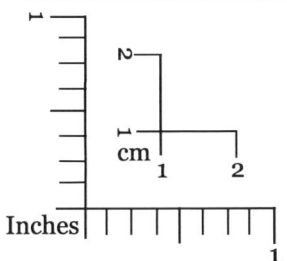

cm
Inches

Glossary

A

Armscye ~ The armhole or the opening in a bodice to which the sleeve is sewn.

B

Backstitch ~ A variation of the running stitch that doubles back on each stitch. It is is the most common hand stitch used as it makes a strong seam.

Backstitch

Back Tack ~To stitch backwards a few stitches to anchor a seam

Baste ~ Temporary stitches made with a running stitch or a long machine stitch used to hold fabric in place before the final stitching.

Bias ~ Bias refers to any line diagonal to the horizontal and vertical grains of the fabric. Woven fabric stretches along the bias. The true bias, 45 degrees to the selvage, allows for the most stretch.

Bodice ~ The part of a garment which runs from the shoulders to the waist.

Button ~ A small disk or knob used as a fastening when passed through a buttonhole or loop.

Buttonhole ~ Holes in fabric that are finished with stitching or fabric which allow buttons to pass through and secure one piece of the fabric to another.

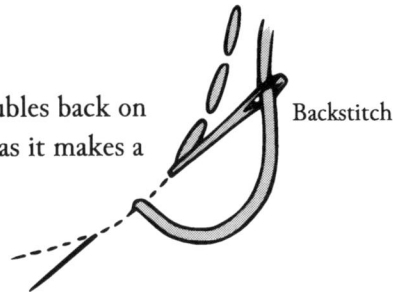

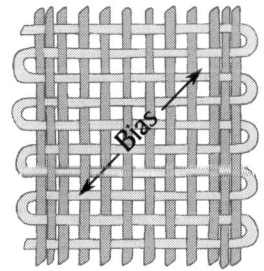

C

Clip ~ To cut small slashes inside the seam allowance of an inside curve to help rounded edges turn and lie neatly.

Clip

Cuff ~ A fold or band that trims or finishes the bottom of a sleeve.

Cutting Line ~ On a pattern, the outermost line that is to be cut.

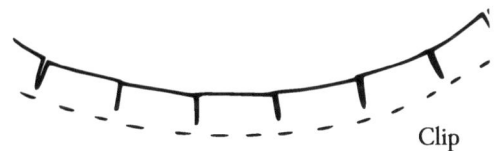

D

Dart ~ A tuck of fabric that tapers into a point. Used to take in ease and give shape to a garment.

Double-fold Hem ~ A hem that is folded once for the hem allowance and a second time to enclose the raw edge.

Double-Fold Hem

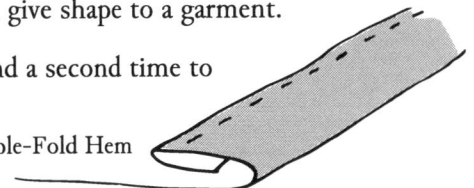

E

Ease ~ The method of fitting a length of fabric into a slightly smaller space without resulting in gathers or puckers. Also, extra room added to a garment beyond the measurements to make the garment less restricting.

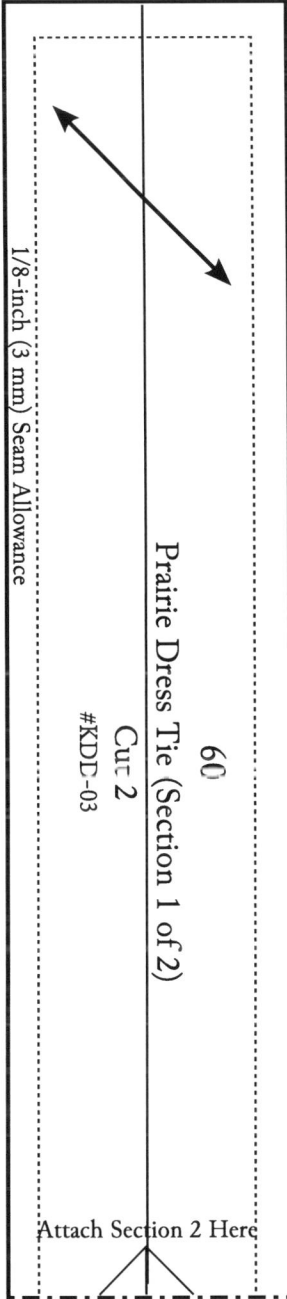

1/8-inch (3 mm) Seam Allowance

60
Prairie Dress Tie (Section 1 of 2)
Cut 2
#KDD-03

Attach Section 2 Here

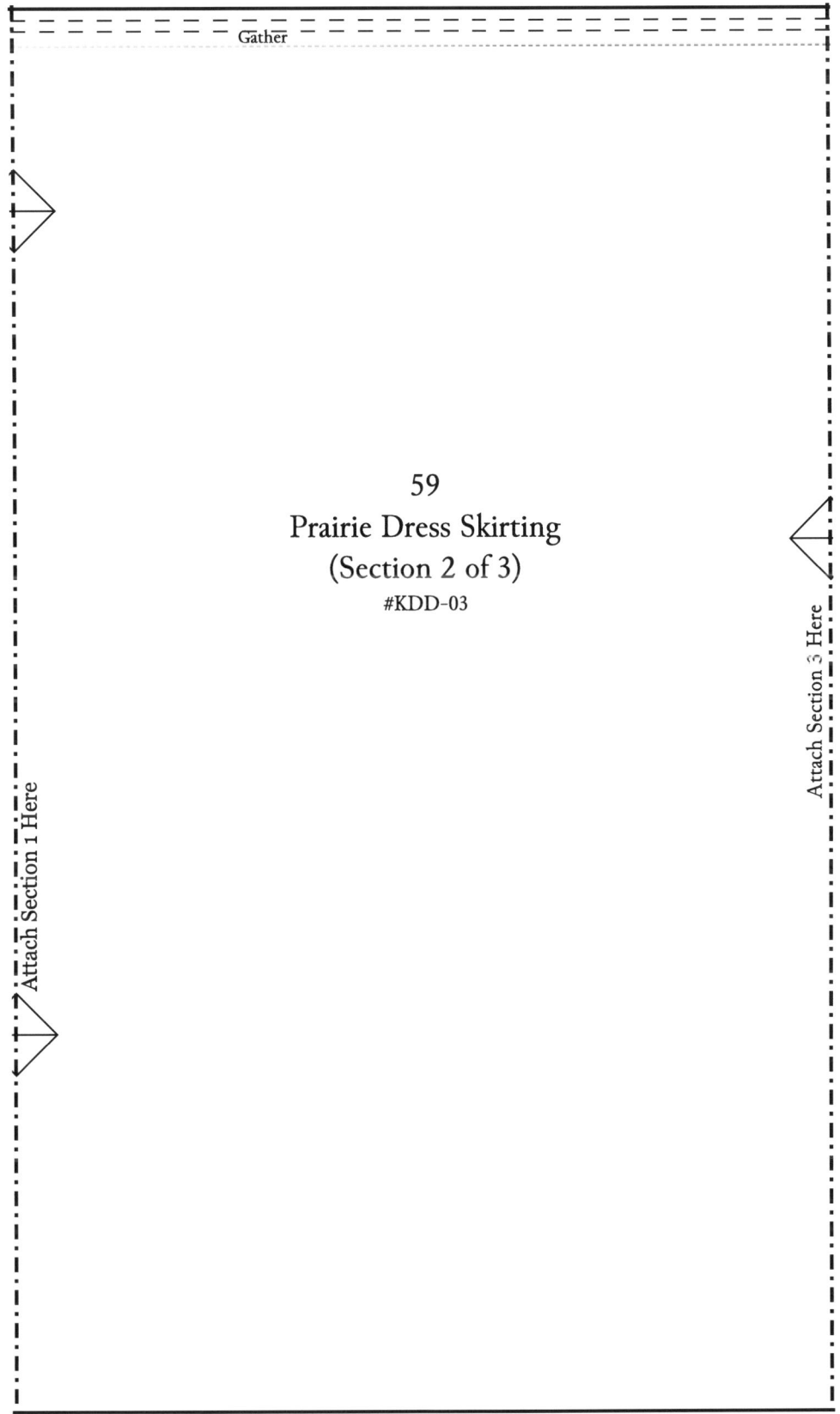

Gather

59
Prairie Dress Skirting
(Section 2 of 3)
#KDD-03

Attach Section 1 Here

Attach Section 3 Here

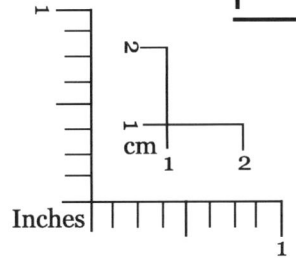

Inches

cm

Attach Section 2 Here

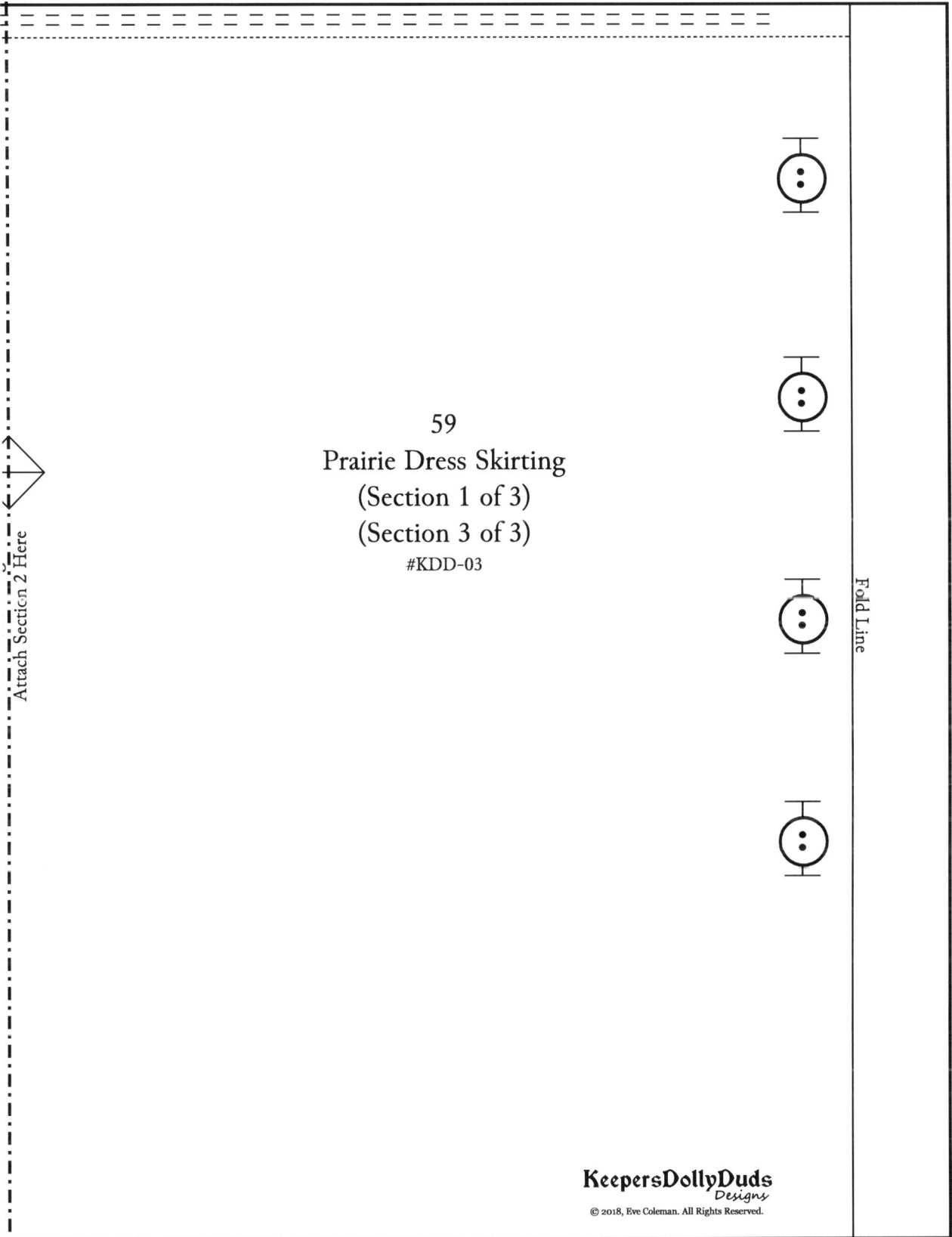

59
Prairie Dress Skirting
(Section 1 of 3)
(Section 3 of 3)
#KDD-03

Fold Line

KeepersDollyDuds
Designs

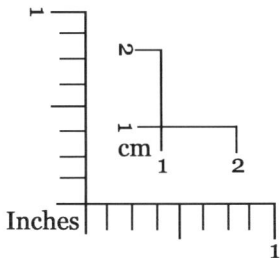

1

2

1

cm   1   2

Inches

1

Easing Stitches ~ Parallel rows of running stitches sewn along the edge of the fabric to be eased. The stitching threads are drawn so that the fabric forms curves slightly along the threads.

F

Facing ~ A section of fabric, used to finish fabric edges and provide extra stability.

Finger Press ~A method of temporarily pressing a seam or creasing fabric using your fingertips.

Finished Seam Allowance ~ A seam allowance where the cut edge has been bound, most commonly done with a zig-zag stitch on a sewing machine or a serger.

Fold Line ~A line along which fabric is or is to be folded.

G

Gathering Stitches ~ Parallel rows of running stitches sewn along the edge of the fabric to be gathered. To create gathers, the stitching threads are drawn so that the fabric forms small folds along the threads.

Grainline ~This refers to the position of the horizontal and vertical threads in a woven piece of fabric. It also refers to the long arrow symbol on a pattern piece that corresponds with the vertical threads on a woven fabric.

H

Hem ~ A garment finishing method, where the edge of a piece of cloth is folded under and sewn to prevent the fabric from unraveling.

Hook and Loop Tape ~ A fastening tape consisting of a strip of nylon with a surface of minute hooks that fasten to a corresponding strip with a surface of uncut pile.

I

Interfacing ~ A secondary woven or non-woven fabric that is fused or sewn onto a primary fabric to add stability, body, reinforcement, or shape.

N

Narrow Hem ~A hem made with a 1/2-inch to 1/4-inch hem allowance that is folded in half twice to form a 1/4-inch to 1/8-inch wide hem. It can be finished with either topstitching or whipstitching.

Neckline ~ The edge of a garment at or below the neck.

Notch ~V shaped clips cut inside the seam allowance of an outside curve that help rounded edges turn out and lie neatly; also refers to pattern markings shaped like diamonds or triangles that are printed on the cutting line of a pattern to indicate where seams should meet.

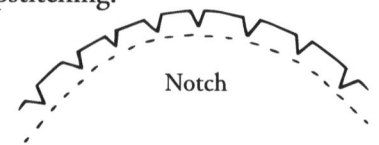

Notch

P

Pattern ~ A template for the pieces of a garment that includes markings for specific details and construction guides.

Placket ~ Overlapping layers of fabric along a garment opening that supports or hides buttons and buttonholes or other closures.

Pocket ~ a bag or envelope like receptacle that is fastened to or inserted in a garment. Earlier in history, a pocket was a separate small pouch.

Proper Left ~ This refers to the wearer's left side.

Proper Right ~This refers to the wearer's right side.

R

Raw Edge ~ A cut edge of fabric that hasn't been finished.

Ribbon ~A long, narrow strip of trim, used for tying things together or for decoration.

Right Side of Fabric ~ This is the side of the fabric with the printed pattern or design. On unprinted or untextured fabrics, both sides may be the same, so the right side is determined by which side will be the visible. In pattern instructions, the right side is shaded in illustrations.

Rolled Hem ~ A hem made with a 1/4-inch hem allowance that is rolled under with the forefinger and thumb to form a 1/8-inch wide hem and finished with a simple blind stitch as the hem is rolled.

Ruffle ~ A strip of fabric, lace, or ribbon pleated or gathered on one edge and applied to a garment or other textile as a form of trimming.

Running Stitch ~ Also known as the straight stitch, the running stitch is the basic hand-sewing stitch on which all other stitches are based. The stitch is worked by passing the needle in and out of the fabric.

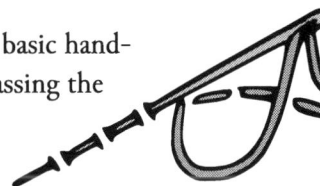

Running Stitch

S

Seam ~A line of stitching that holds two or more pieces of fabric together.

Selvage ~This is the tightly woven factory edge of fabric that runs parallel along each side of the lengthwise grain.

Skirt ~ A part of a garment that fastens around the waist and hangs down around the legs.

Snap ~ A two piece fastener that is engaged by pressing its two halves together.

Stay-Stitch ~ A straight stitch sewn through one layer of fabric that is most often used around a curve to reinforce a seam line and to prevent distortion.

T

Tack ~ To sew a few stitches in one spot, by hand or by machine, to secure one item to another.

Topstitch ~ A straight stitch along fabric edges or seam lines that helps to secure and strengthen an area; It can also be made with a decorative stitch to accentuate seams and style lines

W

Waistband ~ A band of fabric that encircles the waist of a garment.

Whipstitch ~ A sewing stitch that passes over an edge of cloth to join, finish, or gather.

Whipstitch

Wrong Side of Fabric ~ This is the side of the fabric that is unprinted or without intentional design. On unprinted or untextured fabrics, both sides may be the same so the wrong side is determined by which side will be the unseen. In pattern instructions, the wrong side is unshaded in illustrations.

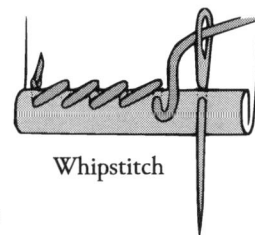

Printed in Great Britain
by Amazon